105³²

AMERICAN HISTORICAL FICTION

Third Edition

by

A. T. Dickinson, Jr.

The Scarecrow Press, Inc.
Metuchen, N.J.   1971

"The Library of Congress Cataloged the Original Printing of
This Title as:".

Dickinson, A   T
    American historical fiction, by A. T. Dickinson, Jr. 3d
ed. Metuchen, N. J., Scarecrow Press, 1971.

    380 p.   22 cm.

    1. Historical fiction, American. 2. Historical fiction, American—
Bibliography. 3. U. S.—History—Fiction—Bibliography.   I. Title.

PS374.H5D5 1971   016.813'03   78–146503
ISBN 0–8108–0370–4   MARC

Library of Congress   71 ₍30–2₎

"Fancy with fact is just one fact the more. "

Robert Browning

PREFACE

American history in fiction is a fascinating and informative field for study, as evidenced by its popularity with the casual reader in library and bookstore, and its increasing use by teachers who recognize that fiction can bring to life for their students a particular period or event in history.

My interest in historical fiction grew out of an early interest in history, blossomed with the reading of Gone With the Wind and The Red Badge of Courage, and bore fruit in the form of a Master's thesis on the subject under the guidance of Professor Leon Carnovsky of the Graduate Library School, The University of Chicago. This book is a descendant of that first effort.

Experience with the first edition revealed that its primary value was as a bibliography. Subsequent editions have been tailored to that usage. The basic list consists of novels published from 1917 to 1969. I have added those authors and titles from the past which have come to be standard names in historical fiction regardless of publication date.

A total of 2,440 novels casting light on some aspect of American history are classified into natural chronological periods from Colonial days to the beginnings of the Space Age. The brief annotations are designed to place the books in historical perspective rather than to make any critical judgment on the quality or the historical accuracy of the writing.

A major change in the Index is introduced for the first time in this edition with the hope that it will be easier and quicker to use. A separate Author-Title Index and a Subject Index are keyed to an entry number assigned to each title in the body of the book.

v

CONTENTS

INTRODUCTION

Just what constitutes a historical novel is a question which either plagues the person who would write about it, or concerns him very little. At any rate, there are as many definitions as there are definers. Perhaps the most succinct statement has been made by Ernest E. Leisy in The American Historical Novel:

> In a sense all fiction has a preterit quality, a sense of having been lived. More specifically, historical fiction is concerned with historical truth, whatever that is. Whether such truth requires a spectacular historical figure or episode is a matter of controversy, as is the question of whether the term includes novels written contemporaneously with the events. Paul Leicester Ford once said, 'An historical novel is one which grafts upon a story actual incidents or persons well enough known to be recognized as historical elements.' This definition appears too restrictive, however, for manners, customs, and ideas may suffice to identify a period... Owen Wister complicated the problem by asserting that 'any narrative which presents a day and a generation is of necessity historical,' a view concurred in by Brander Matthews when he said: 'The really trustworthy historical novels are those which were a-writing while the history was a-making.'

The statements of Owen Wister and Paul Leicester Ford represent opposite extremes in the academic approach to the definition of historical fiction. In practice, few would disagree with Leisy that the historical novel is one in which the action is laid in some identifiable past time. He suggests that a generation seems sufficient to make a preceding period historical, and he ends his discussion with the period of national expansion preceding World War I.

Robert A. Lively, in Fiction Fights the Civil War, is not concerned with past time as a prerequisite for the novels

ix

so ably analyzed in his study of the Civil War in fiction.
His conclusion is that it is the "true residue of fact or
color which determines the value of a work as a report from
the past. "

 The criteria for judging whether a novel will, at a
given point in time, present to the reader a feeling for the
history potentially inherent in any piece of writing are:
identifiable time, either by date or by approximate period;
identifiable place, either by definite locality or general area;
and an historical agent, whether a person, an event, or a
recognizable social, political, or economic phenomenon
characteristic of a period. Such a definition may be inter-
preted with varying degrees of latitude, and offers the reader
interested in viewing our past through the novelist's eyes
wide scope in selection without concern about whether the
author was sufficiently removed from his subject to rate the
title of historical novelist.

 American history, as rich and as varied as it is,
falls into a natural chronological pattern corresponding to
the periods of development of the nation from Colonial days
to the present, and this seems to be a logical arrangement
to follow.

Colonial America to 1775

 The colonial period has been the inspiration for novels
dealing with a variety of themes. The period covered is that
of the colonization and settlement of the original colonies, and
of their political, economic, social, and religious development up to the time of the Revolution. The ill-fated settlement on Roanoke Island, the struggle for survival of the
first settlement at Plymouth, Bacon's Rebellion, the Pontiac
Conspiracy, the Yemassee Wars, the Deerfield raid, the
Salem witchcraft trials, conflict between Quakers and
Puritans, the New Hampshire land grant controversy, the
attack on the French at Louisburg, Braddock's defeat, King
Philip's War, and the siege of Fort Pitt are some of the
more violent episodes in the history of the period which have
been used in historical novels. Other novels have dealt with
less violent, though not less crucial aspects of the period,
such as the founding of Detroit, the French settlement of
Mobile and New Orleans, social life at Williamsburg, the
immigration of French Huguenots into the Carolinas and of
the Scotch-Irish and Germans into Pennsylvania, the life of

George Washington, and the social and mercantile life of the
Dutch and the English in New York.

The American Revolution

The American Revolution has been well documented in
historical fiction, from the tense political situation leading to
the Battles of Lexington and Concord, through the progress
of the war southward to its culmination in Cornwallis' surrender at Yorktown, the war on the frontier, and the development of the American navy under Commodore John Paul
Jones. The Boston Tea Party, the terrible winter at Valley
Forge, Benjamin Franklin's diplomatic mission to France,
the career of Benedict Arnold, the activities of George
Rogers Clark on the frontier and of Francis Marion in South
Carolina, the neutrality of Westchester County, New York and
the conflict between English and rebel loyalties throughout the
colonies, the separatist movement on the frontiers of Kentucky
and Tennessee and the founding of the Transylvania Company
and the state of Franklin, as well as action leading to various battles and campaigns of the war are some of the subjects of novels dealing with this period of history.

The Young Nation, 1783 to 1860

The period covered by this category extends from the
end of the Revolution to the mid-1800's, thus overlapping in
time parts of the two following categories. Novels dealing
with political, social, cultural, and industrial development of
the new young nation following the Revolution contribute to a
fuller understanding of our history. Some of the themes
found in fiction of this period are: the period of Confedera-
tion, the ratification of the Constitution, Shays' Rebellion,
the Tripolitan War, the War of 1812, the beginnings of industrial and financial development, shipbuilding and the shipping industry, national and local politics in the 1830's and
1840's, musical life in New York in the 1830's, and American literary development in the early 1800's.

Expanding Frontiers, 1783 to 1893

The course of westward expansion from the Revolution to the closing of the American frontier in the 1890's
offers the novelist a multitude of settings, periods, and

characters from which to draw: simple tales of family life
in a frontier cabin; heroic treks from the East to the wilderness of Western Pennsylvania, Ohio, Kentucky, and Tennessee; fur trade with the Indians and the founding of the cities
on the Great Lakes and on the Ohio and Mississippi Rivers;
wagon trains pushing westward; the California gold rush;
settlement of the plains states; and the development of the
Old West. Daniel Boone, Buffalo Bill, General Custer,
Aaron Burr, Marcus Whitman, William Bonney, Lewis and
Clark, Abraham Lincoln, J. J. Hill, John Jacob Astor, Kit
Carson, Santa Anna, David Crockett, and the Indians,
Pontiac, Sitting Bull, and Geronimo are among the many
historical figures who appear in novels dealing with this phase
of American history.

Eastern and Southern Frontiers

During the colonial period the frontier was pushed
slowly inland from the settlement along the Atlantic coast by
hunters and fur traders followed by settlers, until at the
time of the Revolution the Appalachian Mountains had been
breached; the Wautauga and Transylvania settlements had
been made in Tennessee and Kentucky. George Rogers
Clark's successful expedition against Hamilton in the Northwest Territory and the treaty setting the western boundary
of the United States at the Mississippi River added impetus
to the westward migration. However, frontier conditions did
not cease to exist as the boundary of the frontier itself ad-
vanced. The New England states, and Western Pennsylvania
and New York still had areas in which pioneer conditions
existed in the mid-1800's. In the South, Florida, Georgia,
the Mississippi Territory, and Louisiana furnish abundant
sources for novels of frontier and pioneer life.

The Middle West

The settlement of the area comprising Ohio, Indiana,
Illinois, Michigan, Wisconsin, Iowa, and Minnesota, has
been treated in a large number of novels covering a wide
range of time from the early settlements on the Ohio River
to the immigration of Norwegians and Irish into Wisconsin
and Minnesota in the 1870's.

The Southwest

The history of the American Southwest--Texas, New
Mexico, Arizona, and Oklahoma--can be summed up in a
relatively few subjects as far as historical fiction is concerned: the struggle for Texas independence and the siege
of the Alamo; the Mexican War; life along the Sante Fe Trail;

conflict with the Indians; Indian life and customs; cattlemen
versus homesteaders; and outlaws and characters.

California and the Pacific Northwest
              California and Oregon became states in 1850 and
1858, respectively, thus being in the position of outposts
separated from the rest of the United States by the Great
American Desert, a vast expanse of mountains and plains
considered unfit for white habitation, and it was to these
outposts that pioneers looked for land to settle before turn-
ing to the plains for their rich soil and to the mountains for
their rich mineral deposits.   Episodes in the history of this
region have been dealt with in novels centering around
Spanish life and missionary activities in Mexico and
California, the California gold rush and politics leading to
statehood, the Lewis and Clark explorations, establishment
of the early fur trading outposts and the settlement of
Oregon, the British-American boundary dispute, and early
Russian efforts to colonize the Northwest.

The Civil War--Before and After

              Among the novels dealing with the period of the
Civil War are, of course, those which deal with specific
battles and campaigns of the war and with the lives of military and government leaders on both sides.   There is, however, a wide range of subject matter far removed from the
battlefields.   There are novels set against a background of
the ante-bellum South, a South of manors, mammies, and
mint juleps; novels of social life in the Eastern and Southern
cities; stories of the abolitionist movement; stories of
families, both North and South, torn between conflicting
ideals and loyalties; and novels depicting the conflict between
Southern sympathizers and those loyal to the Union in the
struggle to influence the Western states.   Blockade running
and international diplomacy, spies, prison camps, and the
activities of Copperheads furnish the motif for others.   And
there are novels dealing with the period of Reconstruction
following the war.   These novels are divided into the following sections: "The Old South, " "Abolition, " "The War
Years, " and "Reconstruction. "

The Old South
              Life in the South before the Civil War, as reflected in
the romantic school of historical fiction, was one of great
plantations, loyal slaves, and a leisurely social life.   During

the 1930's and 1940's, a period during which there was a
stream of reappraisals of Civil War history, a more com-
plete picture of life in the South began to emerge. As a
result of this revisionist trend novelists took a fresh approach to the people of the South, concerning themselves
with the pioneer-like daily existence of the small farmer,
and the economic struggles of the planter and his relation
with the Negroes.

Abolition

Novels of the Abolitionist movement develop some exciting themes: the free-soil struggle for Kansas, John Brown's
raid, the Underground Railroad, and the life and times of
various real and fictitious leaders in the movement.

The War Years

Novels dealing with military and naval engagements
range through the entire course of the war, from Fort
Sumter to Appomattox, and through all phases of the conflict, from the drive down the Mississippi River to the final
push against Richmond which culminated in Lee's surrender,
naval warfare, and the plots to win the West over to one
side or the other.   No less important in the fictional litera-
ture of the period is the effect of the war on the home
front.   The occupation of the old plantation house by Yankee
troops, conflicts in areas of neutrality, Copperhead activity
in the North and in the West, the exciting life of spies on
both sides, the terrible conditions in prison camps, and the
lives of political and military leaders are represented in
novels of the Civil War.

Reconstruction

No less a part of the Civil War is the aftermath of
Reconstruction which followed.   With few exceptions, the
theme running through novels of this phase of history is the
disintegration of an affluent mode of life and the rebuilding
of a new South on the ashes of the old.   The return of the
soldier to his ruined plantation and his struggle to rebuild,
the loyalty of the ex-slaves, political and social upheaval in
the South aggravated by fanatic Southerners, insensitive occupation troops, carpetbaggers, the Ku Klux Klan, and the
belligerence of less intelligent Negroes are threads running
through these novels.

The Nation Grows Up, 1877 to 1917

The last decades of the nineteenth century and the

first decade of the twentieth witnessed a major alteration in
the manner of life in the United States. This changing social,
political, and industrial scene is reflected in the background
of novels set in the period from the end of the Civil War to
World War I. The development of financial and industrial
empires, the era of railroad expansion in the 1870's, the
organization of labor and the growth of unions, local and
national politics, the Spanish-American War, social life of
the wealthy classes and life in the small town at the turn of
the century, and such cultural themes as the birth of the
movie industry, the assimilation of immigrants, Mormon life
and customs, and the great world expositions held during the
period are some of the subjects of novels in this group.

World War I

World War I is the first period in which the major
events took place outside the United States. In addition to
novels depicting actual warfare, however, there are novels
based on the experiences of civilian non-combatants, nurses,
telephone operators, ambulance drivers; novels depicting life
in the training camps; stories of German spy activity and of
anti-German feeling in American communities; novels dealing
with the effects of the war on the home front; and novels
dealing with politics before and during the war.

The Nineteen-Twenties

The United States during the decade of the Twenties
was characterized by an extravagance, a restlessness, and
a lack of purpose which resulted in dramatic excesses, from
the frantic boom in Florida real estate to the witch hunting
of the "red" scare. Several main themes predominate in the
novels dealing with this period: the after-effects of World
War I; prohibition and gangsterism; further industrial expansion and the labor movement; mass hysteria and the red
scare; life in the jazz age; and prosperity, speculation, and
the market crash of 1929.

The Nineteen-Thirties

Novels dealing with the decade of the nineteen-thirties
in United States history cover a wide range of dissimilar
themes: The Depression and New Deal relief measures; labor

union activity; the rise of Nazism and fascism and the approach of war; and contemporary family life in which one of
the larger issues of the period is used as a background.
Another theme unique to this period and closely related to
the rise of fascism in its social implications deals with local
politics and demagoguery, as exemplified, for example, by the
rise to power of Huey Long in Louisiana.

World War II

        United States participation in World War II has been
covered in almost all its phases by the fiction dealing with
that period of our history.   In addition to novels concerned
with specific battles and with naval warfare in both theaters,
there are novels depicting various phases of the war on the
home front and the plight of returning veterans.   Among the
themes developed in these novels are: American indifference
to the war in Europe and the sharp reaction to the attack on
Pearl Harbor; the treatment of Japanese-Americans in
California internment camps; life in training camps and
prisoner-of-war camps; the role of women in the war effort;
the effect of the war on civilian life--the fear of invasion,
civil defense measures, rationing and price controls; and the
efforts of returning veterans to find their place in life under
changed conditions and attitudes.

The Tense Years--1945 to the Sixties

        In the years following World War II a new phase of
American history came into existence.   Domestic and international crises erupted at the same time our complacency and
standard of living rose to new heights.   On the domestic
scene the major force stimulating fiction of the period was
the turmoil of the beginning of the fight for equal rights for
the Negro.   The voice of the conservative was heard again
in the land, and is represented in fiction by novels based on
the effects of the Congressional investigations and the fear
aroused by the search for Communists in our midst.   This
was just one aspect of our involvement in the Cold War,
which has been used by novelists in a variety of settings:
the interaction of U. S. servicemen and native populations in
occupied countries all over the world; the Berlin Airlift; the
Korean War; adventures behind the Iron Curtain; tales of
spying and intrigue, and the operation of our diplomatic
service in the tense spots around the world.   Other novels

set in this period deal with the character of the U. S. Senate, with the history of Alaska and Hawaii leading up to statehood, the development of the United Nations, and the student unrest on college campuses.

Chronicles

This group contains those novels which do not readily fall into a single chronological period of history--the epic novel which depicts a whole slice of American life, or which follows a single family through several generations.

COLONIAL AMERICA TO 1775

1 Alderman, Clifford Lindsey. SILVER KEYS. Putnam,
   1960. The adventures of William Phips in Boston,
   London, and the Caribbean before he became the
   first royal governor of Massachusetts under the
   charter of 1691.

2 Allen, Hervey. THE FOREST AND THE FORT.
   Farrar, 1943. The French and Indian War in the
   forests of Pennsylvania in the 1760's, and the
   founding of Fort Pitt.

3 --- BEDFORD VILLAGE. Farrar, 1944. Picture of
   Pennsylvania frontier life from 1763 to 1764. Sequel
   to "Forest and the Fort. "

4 --- TOWARD THE MORNING. Rinehart, 1948. Life
   on the Pennsylvania frontier and in Philadelphia,
   1764-1765. Sequel to "Bedford Village. "

5 Allis, Marguerite. NOT WITHOUT PERIL. Putnam,
   1941. Pioneer hardships and folkways in the early
   settlement of Vermont.

6 Aswell, Mary Louise. ABIGAIL. Crowell, 1959.
   Background of colonial social and political life in
   Philadelphia in the story of a strong willed woman
   who rebelled against her Quaker environment.

7 Bacheller, Irving. CANDLE IN THE WILDERNESS.
   Bobbs, 1930. Boston in stern colonial days;
   Reverend John Cotton, Sir Harry Vane, and others
   appear.

8 Barker, Shirley. PEACE, MY DAUGHTERS. Crown,
   1949. Story of the witchcraft trials and persecutions
   in Salem in 1691.

9 --- RIVERS PARTING. Crown, 1950. Settlement of
   New Hampshire, and the struggle with Massachusetts
   over control of the area.

19

10   --- TOMORROW THE NEW MOON. Bobbs, 1955.
      Religious conflict in Puritan New England in the days
      of Cotton Mather in the early 1700's.

11   --- SWEAR BY APOLLO. Random, 1958. Picture of
      medical and social life in New Hampshire in the
      years leading up to the Revolution.

12   Barth, John. THE SOT-WEED FACTOR. Doubleday,
      1960. A long, bawdy tale of many facets of life
      in colonial Maryland and England written in the style
      of the 17th century novelists.

13   Borland, Barbara Dodge. THE GREATER HUNGER.
      Appleton, 1962. Story of hardship and romance in
      the life of the early Massachusetts Bay Colony.

14   Boyce, Burke. MORNING OF A HERO. Harper, 1963.
      Picture of George Washington as a young man, sur-
      veying on the frontier, fighting in the French-Indian
      Wars, serving in the Virginia House of Burgesses,
      and bringing his bride home to Mount Vernon.

15   Breslin, Howard. THE SILVER OAR. Crowell, 1954.
      Story based on the revolt against Governor Andros
      in Boston in 1689, with Cotton Mather as one of the
      characters.

16   Buchan, John. SALUTE TO ADVENTURERS. Doran,
      1917. Adventure tale of colonial Virginia in 1690.

17   Cannon, LeGrand. COME HOME AT EVEN. Holt,
      1951. Story of four people who settle in the Puritan
      colony of Salem in the 1630's.

18   Coatsworth, Elizabeth. SWORD OF THE WILDERNESS.
      Macmillan, 1936. Story of the French and Indian
      Wars in 1698 in New England.

19   Colver, Alice. THE MEASURE OF THE YEARS. Dodd,
      1954. Story of the white families who settled at
      Indian Town (later Stockbridge) Massachusetts during
      the French and Indian Wars. Pictures family life,
      religious controversy, Indian-white relations, and
      political events leading up to the Revolution.

20   --- THERE IS A SEASON. Dodd, 1957. Picture of

family life and frontier customs in Stockbridge,
Massachusetts and Charles-Town, South Carolina
from 1756 to 1770. Sequel to "Measure of the
Years."

21   Cooper, James Fenimore. THE DEERSLAYER.
      Scribner, 1841. Story of warfare between the
      Iroquois Indians and white settlers around Lake
      Otsego, New York during King George's War, 1744.
      Followed by "Last of the Mohicans."

22   --- THE LAST OF THE MOHICANS. Scribner, 1826.
      Story of wilderness warfare around Lake George,
      New York during the French and Indian Wars. Fol-
      lowed by "The Pathfinder."

23   --- THE PATHFINDER. Dodd, 1840. Tale of the
      French and Indian War in the area around Lake
      Ontario. Followed by "The Pioneers."

24   --- THE PIONEERS. Dodd, 1822. Pioneer life in
      the wilderness around Lake Otsego, New York in the
      years before the Revolution. Followed by "The
      Prairie" (Expanding Frontiers--Middle West).

25   Cooper, Kent. ANNA ZENGER, MOTHER OF FREE-
      DOM. Farrar, 1946. Story of the first newspaper
      in New York and the first battle for freedom of the
      press, set against a background of life under the
      British governors.

26   Coryell, Hubert. INDIAN BROTHER. Harcourt, 1935.
      Adventures of a young colonist and his sister cap-
      tured by the Indians; Maine in 1713.

27   --- SCALP HUNTERS. Harcourt, 1936. Experiences
      of a young colonist and his Indian brother in Maine
      in the early 1700's.

28   Costain, Thomas B. HIGH TOWERS. Doubleday, 1949.
      Adventures of the LeMoyne brothers who explored
      the Mississippi River and founded New Orleans and
      Mobile in the early 1700's.

29   Cross, Ruth. SOLDIER OF GOOD FORTUNE. Banks
      Upshaw, 1936. Exploits of Louis de St. Denis on a
      trading expedition into Texas and Mexico for the
      French colony at Mobile in 1715.

30   Curwood, James Oliver.   THE PLAINS OF ABRAHAM.
      Doubleday, 1928.   Romance of the French-English
      wars leading up to the capture of Quebec.

31   Davidson, L. S. THE DISTURBER.   Macmillan, 1964.
      Story of Puritan persecution and the founding of
      Merry Mount by Thomas Morton.

32   Devon, John Anthony.   O WESTERN WIND.   Putnam,
      1957.   Story of the founding of Merry Mount and of
      its destruction by Miles Standish; emphasis on the
      bigotry and intolerance of the Puritans of the
      Pilgrim colony at Plymouth.

33   Dodge, Constance.   IN ADAM'S FALL.   Macrae, 1946.
      Story of the Salem witchcraft hysteria of the seven-
      teenth century; recreates the life and spirit of the
      times.

34   Dowdey, Clifford.   GAMBLE'S HUNDRED.   Little,
      1939.   Tidewater Virginia around 1730; scene is
      mostly in Williamsburg.

35   Eaton, Evelyn.   RESTLESS ARE THE SAILS.   Harper,
      1941.   Historical romance centering around the fall
      of Louisburg in 1745.

36   --- THE SEA IS SO WIDE.   Harper, 1943.   Story of
      French Acadians banished from their farmland in
      Nova Scotia during the French-English war who
      settle in the Southern colonies; pictures social life
      in Williamsburg.

37   Etheridge, Willie Snow.   SUMMER THUNDER.
      Coward, 1959.   Founding of Savannah and the early
      colonization of Georgia in the 1730's; picture of
      James Oglethorpe.

38   Farrar, Rowena Rutherford.   BEND YOUR HEADS ALL.
      Holt, 1965.   Emigration to Tennessee in 1770 and
      the settlement of Nashville, through the story of a
      pioneer family; pioneer life and Indian fighting
      before and during the Revolution.

39   Fletcher, Inglis.   ROANOKE HUNDRED.   Bobbs, 1948.
      Story of the first British settlement in America;
      scenes laid in England of Elizabethan time and in the

wilderness of Roanoke Island, 1585-1586; Sir
Richard Grenville, Walter Raleigh, and others
appear. Part of author's series on North Carolina
history. See other novels below and under "American Revolution" and "Young Nation. "

40   --- BENNET'S WELCOME. Bobbs, 1950. Story of
      the first permanent settlement of North Carolina,
      still part of Virginia in 1651-1652.

41   --- ROGUE'S HARBOR. Bobbs, 1964. North
      Carolina neighbors rebel against local British rule
      in 1677.

42   --- MEN OF ALBEMARLE. Bobbs, 1942. The evolu-
      tion of law and order in colonial North Carolina;
      1710-1712.

43   --- LUSTY WIND FOR CAROLINA. Bobbs, 1944.
      Story of the North Carolina plantation owners and
      of their attempts to establish communities and ward
      off pirates destroying their trade; 1718-1725.

44   --- CORMORANT'S BROOD. Lippincott, 1959. Pic-
      tures the struggle of the colonists in the Albemarle
      region of North Carolina against their weak but
      greedy royal governors; 1725-1729.

45   --- THE WIND IN THE FOREST. Bobbs, 1957. Story
      of the Regulator's Insurrection in North Carolina,
      an uprising of frontier farmers against the royal
      governor, William Tyron, and the Tidewater
      planters; ends in the Battle of Alamance in 1771.

46   Forbes, Esther. A MIRROR FOR WITCHES.
      Houghton, 1928. Amusing picture of a Massachu-
      setts village during the witchcraft hysteria.

47   --- PARADISE. Harcourt, 1937. Settlement of
      Canaan, near Boston, in the Massachusetts Bay
      Colony at the time of King Philip's War.

48   Frey, Ruby Frazier. RED MORNING. Putnam, 1946.
      Background of the struggle for the Ohio valley;
      warfare between Indians, French, and English in
      which George Washington began his career;
      Governor Dinwiddie, Franklin, and Braddock appear.

49   Fuller, Iola. THE GILDED TORCH. Putnam, 1957.
       Story of the explorations of LaSalle in the Great
       Lakes and Mississippi River areas and of his at-
       tempt to set up a French empire in America and in
       the 1680's and 1690's.

50   Gebler, Ernest. PLYMOUTH ADVENTURE. Double-
       day, 1950. Story of the Mayflower Pilgrims from
       Southampton across the Atlantic through the first
       few months on the New England coast.

51   Gerson, Noel B. THE HIGHWAYMAN. Doubleday,
       1955. Story built around the expedition against the
       French at Louisburg during the French and Indian
       War, 1744-1748.

52   --- DAUGHTER OF EVE. Doubleday, 1958. Story of
       Captain John Smith and Pocahontas; picture of the
       life and customs of the Indians and the English in
       the early days of the Virginia colony at Jamestown.

53   --- THE LAND IS BRIGHT. Doubleday, 1961. Por-
       trait of William Bradford and the hardships of the
       first years of the Massachusetts Bay Colony.

54   --- YANKEE DOODLE DANDY. Doubleday, 1965.
       Biographical novel of John Hancock, signer of the
       Declaration of Independence and governor of
       Massachusetts.

55   --- GIVE ME LIBERTY. Doubleday, 1966. Bio-
       graphical novel of the life of Patrick Henry.

56   Giles, Janice Holt. HANNAH FOWLER. Houghton,
       1956. Story of pioneer settlers on the Kentucky
       River in the 1770's.

57   Gordon, Caroline. THE GREEN CENTURIES.
       Scribner, 1941. Pre-Revolutionary life in pioneer
       Kentucky and Tennessee; picture of the settlement
       of the Holston River area, and of the negotiations
       between the Indians and Judge Henderson.

58   Hawthorne, Nathaniel. THE SCARLET LETTER.
       Dodd, 1850. Tale of sin and retribution in Puritan
       Boston.

59   Hughes, Rupert. STATELY TIMBER. Scribner, 1939.
      Life in Puritan New England and in Virginia and
      the Barbados Islands in the 1650's.

60   Jennings, John. NEXT TO VALOUR. Macmillan,
      1939. Roger's Rangers in New Hampshire during
      the French and Indian Wars; 1750's.

61   --- GENTLEMAN RANKER. Reynal, 1942. Story of
      an English dandy tricked into joining Braddock's
      expedition against the French in 1755; settles in
      America and adapts himself to frontier life.

62   Johnston, Mary. CROATAN. Little, 1923. Story
      of the ill-fated Roanoke settlement in Virginia in
      1587. Heroine is Virginia Dare.

63   --- TO HAVE AND TO HOLD. Houghton, 1900. Story
      set in Virginia in 1621 centering around the first
      shipload of brides sent to the colony.

64   --- PRISONERS OF HOPE. Houghton, 1898. Colonial
      life in Virginia centering around the deportation of
      convicts to the colony from England; 1649-1651.

65   --- THE SLAVE SHIP. Little, 1924. Story of the
      colonial slave trade; 1660's.

66   --- GREAT VALLEY. Little, 1926. Virginia before
      and during the French and Indian Wars; 1737-1759.

67   Jordan, Mildred. ONE RED ROSE FOREVER. Knopf,
      1941. Pennsylvania of the mid-1700's; hero is
      Baron Stiegel, the German immigrant who became
      known as the maker of Stiegel glass.

68   King, Grace. LA DAME DE SAINTE HERMINE.
      Macmillan, 1924. Story of the settlement of New
      Orleans by Pierre LeMoyne in 1718.

69   Lide, Alice. DARK POSSESSION. Appleton, 1934.
      Charles Town, South Carolina in the early 1700's;
      a tale of slaves and indentured servants, Indian
      wars, sorcery, and passion.

70   Lincoln, Victoria. A DANGEROUS INNOCENCE. Rine-
      hart, 1958. Life in Salem, Massachusetts at the time
      of the witchcraft trials.

71   Linderholm, Helmer. LAND OF THE BEAUTIFUL
      RIVER. St. Martins, 1963. Recollections of life
      in Peter Stuyvesant's settlement of New Amster-
      dam and adventures among the Susquehanna Indians.

72   Lofts, Norah. BLOSSOM LIKE THE ROSE. Knopf,
      1939. Romance of a young Scotsman who joins a
      band of religious fanatics, sails to America, and
      battles Indians and Puritan intolerance.

73   Longstreet, Stephen. WAR IN THE GOLDEN WEATH-
      ER. Doubleday, 1965. French and Indian War in
      the 1750's and its effect on the Dutch settlers in
      New York state; characters are a young Dutch
      painter and Major George Washington as a young
      surveyor. Followed by "Eagles Where I Walk"
      (American Revolution).

74   Lovelace, Maud Hart. CHARMING SALLY. Day,
      1932. Story of the first theatrical company to
      come to America; picture of brilliant social life
      in Virginia and more sedate Quaker life in Phila-
      delphia in 1752.

75   Malvern, Gladys. ERIC'S GIRLS. Messner, 1949.
      New Amsterdam, the Dutch city of Peter Stuyve-
      sant at the time of the English siege and capture.

76   Mann, Helen. GALLANT WARRIOR. William B.
      Eerdmans, 1954. Fictionized biography of Hannah
      Duston, pioneer wife and mother who, with her
      baby and its nurse, was captured by Indians in
      1697; recreates the spirit of the period.

77   Marsh, George. ASK NO QUARTER. Morrow, 1945.
      Newport, Rhode Island at the end of the 17th
      century; reconstructs the speech and details of
      daily life of the period.

78   Marshall, Edison. THE LOST COLONY. Doubleday,
      1964. Recreation of the fate of the settlers on
      Roanoke Island; based on the thesis that they
      fled to Florida to escape an Indian massacre and
      were assimilated into a friendly Indian tribe.

79   Mason, F. Van Wyck. THE YOUNG TITAN. Double-
      day, 1959. Story of the hazards of frontier living

during the French and Indian War; scenes set in
Boston, in Bartholomey Mayhew's settlement on
the Penobscot River, and on the wilderness march
against Louisburg in 1745.

80   -- THE SEA 'VENTURE.   Doubleday, 1961.   Story
      of the early years of Jamestown and the first col-
      ony in Bermuda.

81   -- RASCALS' HEAVEN.   Doubleday, 1964.   Story of
      the settling of Georgia by General James Oglethorpe
      and of the colony's early enemies, the Indians and
      the Spanish settlement at St. Augustine.

82   Matschat, Cecile Hulse.   TAVERN IN THE TOWN.
      Farrar, 1942.   A romance of plantation life in
      colonial Virginia.

83   Miers, Earl Schenck.   VALLEY IN ARMS.   Westmin-
      ster, 1943.   Clearing the land and fighting Indians
      in a Connecticut valley in the 1630's.

84   Miller, Helen Topping.   DARK SAILS.   Bobbs, 1945.
      Oglethorpe's colonization of Georgia in the 1730's
      and 1740's.

85   Moore, Ruth.   A FAIR WIND HOME.   Morrow, 1953.
      Story of Nathan Ellis of Massachusetts, Francis
      Carnavon of Cork, and Maynard Cantril, a ship-
      builder of Somerset, Maine before the Revolution.

86   Murphy, Edward.   A BRIDE FOR NEW ORLEANS.
      Hanover, 1955.   Historical romance of the Casket
      girls sent to New Orleans from Paris in 1727 to
      marry and to help settle Louisiana.

87   Newton, John Edward.   THE ROGUE AND THE
      WITCH.   Abelard, 1955.   Story of religious con-
      flict between Puritans and Quakers in Boston, in-
      volving the Salem witchcraft trials; Increase Mather
      is one of the characters.

88   Oemler, Marie.   THE HOLY LOVER.   Boni and
      Liveright, 1927.   Story of John Wesley, dealing
      with the three years he spent in the Georgia col-
      ony, 1735-1738; based on journals and letters from
      the period.

89   Page, Elizabeth. WILDERNESS ADVENTURE. Rine-
      hart, 1946. A tale of the rescue of a young girl
      captured by Indians; rescuers follow her from Vir-
      ginia to the Mississippi River, to New Orleans,
      and on to France and England.

90   Paradise, Jean. THE SAVAGE CITY. Crown, 1955.
      Story of colonial New York, based on the hysteria
      caused by a servant girl's tale of a Negro-Spanish
      plot to massacre the whites in the city.

91   Parker, Sir Gilbert. THE POWER AND THE GLORY.
      Harper, 1925. Achievements of LaSalle as pioneer
      and explorer; a novel of early Canadian and
      American history.

92   Pendexter, Hugh. WIFE-SHIP WOMAN. Bobbs, 1926.
      Louisiana and Virginia in the early 1700's; heroine
      is one of the Casket girls sent from France to be
      the wives of men in the Louisiana colony at New
      Orleans in 1727.

93   -- THE RED ROAD. Bobbs, 1927. Tale of Brad-
      dock's defeat during the French and Indian War,
      1754-1763.

94   Phillips, Alexandra. FOREVER POSSESS. Dutton,
      1946. Picture of life on the feudal estates on the
      Hudson River in New York in the 17th century at
      the time of an uprising among the tenants.

95   Pinckney, Josephine. HILTON HEAD. Farrar, 1941.
      Story of the tribulations of a young doctor in
      South Carolina in the 1600's.

96   Pound, Arthur. THE HAWK OF DETROIT. Reynal,
      1939. The founding of Detroit, and conflicting
      interests in the government monopoly of trade;
      Chief Cadillac is one of the characters.

97   Rees, Gilbert. I SEEK A CITY. Dutton, 1950.
      Fictional autobiography of Roger Williams, from
      his early life in England, his voyage to the col-
      onies, his work as a minister in Salem, Massa-
      chusetts, his founding of Providence, Rhode Island,
      and his understanding of the Indians.

98   Richter, Conrad. FREE MAN. Knopf, 1943. Story
      of a young emigrant from the Palatinate who sought
      political freedom among the Pennsylvania-Dutch.

99   -- THE LIGHT IN THE FOREST. Knopf, 1953.
      Settlers and Indians in Pennsylvania and Ohio at
      the time of Bouquet's expedition to free the cap-
      tives of the Tuscarawas Indians in 1765. Followed
      by "A Country of Strangers" (Expanding Frontiers--
      Eastern).

100   Ritchie, Cicero T. THE WILLING MAID. Abelard,
      1958. Boston and Nova Scotia during the French
      and Indian War; climax comes at the fall of
      Louisburg; 1740's.

101   Roberts, Kenneth L. NORTHWEST PASSAGE. Dou-
      bleday, 1937. Major Robert Rogers, and his ex-
      pedition against the Indians of St. Francis in 1759.
      His dream was to find an overland passage to the
      Pacific.

102   -- BOON ISLAND. Doubleday, 1956. Story of the
      harrowing experience of the survivors of a ship-
      wreck on an island near Portsmouth, New Hamp-
      shire in 1710.

103   Safford, Henry B. TRISTRAM BENT. Coward,
      1940. Hero is an English agent sent to spy on the
      Dutch colonies in 1640; accurate historical details
      of the period and place.

104   Sass, Herbert R. EMPEROR BRIMS. Doubleday,
      1941. The Yemassee War in South Carolina in
      1715; uprising of the Creek Indian Confederacy
      against the white settlements on the coast.

105   Schachner, Nathan. THE KING'S PASSENGER. Lip-
      pincott, 1942. Colonial Virginia at the time of
      Bacon's Rebellion and the burning of Jamestown in
      1676.

106   Seifert, Shirley. RIVER OUT OF EDEN. M. S.
      Mill, 1940. Trip up the Mississippi River from
      New Orleans to the settlement later known as St.
      Louis in 1763; pictures political and economic
      rivalries on the frontier.

107   Seton, Anya. THE WINTHROP WOMAN. Houghton,
      1958. Story of the Massachusetts Bay Colony and
      Connecticut, based on the life of Governor John
      Winthrop's niece; an account of life in early Bos-
      ton.

108   -- DEVIL WATER. Houghton, 1962. Biographical
      novel about the Radcliffe family and William Byrd
      of Westover in 18th century Virginia and England.

109   Settle, Mary Lee. O BEULAH LAND. Viking, 1956.
      Pictures the hardships of a group of Virginia set-
      tlers in the wilderness beyond the Allegheny
      Mountains and their struggles with the French and
      Indians; 1754-1774.

110   Simms, William Gilmore. THE YEMASSEE. Amer-
      ican Book, 1835. Colonial expansion seen from
      the viewpoint of the Indians; story of the events
      leading up to the Yemassee War in South Caro-
      lina in the early 1700's.

111   Simons, Katherine. ALWAYS A RIVER. Appleton,
      1956. Story of the clash of temperaments be-
      tween a Puritan schoolmaster, who leaves Massa-
      chusetts during the witchcraft hysteria, and the
      French Huguenots in the Carolinas in 1695.

112   -- THE LAND BEYOND THE TEMPEST. Coward,
      1960. Story of a hazardous voyage from England
      to colonial Jamestown, Virginia.

113   Singmaster, Elsie. A HIGH WIND RISING. Houghton,
      1942. Story of life in a Pennsylvania German-Dutch
      settlement at the time of the French and Indian War;
      based on the life of Conrad Weiser and his relations
      with the Indians.

114   Smith, Arthur Douglas. THE DOOM TRAIL. Bren-
      tano, 1922. Story built on the struggle for supre-
      macy in the fur trade between the French and the
      English.

115   Snedeker, Caroline. UNCHARTED WAYS. Doubleday,
      1935. Based on the life of Mary Dyer, a Quaker con-
      vert in Boston in the 1650's; pictures the religious
      tension of the period, and John Cotton's persecution

of the Quakers.

116 Speare, Elizabeth. THE PROSPERING. Houghton,
1967. Story of the settling of Stockbridge, Massachusetts in the early 1700's by young missionary
John Sergeant whose dream was to integrate the
Indians and whites.

117 Stanford, Alfred B. THE NAVIGATOR. Morrow,
1927. Biography of Nathaniel Bowditch, creator
of "The American Practical Navigator" in Salem in
the 1770's.

118 Stone, Grace Zaring. THE COLD JOURNEY. Morrow,
1934. Story of the 1704 raid on Deerfield, Massachusetts by French and Indians and the long journey
of the captives to Quebec; contrasts life and man-
ners of the French and the Puritans.

119 Stover, Herbert. SONG OF THE SUSQUEHANNA.
Dodd, 1949. Story of a Pennsylvania-German's
battle with Indians during the French and Indian
War; Governeur Morris, John Bartram, and
Conrad Weiser appear in the story.

120 Stowman, Knud. WITH CRADLE AND CLOCK. Harper, 1946. Struggles of a young doctor to estab-
lish an obstetrical practice in New York in 1702;
background of New York social life and customs.

121 Sublette, Clifford. SCARLET COCKEREL. Little,
1925. Historical romance based on the French
Huguenot colonization of the Carolinas in the
1690's.

122 -- THE BRIGHT FACE OF DANGER. Little, 1926.
Life in Henrico County, Virginia in the days of
Bacon's Rebellion; 1676.

123 Swanson, Neil. THE JUDAS TREE. Putnam, 1933.
Pittsburg besieged by the Indians during the Pontiac Conspiracy of 1763.

124 -- THE FIRST REBEL. Farrar, 1937. Story of
the uprising of the Scotch-Irish in Pennsylvania,
led by James Smith, against the British and of
Smith's capture by the Indians; 1763-1767.

125 -- THE SILENT DRUM. Farrar, 1940. Life on the
     Pennsylvania frontier during the pre-Revolutionary
     period.

126 -- THE UNCONQUERED. Doubleday, 1947. Story
     of the Pontiac Conspiracy of 1763 in the Ohio
     River region of the Pennsylvania frontier.

127 Van Every, Dale. BRIDAL JOURNEY. Messner,
     1950. Story of life in the Ohio River valley when
     Indians, English, and Americans were fighting for
     the frontier lands prior to the Revolution.

128 Vaughan, Carter. THE INVINCIBLES. Doubleday,
     1958. Financial scheming and frontier warfare
     during the French and Indian Wars, set in and
     around Boston and in the wilderness on the expedi-
     tion against Louisburg; 1744-1745.

129 -- THE SILVER SABER. Doubleday, 1967. Swash-
     buckling romance of an indentured servant in
     colonial Delaware and in Quebec.

130 -- THE SENECA HOSTAGE. Doubleday, 1969. Life
     and adventures on the American frontier and as
     captive of the Seneca Indians in 1753.

131 White, Ethel. BEAR HIS MILD YOKE. Abingdon,
     1966. Persecution of the Quakers pictured in the
     story of Mary Dyer, a Quaker convert, who was
     hanged in Massachusetts in 1660; social and reli-
     gious customs.

132 Widdemer, Margaret. LADY OF THE MOHAWKS.
     Doubleday, 1951. Story of French and English
     rivalry in the Mohawk Valley; the heroine is
     Molly Brant, who became the wife of Sir William
     Johnson, English Indian Commissioner.

133 -- THE GOLDEN WILDCAT. Doubleday, 1954. His-
     torical romance depicting the struggle between
     British and French for the loyalty of the Mohawks
     and Iroquois Indians in upstate New York in the
     1750's.

134 -- BUCKSKIN BARONET. Doubleday, 1960. Story
     of an English traveler in and around Albany, New

York on the eve of the Revolution; picture of
Indian customs and the political intrigues of the
time.

135 Winwar, Frances. GALLOWS HILL. Holt, 1937.
Story of early times in old Salem, chiefly concerned with the religious frenzy which took
possession of the colony leading to the witchcraft
trials and hangings; Cotton Mather appears.

136 Zara, Louis. BLESSED IS THE LAND. Crown,
1954. Set in the days of Peter Stuyvesant when
the first Jewish settlers came from Brazil to
settle in New Amsterdam; picture of Jewish customs, language, and religion in the colonial period.

THE AMERICAN REVOLUTION

137 Allen, Merritt Parmalee. BATTLE LANTERNS.
Longmans, 1949. Exploits of Francis Marion,
the Swamp Fox, and the war in South Carolina.

138 Bacheller, Irving. IN THE DAYS OF POOR RICH-
ARD. Bobbs, 1922. Shows the work of Franklin in the colonies, in England, and in France;
comprehensive picture of the Revolution.

139 -- MASTER OF CHAOS. Bobbs, 1932. Early days
of the Revolution; George Washington and
others appear.

140 Barker, Shirley. FIRE AND THE HAMMER.
Crown, 1953. Story of Quaker outlaws in
Bucks County, Pennsylvania harrassing the
Revolutionists.

141 -- THE LAST GENTLEMAN. Random, 1960.
Story of the conflicts facing the colonial born
Sir John Wentworth, royal governor of New
Hampshire in 1774; climax comes when he
sends aid to General Gage in Boston in 1775.

142 -- THE ROAD TO BUNKER HILL. Duell, 1962.
Two girls and their grandmother witness events
leading up to the Battle of Bunker Hill.

143 -- STRANGE WIVES. Crown, 1963. Life in the
Jewish settlement at Newport, Rhode Island;
persecution and hardship suffered before George
Washington promised freedom of religion to the
Jews.

144 Barry, Jane. THE CAROLINIANS. Doubleday,
1959. A Loyalist family in South Carolina
becomes involved in the war when they help
one of General Dan Morgan's men; action includes the Battles of Cowpens and King's
Mountain.

145   -- THE LONG MARCH. Appleton, 1955. Portrait
        of General Dan Morgan in the campaign cul-
        minating in the Battle of Cowpens.

146   Beebe, Elswyth Thane. DAWN'S EARLY LIGHT.
        Duell, 1943. The Carolina campaigns of the
        war, and politics and society in Williamsburg;
        1774-1779.

147   Benét, Stephen Vincent. SPANISH BAYONET.
        Doran, 1926. Adventure tale set in New York
        and Spanish Florida at the time of the Revolu-
        tion.

148   Beverley-Giddings, Arthur Raymond. THE RIVAL
        SHORES. Morrow, 1956. Story of an English-
        man sent to the colonies to aid the escape of
        Loyalists from Tidewater Maryland in 1774.

149   Boyce, Burke. THE PERILOUS NIGHT. Viking,
        1942. The war as it affected the prosperous
        Hudson River Valley farmers, with firm con-
        victions of loyalty either to king or to the
        colonies.

150   -- MAN FROM MT. VERNON. Harper, 1961.
        Personal and family life of George Washington
        from his appointment as Commander-in-Chief
        of the Continental army to the surrender of the
        British at Yorktown.

151   Boyd, James. DRUMS. Scribner, 1925. The war
        in the southern colonies; John Paul Jones,
        Generals Dan Morgan and Tarleton appear.

152   Boyd, Thomas Alexander. SHADOW OF THE
        LONG KNIVES. Scribner, 1928. Story of the
        Ohio frontier during the Revolution.

153   Brick, John. THE RAID. Farrar, 1951. The
        Mohawk chief, Joseph Brant, leading his tribe
        in raids against the settlers in upstate New
        York.

154   -- THE RIFLEMAN. Doubleday, 1953. Story of
        Tim Murphy, one of Morgan's riflemen, and of
        his grudge against the Indians; description of the

Battle of Saratoga.

155   -- THE KING'S RANGERS. Doubleday, 1954.
      Story of Butler's Rangers and Loyalists in the
      western Mohawk Valley area of New York.

156   -- STRONG MEN. Doubleday, 1959. Story of a
      company of rangers with Washington at Valley
      Forge in the winter of 1777-1778, and of Baron
      von Steuben's efforts to mold the survivors into
      an effective army.

157   Bristow, Gwen. CELIA GARTH. Crowell, 1959.
      Story of an orphan girl who witnessed the siege
      of Charleston by the British, and became a spy
      for the rebels during the occupation of the city;
      description of the fighting between General
      Tarleton and Francis Marion's raiders.

158   Cannon, LeGrand. LOOK TO THE MOUNTAIN.
      Holt, 1942. Frontier days in New Hampshire
      just before and after the Revolution.

159   Chambers, Robert W. CARDIGAN. Harper, 1901.
      First of a series of novels of frontier life in
      upstate New York, relations with the British
      and the Indians before and during the war, and
      life in New York City during the war; 1774 to
      1782.

160   -- MAID-AT-ARMS. Harper, 1902. Part of the
      author's New York series. See above.

161   -- HIDDEN CHILDREN. Appleton, 1914. One of
      the author's New York novels. See above.

162   -- LITTLE RED FOOT. Doran, 1921. Indian
      warfare in northeastern New York; 1774-1782.

163   -- THE PAINTED MINX. Appleton, 1930. Life in
      New York City during the war; 1777-1781. See
      "Cardigan" above.

164   Chapman, Maristan (pseud.). ROGUE'S MARCH.
      Lippincott, 1949. Skirmishing in western
      Carolina and Tennessee culminating in the
      Battle of King's Mountain in 1780.

165   Chidsey, Donald Barr. THE EDGE OF PIRACY.
       Crown, 1964. New England sea captain, em-
       pressed into service aboard a British man-of-
       war, escapes and takes up smuggling in the
       West Indies.

166   Churchill, Winston. RICHARD CARVEL. Mac-
       millan, 1899. Set in Maryland and London be-
       fore and during the Revolution. Hero fights
       with John Paul Jones in the battle between the
       "Bonhomme Richard" and the "Serapis."

167   -- THE CROSSING. Macmillan, 1904. Life on the
       Kentucky frontier during the Revolution; George
       Rogers Clark's expedition against Vincennes and
       Kaskaskia; life in early Louisville; and a pic-
       ture of New Orleans during an epidemic.

168   Coatsworth, Elizabeth. A TOAST TO THE KING.
       Coward, 1940. Boston at the time of the Bos-
       ton Tea Party, seen from the Loyalists' view-
       point.

169   Cooper, James Fenimore. THE SPY. Dodd, 1821.
       Story of conflicting loyalties in New York City
       and the Hudson valley.

170   -- THE PILOT. Dodd, 1824. Story of John Paul
       Jones and naval warfare during the Revolution.

171   -- THE RED ROVER. Putnam, 1827. An adven-
       ture story of a former pirate fighting for his
       country during the Revolution.

172   Cormack, Maribelle, and William P. Alexander.
       LAND FOR MY SONS. Appleton, 1939. A
       surveyor and wilderness scout on the Pennsyl-
       vania frontier sees action as a member of the
       local militia when war breaks out.

173   Davis, Burke. THE RAGGED ONES. Rinehart,
       1951. Southern campaign of 1781 with Generals
       Morgan and Nathanael Greene engaging the
       forces under Cornwallis.

174   -- YORKTOWN. Rinehart, 1952. Portrait of Wash-
       ington, Lafayette, Clinton, and Cornwallis in the

campaign leading up to Cornwallis' surrender
at Yorktown.

175   Davis, William Stearns.   GILMAN OF REDFORD.
Macmillan, 1927.   Story of Boston and Harvard College on the eve of the Revolution,
1770-1775; pictures life and customs in town
and country, and revolves around famous men
and events of the period; Paul Revere,
Samuel Adams, and others appear.

176   Decker, Malcolm.   THE REBEL AND THE TURN-
COAT.   McGraw, 1949.   A young colonist
torn between loyalty to the British and the
American cause chooses sides with the help
of Nathan Hale.

177   Dodge, Constance.   DARK STRANGER.   Penn,
1940.   Son of Scotch settlers fights under
John Paul Jones on the "Bon Homme Richard. "

178   Eaton, Evelyn.   GIVE ME YOUR GOLDEN HAND.
Farrar, 1951.   Eighteenth century England
and America; events leading up to the Revolution are seen through the eyes of the hero
who comes to the colonies as a bonded ser-
vant during the Revolution.

179   Edmonds, Walter D.   DRUMS ALONG THE MOHAWK.
Little, 1936.   Effects of the Revolution on the
farmers of the Mohawk Valley in upstate New
York; 1776-1784.

180   -- WILDERNESS CLEARING.   Dodd, 1944.   Story
of conflict and divided loyalties in the Mohawk
Valley in 1777.

181   -- IN THE HANDS OF THE SENECAS.   Little,
1947.   Indian warfare on the frontier in 1778;
story of the captivity of a group of children
held by the Senecas.

182   Ellsberg, Edward.   CAPTAIN PAUL.   Dodd, 1941.
John Paul Jones from his days as a privateer
to the engagement with the "Serapis. "

183   Erskine, John.   GIVE ME LIBERTY.   Stokes, 1940.

Patrick Henry, George Washington, and Thomas Jefferson appear in a story of a young Virginian from 1759 to the outbreak of the Revolution.

184   Fast, Howard. CONCEIVED IN LIBERTY. Simon and Schuster, 1939. Alexander Hamilton, von Stueben, Valley Forge; picture of the contrast between the ragged soldiers and the wealthy aristocrats in the Continental army.

185   -- THE UNVANQUISHED. Duell, 1942. Portrays Washington, Knox, Putnam, Greene, and Hamilton and their part in the fight for freedom from the retreat from Brooklyn to the crossing of the Delaware and the Battle of Trenton.

186   -- CITIZEN TOM PAINE. Duell, 1943. Portrait of Tom Paine as a rabble-rouser.

187   -- THE PROUD AND THE FREE. Little, 1950. Based on a revolt in the Continental army against injustices by the officers of the Pennsylvania militia.

188   -- APRIL MORNING. Crown, 1961. Experiences of a 15 year old farm boy in the Battles of Lexington and Concord; April, 1775.

189   Fletcher, Inglis. RALEIGH'S EDEN. Bobbs, 1940. Life in North Carolina from 1765 to 1782; one of the author's series on the history of North Carolina ("Colonial America" and "The Young Nation").

190   -- TOIL OF THE BRAVE. Bobbs, 1946. The Albemarle district of North Carolina in the last years of the war, 1779-1780.

191   -- THE SCOTSWOMAN. Bobbs, 1954. Flora McDonald, who rescued Bonnie Prince Charlie after the Battle of Culleden, settles in the Carolinas and becomes involved in the American Revolution.

192   Flood, Charles Bracelen. MONMOUTH. Houghton, 1961. Story of events leading up to the Battle of Monmouth; some characters are George

Washington, Alexander Hamilton, and Generals
Howe, Pulaski, and Lafayette.

193   Forbes, Esther. THE GENERAL'S LADY. Har-
       court, 1938. Girl of a New England Tory
       family marries a rebel general to save her
       family's fortune, then falls in love with a
       British officer.

194   -- JOHNNY TREMAIN. Houghton, 1943. Boston
       at the beginning of the Revolution; the Boston
       Tea Party, the Battle of Lexington; young hero
       is a courier for the rebel Committee of Public
       Safety.

195   Ford, Paul Leicester. JANICE MEREDITH. Dodd,
       1899. Beginning in New Jersey in 1774, this
       spans the years of the Revolution and includes
       a picture of the character of George Washington.

196   Fox, John. ERSKINE DALE, PIONEER. Scribner,
       1920. Life on the Virginia and Kentucky fron-
       tier at the time of the Revolution.

197   Frye, Pearl. GALLANT CAPTAIN. Little, 1956.
       Story of John Paul Jones, from his days as an
       obscure British ship commander to the hero of
       the American navy; authentic picture of the
       times.

198   Gerson, Noel B. I'LL STORM HELL. Doubleday,
       1967. Life and career of General "Mad An-
       thony" Wayne.

199   -- THE SWAMP FOX. Doubleday, 1967. Life of
       Francis Marion, the Swamp Fox, fighting the
       Cherokee Indians and leading his guerrilla band
       in the battle for the Carolinas; scenes in
       Charleston, Boston, and Philadelphia.

200   Gessner, Robert. TREASON. Scribner, 1944.
       Fictional biography of Benedict Arnold.

201   Giles, Janice Holt. THE KENTUCKIANS. Hough-
       ton, 1953. Story of pioneer Kentucky when the
       Transylvania Company was agitating for separate
       statehood; 1769-1777.

202   Gordon, Charles William. THE REBEL LOYALIST.
        Dodd, 1935. Story of a Loyalist who fought on
        the side of the British in the war, and after-
        ward took his bride to Canada.

203   Graves, Robert. SERGEANT LAMB'S AMERICA.
        Random, 1940. Experiences of an English sol-
        dier in the early years of the war.

204   -- PROCEED, SERGEANT LAMB. Random, 1941.
        English soldier's experiences as a prisoner,
        his escape, service under Cornwallis, and the
        surrender at Yorktown. Sequel to "Sergeant
        Lamb's America. "

205   Gray, Elizabeth Janet. MEGGY MacINTOSH.
        Doubleday, 1930. Story of a young Scotch
        girl who joins Flora MacDonald in North Caro-
        lina in 1775.

206   -- THE VIRGINIA EXILES. Lippincott, 1955. Story
        of the exile of a group of Philadelphia Quakers
        to Virginia when they refuse to sign a loyalty
        oath.

207   Grey, Zane. BETTY ZANE. Grosset, 1903. Tale
        of hardships of life beyond the Allegheny Moun-
        tains on the Virginia frontier; fights with the
        Indians and the destruction of the settlement
        during the Revolution.

208   Haines, Edwin. THE EXQUISITE SIREN. Lippin-
        cott, 1938. Historical novel about Peggy Ship-
        pen, Tory wife of Benedict Arnold, and her
        relations with Major André.

209   Haislip, Harvey. SAILOR NAMED JONES. Double-
        day, 1957. Story of John Paul Jones and of
        his financial difficulties and lack of support
        from the government; vivid re-creation of naval
        warfare, culminating in the battle of the "Bon
        Homme Richard" and the "Serapis. "

210   -- THE PRIZE MASTER. Doubleday, 1959. Story
        of sea warfare during the Revolution through
        the adventures of a young seaman introduced in
        "Sailor Named Jones" (above).

211   -- SEA ROAD TO YORKTOWN.   Doubleday, 1960.
       Further adventures of the hero of "The Prize
       Master" (above) as a privateer and on duty
       with the fleet of Admiral de Grasse in Chesa-
       peake Bay blocking Cornwallis' escape from
       Yorktown.

212   Harris, Cyril.   TRUMPET AT DAWN.   Scribner,
       1938.   New York social life and politics,
       1776-1783.

213   -- RICHARD PRYNE.   Scribner, 1941.   Story of a
       spy for General Washington in and around
       New York City.

214   Henri, Florette.   KINGS MOUNTAIN.   Doubleday,
       1950.   Story of the war in the southern
       colonies; Battle of King's Mountain, South
       Carolina in 1780.

215   Hopkins, Joseph G. E.   PATRIOT'S PROGRESS.
       Scribner, 1961.   A Harvard educated physician
       in a rural Massachusetts village is won over to
       the rebel cause while serving as a surgeon for
       the Continental militia at Lexington, Concord,
       and the seige of Boston.

216   -- RETREAT AND RECALL.   Scribner, 1966.
       Story of an American surgeon who is captured
       by the British, escapes from prison and be-
       comes a secret agent operating in New York.
       Sequel to "Patriot's Progress. "

217   Horan, James David.   THE KING'S REBEL.   Crown,
       1953.   Story of a British officer sent to study
       the Indians; captured by the backwoodsmen, he
       comes to know them and joins their cause.

218   Horne, Howard.   CONCORD BRIDGE.   Bobbs, 1952.
       Story of the events preceding the Battles of
       Lexington and Concord; sympathetic portrait of
       General Gage, commander of the English forces
       at Boston.

219   Hough, Frank Olney.   RENOWN.   Lippincott, 1938.
       Sympathetic account of Benedict Arnold, showing
       him as a brilliant, extravagant, and frustrated
       man of action.

man of action.

220   -- IF NOT VICTORY. Lippincott, 1939. The war
       from the viewpoint of the common man; setting
       is the Hudson River valley of New York.

221   -- THE NEUTRAL GROUND. Lippincott, 1941.
       The effects of the war on the neutral West-
       chester County region of New York.

222   Jahoda, Gloria. DELILAH'S MOUNTAIN. Hough-
       ton, 1963. Light romance set on the Tennessee
       frontier in the Clinch River valley where the
       settlers suffer from British and Indian raids
       and the heroine is captured by the Cherokees.

223   Jennings, John. THE SHADOW AND THE GLORY.
       Reynal, 1943. Centers around the campaigns
       leading up to the Battle of Bennington, 1774-
       1777.

224   -- THE SEA EAGLES. Doubleday, 1950. Story of
       the young American navy and its part in the
       war.

225   Johnston, Mary. HUNTING SHIRT. Little, 1931.
       Life in a Cherokee Indian village in the Vir-
       ginia wilderness, 1775-1780.

226   Karig, Walter and Horace Bird. DON'T TREAD ON
       ME. Rinehart, 1954. Exploits of Commodore
       John Paul Jones; picture of early American
       politics, naval warfare, and social life.

227   Kelly, Eric. THREE SIDES OF AGIOCHOOK.
       Macmillan, 1935. Life on the New England
       frontier in 1775.

228   Lancaster, Bruce. GUNS OF BURGOYNE. Stokes,
       1939. Story of the defeat of Burgoyne at the
       Battle of Saratoga from the viewpoint of a
       Hessian officer.

229   -- TRUMPET TO ARMS. Little, 1944. Story of
       local militia companies in the campaigns of the
       war up to the Battle of Trenton.

230   -- THE PHANTOM FORTRESS. Little, 1950.
      Story of the guerrilla warfare of Francis Marion,
      the Swamp Fox, in the Carolinas.

231   -- THE SECRET ROAD. Little, 1952. Story of
      the part Washington's secret service played in
      exposing Benedict Arnold's treason and in the
      capture of Major André; picture of wartime
      life in New York City under British occupation.

232   -- THE BLIND JOURNEY. Little, 1953. Benjamin
      Franklin sends money and supplies from France
      by a courier who lands near Yorktown in time
      for the campaign against Cornwallis.

233   -- THE BIG KNIVES. Little, 1964. Lancaster's
      last novel follows a member of George Rogers
      Clark's expedition against the Indians and the
      British culminating in the capture of Vincennes.

234   Leland, John Adams. OTHNEIL JONES. Lippincott,
      1956. The war in the Carolinas as seen by a
      member of Francis Marion's raiders.

235   Linington, Elizabeth. THE LONG WATCH. Viking,
      1956. Story of two colonial newspaper editors
      and of their struggle to keep their newspapers
      operating during the war; picture of life in
      New York City in the 1770's before the war
      and during the British occupation.

236   Longstreet, Stephen. EAGLES WHERE I WALK.
      Doubleday, 1961. Story of Dutch land-owning
      families in New York during the war; a young
      surgeon in Washington's army sees much of
      the war in New York state; ends with Benedict
      Arnold's treachery and the capture and execu-
      tion of Major André. Sequel to "War in the
      Golden Weather" (Colonial).

237   -- A FEW PAINTED FEATHERS. Doubleday, 1963.
      The war in the South through Yorktown to
      Washington's resignation from the Continental
      Army. One of the main characters is Oxford
      educated Peter Blue Feather, adopted son of
      Thomas Jefferson, who serves as a spy for the
      Americans. Sequel to "Eagles Where I Walk."

238   Lynde, Francis. MR. ARNOLD. Bobbs, 1923.
        Story of Benedict Arnold centering around an
        attempt to kidnap Arnold and bring him back
        for trial after his escape.

239   Mason, F. Van Wyck. THREE HARBORS. Lippin-
        cott, 1938. First in the author's series on the
        role of the American navy in the war; setting
        is Norfolk and Boston; 1774-1775.

240   -- STARS ON THE SEA. Lippincott, 1940. Pic-
        ture of the war in Rhode Island, Charleston,
        and the Bahamas; 1776-1777.

241   -- RIVERS OF GLORY. Lippincott, 1942. Story
        centering around the seige of the British forces
        in Savannah;   1778-1779.

242   -- EAGLE IN THE SKY. Lippincott, 1948. The
        role of the navy in the final campaign at York-
        town; 1780-1781.

243   -- WILD HORIZON. Little, 1966. Story of life on
        the Tennessee frontier; pictures hardships of
        pioneer life, Indian raids, raids by the English
        under Col. Banastre Tarleton, and events
        leading to the American victory at the Battle
        of King's Mountain in 1780.

244   Melville, Herman. ISRAEL POTTER. Putnam,
        1855. Based on the life of a Revolutionary War
        hero who fought at Bunker Hill, served as
        messenger to Benjamin Franklin, and served
        under John Paul Jones in the battle of the
        "Bon Homme Richard" and the "Serapis. "

245   Mercer, Charles. ENOUGH GOOD MEN. Putnam,
        1960. Picture of the political background of
        the war, and of social life in Philadelphia.

246   Miller, Helen Topping. THE SOUND OF CHARIOTS.
        Bobbs, 1947. A Loyalist family flees from
        Augusta, Georgia to John Sevier's state of
        Franklin on the frontier after the Battle of
        King's Mountain.

247   -- SLOW DIES THE THUNDER. Bobbs, 1955.

Romance set against a background of the war
in South Carolina in 1780; the bombardment of
Charleston, Francis Marion's guerrilla warfare,
and the Battle of King's Mountain.

248   -- CHRISTMAS AT MOUNT VERNON. Longmans,
1957.   Short novel picturing the homecoming
and Christmas celebration of George and
Martha Washington at Mount Vernon in December, 1783.

249   Minnegerode, Meade. THE BLACK FOREST.
Farrar, 1937.   Story of life in the Northwest
Territory from 1754 through the Revolution.

250   Mitchell, S. Weir. HUGH WYNNE, FREE QUAKER.
Century, 1897.   Life in Philadelphia during the
war; hero serves as a spy for Washington and
Lafayette.

251   Nutt, Frances. THREE FIELDS TO CROSS.
Stephen-Paul, 1947.   Spy story set in Staten
Island, New York.

252   Page, Elizabeth. TREE OF LIBERTY. Farrar,
1939.   A panorama of national events from
1754 to 1806.

253   Patterson, Emma. MIDNIGHT PATRIOT. Longmans, 1949.   Heroic activities of a young colonist in the early days of the Revolution.

254   Pridgen, Tim. TORY OATH. Doubleday, 1941.
Highland Scots of the Carolinas take the King's
side in the Revolution.

255   Raddall, Thomas. HIS MAJESTY'S YANKEES.
Winston, 1943.   New Englanders living in
Nova Scotia at the outbreak of the Revolution
are torn between allegiance to the Crown and
to the cause of the colonies.

256   Ripley, Clements. CLEAR FOR ACTION. Appleton, 1940.   John Paul Jones and the "Bon
Homme Richard. "

257   Roberts, Kenneth L. ARUNDEL. Doubleday, 1930.

Setting is Arundel, Maine; describes Benedict Arnold's expedition against Quebec.

258   -- RABBLE IN ARMS. Doubleday, 1933. Story of the campaign leading up to the Battle of Saratoga; hero is Benedict Arnold; villain is Continental Congress.

259   -- OLIVER WISWELL. Doubleday, 1940. Presents the Loyalists' side of the war.

260   Sabatini, Rafael. THE CAROLINIAN. Houghton, 1925. Historical romance set in South Carolina during the war.

261   Safford, Henry B. THAT BENNINGTON MOB. Messner, 1935. Story of the settlers in the New Hampshire grants, their relations with the Indians, and the actions leading to the Battle of Bennington in 1777.

262   Schoonover, Lawrence. THE REVOLUTIONARY. Little, 1958. Biographical novel of John Paul Jones, from boyhood in Scotland, through the Revolution, service in Russia under Catherine the Great, to his death in Paris in 1792.

263   Seifert, Shirley. WATERS OF THE WILDERNESS. Lippincott, 1941. Story of George Rogers Clark's expeditions in the Ohio wilderness and life in Spanish St. Louis; 1778-1780.

264   -- LET MY NAME STAND FAIR. Lippincott, 1956. Light romance of the Revolution in which General Nathanael Greene, Light-Horse Harry Lee, Anthony Wayne, Alexander Hamilton, and George Washington appear.

265   Simons, Katherine. THE RED DOE. Appleton, 1953. Exploits of Francis Marion, the Swamp Fox.

266   Sinclair, Harold. WESTWARD THE TIDE. Doubleday, 1940. The war on the frontier; action centers around Fort Pitt and George Rogers Clark's expedition against Vincennes.

267   Singmaster, Elsie. RIFLES FOR WASHINGTON.
       Houghton, 1938. Story of a young colonist who
       joins Washington's ragged army.

268   Slaughter, Frank. FLIGHT FROM NATCHEZ.
       Doubleday, 1955. Describes the flight of a
       group of Loyalists from Natchez in 1781.

269   Spicer, Bart. BROTHER TO THE ENEMY. Dodd,
       1958. Based on the attempt of Light-Horse
       Harry Lee's sergeant-major, John Champe, to
       capture Benedict Arnold by slipping into British
       occupied New York.

270   Stackpole, Edouard A. NANTUCKET REBEL.
       Washburn, 1963. A neutral Quaker joins the
       colonial cause and becomes a successful pri-
       vateer.

271   Stanley, Edward. THOMAS FORTY. Duell, 1947.
       Follows the career of a neutral Westchester
       County journeyman-printer through the war.

272   Sterne, Emma Gelders. DRUMS OF THE MON-
       MOUTH. Dodd, 1935. Set in New Jersey and
       New York. Shows the part played by the
       Huguenots and Quakers in the war; central
       character is Philip Freneau.

273   Stone, Irving. THOSE WHO LOVE. Doubleday,
       1965. Biographical novel of courtship and
       marriage of Abigail and John Adams.

274   Swanson, Neil. THE FORBIDDEN GROUND.
       Farrar, 1938. Detroit fur trade at the time of
       the Revolution.

275   Taylor, David. LIGHTS ACROSS THE DELAWARE.
       Lippincott, 1954. Story of a spirited farm girl
       torn between her devotion to the American
       cause and her pacifist Quaker lover; centers
       around Washington's campaign against Trenton;
       1776-1777.

276   -- FAREWELL TO VALLEY FORGE. Lippincott,
       1955. General Charles Lee's plot to betray
       the colonial forces; the British evacuation of

Philadelphia; and the Battle of Monmouth.

277   -- SYCAMORE MEN. Lippincott, 1958. The war
        in South Carolina in 1880-1881; Francis Marion,
        the Swamp Fox, fights Cornwallis and Tarleton
        at the Battles of Camden, King's Mountain, and
        Eutaw Springs.

278   -- STORM THE LAST RAMPART. Lippincott,
        1960. Adventures of a colonial agent spying
        on the British in Tarrytown, New York from
        the time of Arnold's treason to the surrender
        of Cornwallis at Yorktown; 1780-1781.

279   Thompson, Maurice. ALICE OF OLD VINCENNES.
        Bobbs, 1900. Indian warfare and pioneer life
        in the northwest territory in and around Vin-
        cennes in 1778.

280   Turnbull, Agnes. THE DAY MUST DAWN. Mac-
        millan, 1942. Western Pennsylvania and fron-
        tier warfare in the days of the Revolution.

281   Vail, Philip (pseud.). THE TWISTED SABRE.
        Dodd, 1963. Story of Benedict Arnold from his
        youth to his retirement; focuses on the mili-
        tary genius of his campaigns at Ticonderoga,
        Quebec, and Saratoga.

282   Van de Water, Frederick. THE RELUCTANT
        REBEL. Duell, 1948. Story of Ethan Allen
        and the Green Mountain boys of New Hamp-
        shire; the Battle of Ticonderoga; fight over
        reapportionment of the New Hampshire grants.

283   -- CATCH A FALLING STAR. Duell, 1949. Ver-
        mont in 1780; story of conflict and divided
        loyalties.

284   -- WINGS OF THE MORNING. Washburn, 1956.
        Story of the struggle for independence and
        unity in Vermont; 1774-1791; picture of the
        political issues involved.

285   -- DAY OF BATTLE. Washburn, 1958. Story of
        the rebel forces in Vermont from the Battle
        of Ticonderoga to the Battle of Bennington; 1777.

286   Vaughan, Carter (pseud). SCOUNDREL'S BRIGADE.
       Doubleday, 1962. A former indentured servant
       becomes a spy to uncover a plot to undermine
       the colonial currency with counterfeit paper
       money.

287   -- THE YANKEE RASCALS. Doubleday, 1963.
       Tale of espionage and intrigue in the Revolu-
       tionary War.

288   -- DRAGON COVE. Doubleday, 1964. Romantic
       novel of action centering around Newport,
       Rhode Island during the war.

289   Wallace, Willard M. EAST TO BAGADUCE. Reg-
       nery, 1963. Based on a little known episode,
       the seige of Bagaduce (now Castine), Maine,
       in 1779.

290   Wheelwright, Jere. KENTUCKY STAND. Scribner,
       1951. A Baltimore boy on the Kentucky frontier,
       1777, involved in politics and frontier warfare.
       Daniel Boone, Simon Kenton, and Thomas Jeffer-
       son appear.

291   Williams, Ben Ames. COME SPRING. Houghton,
       1940. Life in a remote Maine settlement
       during the Revolution.

292   Wyckoff, Nicholas E. THE BRAINTREE MISSION.
       Macmillan, 1957. Based on the idea that
       England hoped to offer a title and a seat in
       Parliament to six colonial leaders to placate
       the colonies; this is the story of the offer
       made to John Adams.

293   Adams, Samuel Hopkins.   THE GORGEOUS HUSSY.
       Houghton, 1934.   Washington social and politi-
       cal life from 1812 to the Civil War; story of
       Peggy Eaton, protege of Andrew Jackson.

294   -- CANAL TOWN. Random, 1944.   Struggles of a
       young physician fighting ignorance and super-
       stition in New York state in the 1820's; medi-
       cal lore and customs of the times.

295   -- BANNER BY THE WAYSIDE. Random, 1947.
       A group of itinerant players tour the Erie
       Canal country of New York in the 1830's.

296   -- SUNRISE TO SUNSET. Random, 1950. Early
       days in the shirt-making industry in Troy,
       New York in the 1830's; centers around the
       struggle for better working conditions.

297   Allis, Marguerite.   THE SPLENDOR STAYS.   Put-
       nam, 1942.   Social and political developments
       during the first decades of the nineteenth cen-
       tury; birth of the Monroe Doctrine; Isaac Hull,
       Simon Bolivar, and others appear; setting is
       Boston and New York.

298   -- ALL IN GOOD TIME.   Putnam, 1944.   Begin-
       nings of American industry at the turn of the
       century; a Connecticut clockmaker initiates the
       first steps toward mass production, and faces
       the hard times of the Embargo Act of 1807.

299   -- CHARITY STRONG.   Putnam, 1945.   Picture of
       the New York musical world in the 1830's.

300   -- WATER OVER THE DAM.   Putnam, 1947.
       Story of the fight for the Farmington Canal
       project in Connecticut in the 1820's.

301   -- THE LAW OF THE LAND.   Putnam, 1948.

Story of the prejudice against public performers
in early nineteenth century New England.

302   Bacheller, Irving.   LIGHT IN THE CLEARING.
       Bobbs, 1917.   Career of Silas Wright,
       governor of New York; 1840's and 1850's.

303   Bosworth, Allan R.   STORM TIDE.   Harper, 1965.
       An adventure tale of New England whaling ships
       at the turn of the century.

304   Breslin, Howard.   TAMARACK TREE.   McGraw,
       1947.   Story of the effects of a political con-
       vention on a small New England town, Stratton,
       Vermont, in 1840.   William Henry Harrison
       and Daniel Webster appear.

305   -- SHAD RUN.   Crowell, 1955.   Life of the shad
       fishermen in the Hudson River valley near
       Poughkeepsie at the time New York ratified
       the Constitution in 1788.

306   Caldwell, Janet Taylor.   THE WIDE HOUSE.
       Scribner, 1945.   Family story set against a
       background of social and political developments
       in a small New York town torn by the conflicts
       of the "Know-Nothing" party in the 1850's.

307   Carmer, Carl.   GENESEE FEVER.   Farrar, 1941.
       Background of fairs, horse racing, and political
       conflict when the Scotch-Irish in the Genesee
       Valley of New York rebelled against Hamilton's
       excise law; Colonel Williamson, with Robert
       Morris and Aaron Burr, planned to establish
       landed estates in the valley.

308   Carr, John Dickson.   PAPA LA-BAS.   Harper,
       1968.   A mystery story set in New Orleans in
       1858, involving Judah P. Benjamin, the Bri-
       tish Consul, and some French voodoo.

309   Carse, Robert.   GREAT CIRCLE.   Scribner,
       1956.   Story of a whaling voyage out of
       Salem in the 1840's.

310   Case, Josephine.   WRITTEN IN SAND.   Houghton,
       1945.   Story of the Tripolitan War, 1801-1805;

centering around General Eaton's campaigns in
Africa.

311   Chapman, Maristan (pseud). TENNESSEE HAZARD.
       Lippincott, 1953. Tennessee frontier in 1788
       in a story of the effort to ratify the Constitu-
       tion and of General Wilkinson's conspiracy to
       turn the frontier lands over to the Spanish
       in Louisianna.

312   Chase, Mary Ellen. SILAS CROCKETT. Macmil-
       lan, 1935. Chronicle of a Maine seafaring
       family as steam begins to replace sail, and the
       New England shipbuilding industry declines.

313   Coatsworth, Elizabeth. HERE I STAY. Coward,
       1938. Story of Maine in 1817, and the begin-
       ning of the rush to the Ohio wilderness.

314   Cochran, Louis. THE FOOL OF GOD. Duell,
       1958. Fictional biography of the life and times
       of Alexander Campbell, founder of the Disci-
       ples of Christ, president of Bethany College,
       and friend of John Brown, Henry Clay, James
       Madison, and Thomas Jefferson.

315   Coffin, Robert Peter Tristram. JOHN DAWN.
       Macmillan, 1936. Maine during the shipbuilding
       era following the Revolution.

316   Colver, Anne. LISTEN FOR THE VOICES. Farrar,
       1939. Concord during the years 1848 to 1851;
       picture of small town life and literary activity;
       Thoreau, Emerson, and the Alcotts mingle
       with the characters.

317   Cowdrey, A. E. ELIXIR OF LIFE. Doubleday,
       1965. Story of a patent medicine hawker who
       develops a remedy for the yellow fever during
       the epidemic in New Orleans in 1850.

318   Crabb, Alfred Leland. HOME TO THE HERMITAGE.
       Bobbs, 1948. Story of Andrew and Rachel
       Jackson, from his return from the War of 1812
       to the time he leaves for Washington and the
       Presidency.

319   -- HOME TO KENTUCKY. Bobbs, 1953. Fic-
       tional biography of Henry Clay.

320   David, Evan John. AS RUNS THE GLASS. Har-
       per, 1943. Story of a Maine seafaring family
       at the time of the French revolution.

321   Davidson, Louis B. and Edward J. Doherty.
       CAPTAIN MAROONER. Crowell, 1952.
       Based on an actual mutiny on the whaler
       "Globe" out of Nantucket in 1822.

322   Davis, Dorothy. MEN OF NO PROPERTY. Scrib-
       ner, 1956. Irish immigrants in conflict with
       the "Know-Nothing" faction in New York City
       in the 1850's.

323   Degenhard, William. THE REGULATORS. Dial,
       1943. Story of Shays' Rebellion in Massachu-
       setts.

324   Dolbier, Maurice. BENJY BOONE. Dial, 1967.
       Life among a traveling theatrical troupe in the
       early 1800's with scenes in New England,
       Philadelphia, and in the frontier country.

325   Edmonds, Walter D. YOUNG AMES. Little, 1942.
       Social, political, and economic life in New York
       City in the 1830's.

326   Ehle, John. THE ROAD. Harper, 1967. Story
       of the first railroad construction in the North
       Carolina mountains in the 1870's; characters
       are descendants of "The Land Breakers"
       (Frontier-Southern).

327   Falkner, Leonard. PAINTED LADY. Dutton,
       1962. Story of Eliza Jumel, wife of Aaron
       Burr, against a background of social life in
       New York and Paris in the early 1800's.

328   Field, Rachel. ALL THIS AND HEAVEN TOO.
       Macmillan, 1938. Novel of the American
       literary scene in the 1850's. Harriet Beecher
       Stowe, Samuel Morse, William Cullen Bryant,
       and others appear.

329   Fletcher, Inglis. THE QUEEN'S GIFT. Bobbs,
        1952. Albemarle County, North Carolina in
        1788. Story of the debates about the ratifica-
        tion of the Constitution.

330   Forbes, Esther. THE RUNNING OF THE TIDE.
        Houghton, 1948. Novel of Salem's great
        ship building days and the beginning of its
        decline.

331   -- RAINBOW ON THE ROAD. Houghton, 1954.
        Story of an itinerant portrait painter in New
        England in the 1830's.

332   Gerson, Noel B. OLD HICKORY. Doubleday,
        1964. Biographical novel of the life and
        career of Andrew Jackson.

333   -- THE SLENDER REED. Doubleday, 1965.
        Biographical novel of James K. Polk, 11th
        president of the U.S.; covers the period of
        The Mexican War, the annexation of Texas,
        and the Oregon boundary dispute. Martin Van
        Buren, Daniel Webster, and John Tyler appear.

334   Grebenc, Lucile. THE TIME OF CHANGE. Dou-
        bleday, 1938. Customs and daily life of a
        Connecticut family in the years following 1812.

335   Hackney, Louise. WING OF FAME. Appleton,
        1934. Fictional biography of the founder of
        the Smithsonian Institution. Historical charac-
        ters are Smithson, Franklin, Blake, Cavendish,
        and Lavoisier.

336   Hawthorne, Nathaniel. THE BLITHEDALE RO-
        MANCE. Dutton, 1852. Story of George Rip-
        ley's Brook Farm socialistic experiment in
        1841; associated with the venture were Emerson,
        Hawthorne, Margaret Fuller, and other Trans-
        cendentalists.

337   Hergesheimer, Joseph. JAVA HEAD. Knopf, 1919.
        Story of a Salem shipowning family in the 1840's.

338   -- BALISAND. Knopf, 1924. Political developments
        in Virginia from Washington's second inaugura-

tion to Jefferson's election.

339   Hough, Henry Beetle. THE NEW ENGLAND STORY.
        Random, 1958. Three generations of a New
        England whaling family in the 1800's.

340   Hulme, Kathryn. ANNIE'S CAPTAIN. Little,
        1961. Story of the long happy marriage of the
        author's grandparents as a background for the
        description of the progress from sail to steam
        in the 1800's.

341   Idell, Albert. ROGER'S FOLLY. Doubleday, 1957.
        New Jersey, 1844; picture of social and eco-
        nomic life in the period when steam was re-
        placing sail and the railroad empires were being
        formed. Followed by "Centennial Summer"
        (Nation Grows Up).

342   James, Henry. WASHINGTON SQUARE. Modern
        Library, 1881. Social life in New York City
        in the early 1800's.

343   Jennings, John. SALEM FRIGATE. Doubleday,
        1946. Adventurous sea story of the early
        years of the young nation; action centers around
        the African coast during the Tripolitan War.

344   -- BANNERS AGAINST THE WIND. Little, 1954.
        Biographical novel of Dr. Samuel Gridley Howe,
        his interest in the struggle for Greek indepen-
        dence, founding a school for the blind, and
        marriage to Julia Ward.

345   Kane, Harnett. NEW ORLEANS WOMAN. Double-
        day, 1946. Biographical novel of Myra Clark
        Gaines and a picture of the New Orleans scene.

346   -- THE AMAZING MRS. BONAPARTE. Doubleday,
        1963. Story based on the life of Betsy Patter-
        son, Jerome Bonaparte's Baltimore-born wife;
        setting in America and Europe.

347   Kelland, Clarence Buddington. HARD MONEY.
        Harper, 1930. Son of a Dutch peddler becomes
        one of the financial leaders in New York. First
        in the author's series on the economic develop-

ment of the United States (Civil War and The
Nation Grows Up).

348   Kennedy, Lucy. MR. AUDUBON'S LUCY. Crown,
       1957. Story of Lucy Bakewell Audubon and of
       her life with the naturalist, painter, John James
       Audubon.

349   Laing, Alexander. JONATHAN EAGLE. Duel,
       1955. Picture of American politics from 1786
       to 1801; banking policies of Hamilton, reaction
       to the Alien and Sedition Laws, and the elec-
       tion of Jefferson.

350   -- MATHEW EARLY. Duell, 1957. Story of New
       England and the slave trade; heroine is active
       in a move to abolish slavery.

351   LeMay, Alan. PELICAN COAST. Doubleday, 1929.
       New Orleans with its varied characters and the
       contrast of sea, town, and river life in the
       early 1800's.

352   Longstreet, Stephen. A MAST TO SPEAR THE
       STARS. Doubleday, 1967. Story of ship
       building days in Nantucket, and sailing in the
       China trade.

353   McKee, Ruth Eleanor. THE LORD'S ANOINTED.
       Doubleday, 1934. Story of the missionaries
       from Boston who sailed to Hawaii in 1820.

354   Malm, Dorothea. THE WOMAN QUESTION.
       Appleton, 1958. Amusing novel of the woman's
       rights movement culminating in a woman's
       rights convention in New York in 1853. Lu-
       cretia Mott, Lucy Stone, and others appear.

355   Mason, F. Van Wyck. HARPOON IN EDEN.
       Doubleday, 1969. A seafaring tale of whaling
       ships out of Nantucket in the 1830's, involving
       adventures in Mexico and New Zealand.

356   Miller, Heather Ross. GONE A HUNDRED MILES.
       Harcourt, 1968. Story of a German doctor who
       settles in rural North Carolina and raises his
       only daughter alone after his wife dies.

357   Minnigerode, Meade. COCKADES. Putnam,
              1927. New York and New Orleans at the
              time of the French Revolution; story of the
              Dauphin's supposed escape to America.

358   Morrow, Honoré. BLACK DANIEL. Morrow,
              1931. Romance of Daniel Webster and Caro-
              line LeRoy and of her influence on his career.

359   Muir, Robert. THE SPRIG OF HEMLOCK. Long-
              mans, 1957. Story of Shays' Rebellion in
              Massachusetts in 1786-1787, when Daniel
              Shays led an uprising against high land taxes
              and debtors prisons.

360   Murphy, Edward. ANGEL OF THE DELTA. Hano-
              ver, 1958. Based on the life of Margaret
              Haughery, who worked to establish a home
              for orphan children in New Orleans; follows
              her struggles during the Union occupation
              after the Civil War.

361   O'Neal, Cothburn. THE VERY YOUNG MRS. POE
              Crown, 1956. Based on the life of Virginia
              Clemm, wife of Edgar Allen Poe; describes
              the unsettled, emotional life of the poet and
              his dependence upon his wife.

362   O'Neill, Charles. MORNING TIME. Simon and
              Schuster, 1949. Based on the supposed plot
              of General Wilkinson to sell out to the Span-
              ish at New Orleans during the period of the
              Confederation, 1783-1789.

363   Paradise, Viola. TOMORROW THE HARVEST.
              Morrow, 1952. Small town life in Maine just
              after the Revolution.

364   Parker, Cornelia Stratton. FABULOUS VALLEY.
              Putnam, 1956. Romance set against a back-
              ground of the oil rush in Western Pennsylvania
              in the mid-1800's.

365   Partridge, Bellamy. THE BIG FREEZE. Crowell,
              1948. Story of the political skulduggery con-
              nected with the development of New York's
              water supply in the 1840's.

366   Roark, Garland. THE LADY AND THE DEEP BLUE
       SEA. Doubleday, 1958. A sea story set around
       the clipper ship trade out of Boston; plot re-
       volves around a race from Melbourne to Boston.

367   Roberts, Kenneth L. LYDIA BAILEY. Doubleday,
       1947. Story of Americans in the Haitian revo-
       lution and in the Tripolitan War.

368   Seifert, Shirley. THE THREE LIVES OF ELIZA-
       BETH. Lippincott, 1952. Follows the heroine
       from her youth on the Missouri River frontier
       in the 1820's to maturity as a leader in
       Washington society just before the Civil War.

369   Seton, Anya. DRAGONWYCK. Houghton, 1944.
       Manners and customs of the early 1800's in a
       baronial family home in the Hudson River
       valley.

370   Stewart, Ramona. CASEY. Little, 1968. Picture
       of life among the immigrant Irish in New York
       City in the 1850's and '60's; politics in the
       Tweed ring, Boss Kelly, the Draft Riots of
       1863, the Molly Maguires, and fire fighting.

371   Stone, Irving. THE PRESIDENT'S LADY. Double-
       day, 1951. Sympathetic account of Rachel and
       Andrew Jackson against a background of Ameri-
       can politics at the beginning of the nineteenth
       century.

372   Stowe, Harriet Beecher. OLDTOWN FOLKS.
       Belknap, 1966. Saga of life in Oldtown (South
       Natick), Massachusetts in the years following
       the Revolutionary War. First published in
       1869.

373   Taylor, David. MISTRESS OF THE FORGE.
       Lippincott, 1964. Social and political life and
       industrial development in Pennsylvania in the
       1790's, at the time of the Alien and Sedition
       Laws.

374   Turnbull, Agnes. THE KING'S ORCHARD. Hough-
       ton, 1963. Fictional biography of James O'Hara,
       Irish immigrant, who settled at Fort Pitt,

served as an officer in the Revolution, Indian
agent, and as Quartermaster General of the
U. S.   Saga of the social, political, and industrial development of the period.

375   Wellman, Paul L.   THE BUCKSTONES.   Trident,
          1967.   A light tale of a picaresque scoundrel
          whose daughter seeks his release from a
          Tennessee debtor's prison by appealing to
          President Andrew Jackson.

376   Whitney, Janet.   JUDITH.   Morrow, 1943.   Phila-
          delphia in 1792 is the background for the love
          story of two young people; Washington's second
          inauguration, Blanchard's balloon ascent,
          troubled international relations, and the
          yellow fever epidemic are historical high lights.

377   Whitney, Phyllis A.   SEA JADE.   Appleton, 1965.
          Romantic tale of life in a New England seaport
          town, with glimpses of the sailing and shipping
          industry.

378   Widdemer, Margaret.   THE RED CASTLE WOMEN.
          Doubleday, 1968.   Life, manners, dress and
          customs in a mansion on the Hudson River and
          in New York City in the period between the
          Mexican War and the Civil War.

War of 1812

379   Banks, Polan.   BLACK IVORY.   Harper, 1926.
          Story of Jean Lafitte, pirate and slave runner,
          and of the conflict involved in his decision to
          join the Americans in the defense of New Or-
          leans against the British in the War of 1812.

380   Beebe, Ralph.   WHO FOUGHT AND BLED.   Coward,
          1941.   Pioneering in Ohio and General Isaac
          Hull's campaigns around Detroit.

381   Bell, Sallie.   MARCEL ARMAND.   Page, 1935.
          Intrigue of Lafitte's lieutenant with the British.

382   Chambers, Robert W.   THE HAPPY PARROT.
          Appleton, 1929.   Story of naval warfare during

the War of 1812.

383   -- THE RAKE AND THE HUSSY. Appleton, 1930.
       Story of Jackson's defense of New Orleans.

384   Chidsey, Donald Barr. STRONGHOLD. Doubleday,
       1948. Connecticut and Martinique during the
       War of 1812. Hero is impressed into the Bri-
       tish navy.

385   Finger, Charles. CAPE HORN SNORTER. Hough-
       ton, 1939. New England shippers in the years
       leading up to the War of 1812.

386   Forester, C. S. CAPTAIN FROM CONNECTICUT.
       Little, 1941. Blockade running out of Long
       Island during Jefferson's administration.

387   Gordon, Charles William. THE RUNNER. Double-
       day, 1929. Fighting around the Niagara penin-
       sula.

388   -- ROCK AND THE RIVER. Dodd, 1931. Set in
       Quebec and on the Canadian-American border
       during the War of 1812. Canadian point of view.

389   Harper, Robert S. TRUMPET IN THE WILDERNESS.
       M. S. Mill, 1940. Story of frontier warfare,
       the surrender of Detroit, the Battle of Erie,
       and pioneer newspaper work in Ohio.

390   Hepburn, Andrew. LETTER OF MARQUE. Little,
       1959. Vivid account of sea warfare; story of
       an American privateer in the War of 1812.

391   Hodge, Jane Aiken. HERE COMES A CANDLE.
       Doubleday, 1967. A young British widow is
       taken into the home of a Boston merchant who
       saved her from American militiamen in the
       raids against Canada in the War of 1812.

392   Jennings, John. THE TALL SHIPS. McGraw,
       1958. Story of the American Navy in the
       period before and during the War of 1812.

393   La Farge, Oliver. THE LONG PENNANT. Hough-
       ton, 1933. Rhode Island privateer harrasses

British shipping in the Caribbean.

394   Lane, Carl. THE FLEET IN THE FOREST.
        Coward, 1943. Life around Erie, Pennsylvania;
        the building of Perry's fleet at Presque Isle,
        and the Battle of Erie.

395   Lincoln, Joseph Crosby and Freeman Lincoln.
        THE NEW HOPE. Coward, 1941. Cape Cod-
        ders launch a privateer through the British
        blockade.

396   Marshall, Bernard Gay. OLD HICKORY'S PRIS-
        ONER. Appleton, 1925. Story of a boy too
        young to join the army in the War of 1812 who
        serves as a messenger, earning the commen-
        dation and a promotion from General Andrew
        Jackson.

397   Moore, John. HEARTS OF HICKORY. Cokesbury,
        1926. The defense of New Orleans, Andrew
        Jackson, David Crockett, Jean Lafitte.

398   Mudgett, Helen. THE SEAS STAND WATCH.
        Knopf, 1944. Follows the ups and downs of
        the New England sea trade and politics from
        the Revolution through the War of 1812.

399   O'Daniel, Janet. O GENESEE. Lippincott, 1957.
        A tale of pioneer settlers in the Genesee Valley
        near present Rochester, New York and the
        conflicts building up to the War of 1812.

400   Orr, Myron. THE CITADEL OF THE LAKES.
        Dodd, 1952. Story of Astor's fur trading em-
        pire around Mackinac Island during the War of
        1812.

401   Roberts, Kenneth L. THE LIVELY LADY. Double-
        day, 1931. Privateering against British ship-
        ping and life in Dartmoor prison.

402   -- CAPTAIN CAUTION. Doubleday, 1934. Maine
        merchant ship captured by the British; seamen
        impressed into British service.

403   Root, Corwin. AN AMERICAN, SIR. Dutton, 1940.

Privateering, impressment into British service,
and life in Boston split between Federalists and
Republicans during the War of 1812.

404   Rowland, Henry C.   HIRONDELLE.   Harper, 1922.
        Adventure on the high seas.   Privateering on
        the eve of the war.

405   Shepard, Odell and Willard Shepard.   HOLDFAST
        GAINES.   Macmillan, 1946.   Panorama of
        national events from the end of the Revolution
        to the War of 1812; includes the Fort Mims
        Massacre, Battle of New Orleans; Tecumseh,
        Jean Lafitte, and Andrew Jackson appear.

406   Speas, Jan Cox.   MY LOVE, MY ENEMY.   Morrow,
        1961.   Light story of a young American girl in
        love with a British spy; background of politics
        and battles culminating in the burning of Wash-
        ington.

407   Sperry, Armstrong.   THE BLACK FALCON.   Win-
        ston, 1949.   Son of a New Orleans planter sails
        with Jean Lafitte in his privateering raids
        against the English in 1814.

408   Tracy, Don.   CRIMSON IS THE EASTERN SHORE.
        Dial, 1953.   The war around the shores of
        Eastern Maryland.

409   Vail, Philip (pseud.).   THE SEA PANTHER.   Dodd,
        1962.   Fictionalized account of the life of
        William Bainbridge, commander of the U.S.S.
        Constitution; action centers around Stephen
        Decatur's campaign against Algiers in 1815.

410   Wallace, Willard M.   JONATHAN DEARBORN.
        Little, 1967.   Story of a young law student
        who ships as a privateer in the War of 1812.

411   Williams, Ben Ames.   THREAD OF SCARLET.
        Houghton, 1939.   Nantucket privateer fights a
        British frigate during the War of 1812.

412   Wilson, Margaret.   THE VALIANT WIFE.   Double-
        day, 1934.   Story of the imprisonment of a
        young American in Dartmoor prison in 1812.

EXPANDING FRONTIERS, 1783 TO 1893

Eastern and Southern Frontiers

413   Atkinson, Oriana. THE TWIN COUSINS. Bobbs, 1951. The Catskill country of New York in the days when it was still frontier; story of the construction of the Susquehanna Turnpike.

414   Barnes, Percy Raymond. CRUM ELBOW FOLKS. Lippincott, 1938. Country life and customs of a Quaker settlement on the Hudson River in 1838.

415   Best, Allena. HOMESPUN. Lothrop, 1937. Family life on the New York frontier in the 1820's.

416   Best, Herbert. YOUNG'UN. Macmillan, 1944. Picture of daily living in the frontier region of Northern New York state in the early 1800's.

417   Boyd, James. THE LONG HUNT. Scribner, 1930. Life on the frontier from North Carolina to the Mississippi River at the time of Daniel Boone.

418   Bristow, Gwen. DEEP SUMMER. Crowell, 1937. Evolution of a great Louisiana plantation from a frontier cabin in the wilderness. Followed by "The Handsome Road" (Civil War).

419   Clagett, John. BUCKSKIN CAVALIER. Crown, 1954. Story of a young woman captured by Indians near Fort Pitt; covers much of the frontier region including a description of the Wilderness Road.

420   Cochran, Louis. RACCOON JOHN SMITH. Duell, 1963. Authentic frontier background in a fictional biography of the Campbellite preacher in Kentucky in the early 1800's.

421   Colver, Anne.   THEODOSIA, DAUGHTER OF AARON
           BURR.   Farrar, 1941.   Fictionized biography
           in which his schemes are treated casually.

422   Crabb, Alfred Leland.   JOURNEY TO NASHVILLE.
           Bobbs, 1957.   Story of the founding of Nash-
           ville, retracing the journey of a group of set-
           tlers from the Wautauga Settlement of East
           Tennessee through the wilderness to the site
           of the new town.

423   Davis, Julia.   EAGLE ON THE SUN.   Rinehart,
           1956.   Story of Virginia plantation life and
           the Mexican War.   Sequel to "Bridle the Wind"
           (Civil War--Abolition).

424   Dowdey, Clifford.   TIDEWATER.   Little, 1943.
           Panoramic story of the migration from the
           old Virginia tidewater plantations to new lands
           in the West in 1837.

425   Downes, Anne Miller.   THE PILGRIM SOUL.
           Lippincott, 1952.   Life in the wilderness area
           of New Hampshire in 1820.

426   -- THE QUALITY OF MERCY.   Lippincott, 1959.
           Family affairs and politics in Philadelphia and
           on the Tennessee frontier at the time of
           Andrew Jackson's war against the Creek
           Indians in 1813.

427   Edmonds, Walter D.   ROME HAUL.   Little, 1929.
           Life and manners along the banks of the Erie
           Canal in the 1850's.

428   -- THE BIG BARN.   Little, 1930.   Story of farm
           life in the Black River valley of New York in
           the 1860's.

429   -- ERIE WATER.   Little, 1933.   Story of the
           building of the Erie Canal from 1817 to 1825.

430   -- CHAD HANNA.   Little, 1940.   A circus story
           set in the Erie Canal region of New York in
           the 1850's; depicts the struggle of small busi-
           ness in competition with big business.

431   -- WEDDING JOURNEY. Little, 1947. Story of a
       honeymoon couple traveling through the Erie
       Canal on the way to Buffalo and Niagara Falls
       in the 1830's.

432   Ehle, John. THE LAND BREAKERS. Harper,
       1964. Life and hardships of the settlers in a
       remote mountain valley in North Carolina in
       1779.

433   Fleischmann, Glen. WHILE RIVERS FLOW. Mac-
       millan, 1963. Story of the removal of the
       Cherokee Indians from their home in Georgia
       and Tennessee in the 1830's.

434   Forrest, Williams. TRAIL OF TEARS. Crown,
       1958. Story of the Cherokee Indians and of
       their leader, John Ross, at the time of their
       enforced migration from their home in Georgia
       to new lands in Oklahoma Territory in the
       1830's.

435   Fort, John. GOD IN THE STRAW PEN. Dodd,
       1931. Story of a Methodist revival meeting
       in a Georgia backwoods community in the
       1830's.

436   Gabriel, Gilbert Wolf. I THEE WED. Macmillan,
       1948. Story of a group who came to America
       during the French Revolution to build a refuge
       for Marie Antoinette at the site of Asylum in
       Pennsylvania.

437   Gerson, Noel B. THE CUMBERLAND RIFLES.
       Doubleday, 1952. Story of the frontier state
       of Franklin, its struggle for recognition, and
       the admission of Tennessee as a state in 1796.

438   Giles, Janice Holt. THE BELIEVERS. Houghton,
       1957. Story of religious beliefs and social
       customs of a Shaker colony in Kentucky in the
       early 1800's.

439   -- LAND BEYOND THE MOUNTAINS. Houghton,
       1958. Story of the settling of Kentucky from
       1783 to 1792 and the fight for separate state-
       hood, introducing General James Wilkinson's

schemes for an empire on the frontier.

440   Ham, Tom. GIVE US THIS VALLEY. Macmillan,
      1952. Story of a Pennsylvania couple moving
      to new land in a Georgia valley in 1837.

441   Harris, Cyril. STREET OF KNIVES. Little, 1950.
      Follows Aaron Burr's journey westward on his
      way to Mexico.

442   Hatcher, Harlan H. THE PATTERNS OF WOLFPEN.
      Bobbs, 1934. Family chronicle from pioneer
      days in Eastern Kentucky to the encroachment
      of industry after about 1885.

443   Holt, Felix. THE GABRIEL HORN. Dutton, 1951.
      Frontier life along the Tennessee River.

444   Johnson, Gerald White. BY REASON OF STRENGTH.
      Minton, 1930. Chronicle of the Campbell clan
      of North Carolina from just after the Revolution
      through the Civil War.

445   Jones, Madison. FOREST OF THE NIGHT. Har-
      court, 1960. Story of an idealistic school
      teacher facing the brutal reality of frontier life
      in Tennessee in the early 1800's.

446   Jordan, Mildred. ASYLUM FOR THE QUEEN.
      Knopf, 1948. Story of a group of aristocrats
      who plot to rescue the French Royal family
      imprisoned in Paris and bring them to a
      Pennsylvania colony which they named Asylum.

447   Kendrick, Baynard H. THE FLAMES OF TIME.
      Scribner, 1948. Story of life in Northern
      Florida preceding its acquisition by the United
      States.

448   Kroll, Harry Harrison. ROGUE'S COMPANION.
      Bobbs, 1943. Story of John Murrell's out-
      law band and life on the Natchez Trace in the
      1820's and 1830's.

449   -- DARKER GROWS THE VALLEY. Bobbs, 1947.
      Pioneer life in the Tennessee River valley from
      1778 to the advent of T. V. A. in the 1930's.

450   Linney, Romulus. HEATHEN VALLEY. Atheneum,
            1962. Story of the religious mission of Bishop
            Ames and William Starns and their effect on the
            isolated inhabitants of a mountain valley in
            North Carolina in the 1850's.

452   McCutcheon, George B. VIOLA GWYN. Dodd,
            1922. Frontier Kentucky and Indiana in the
            early 1800's.

453   MacKinnon, Mary Linehan. ONE SMALL CANDLE.
            Crown, 1956. Story of family life in a New
            York farming community during the mid-1800's.

454   McMeekin, Clark (pseud). RECKON WITH THE RIV-
            ER. Appleton, 1941. Life on the Kentucky
            frontier and on the Ohio River; Johnny Apple-
            seed, Aaron Burr, and the Blennerhassetts and
            others appear.

455   Markey, Gene. THAT FAR PARADISE. McKay,
            1960. Story of the eventful journey of a Vir-
            ginia Blue Ridge family to the Kentucky wilder-
            ness beyond the Alleghenies in 1794.

456   Meigs, Cornelia. CALL OF THE MOUNTAIN.
            Little, 1940. Vermont backwoods in the
            1830's.

457   Miller, Caroline. LEBANON. Doubleday, 1944.
            Story of Pioneer life, of hunting and trapping
            in the Georgia swamplands and on the Missis-
            sippi River frontier.

458   Myers, John. THE WILD YAZOO. Dutton, 1947.
            Life on the Mississippi frontier as lived by a
            Virginia aristocrat in the Indian Lands above
            the Yazoo River in the 1780's and 1790's.

459   Nicholson, Meredith. THE CAVALIER OF
            TENNESSEE. Bobbs, 1928. Story of Andrew
            Jackson, 1789 to 1824; Tennessee in pioneer
            days.

460   Palmer, Bruce and John Clifford Giles. HORSE-
            SHOE BEND. Simon and Schuster, 1962.
            Authentic reconstruction of events leading up

to the Battle of Horseshoe Bend during the
Creek Indian Wars in Alabama in 1814; charac-
ters include Andrew Jackson, Sam Houston,
Davy Crockett, and William Weatherford, Chief
Red Eagle of the Creek Indians.

461   Pendexter, Hugh. RED BELTS. Doubleday, 1920.
       Story of the settling of the Tennessee frontier.

462   -- A VIRGINIA SCOUT. Bobbs, 1922. Story of
       Indian warfare on the Virginia frontier.

463   Poole, Ernest. THE NANCY FLYER. Crowell,
       1949. A New Hampshire lad witnesses the end
       of an era as railroads replace the stagecoach;
       1835 through the Civil War.

464   Pope, Edith. RIVER IN THE WIND. Scribner,
       1954. Scouting, fighting, and social life in
       the Florida towns during the Seminole Wars,
       1835-1842.

465   Pridgen, Tim. WEST GOES THE ROAD. Double-
       day, 1944. Story of a frontiersman fighting
       Indians, Spaniards, and Frenchmen for the
       lands between the Alleghenies and the Mississippi
       River, and opposing Wilkinson and Burr's scheme.

466   Pryor, Elinor. THE DOUBLE MAN. Norton, 1957.
       Story of Indian life on the American frontier
       and England in the mid-1800's, as seen by a
       white man raised by the Cherokees, educated in
       England, who returns to live with the Indians.

467   Richter, Conrad. A COUNTRY OF STRANGERS.
       Knopf, 1966. Story of a white girl who grows
       up as a captive of the Tuscarawas Indians and
       is rejected by her own family when she is un-
       willingly returned to Pennsylvania, following
       Bouquet's expedition in 1765. Sequel to "Light
       in the Forest" (Colonial).

468   Roberts, Elizabeth Maddox. THE GREAT MEADOW.
       Viking, 1930. Pioneer life as settlers move
       from Virginia over the Wilderness Road to
       Harrod's Fort, Kentucky.

469   Seifert, Shirley. NEVER NO MORE.   Lippincott,
          1964.   Rebecca Boone endures Indian raids,
          the death of her oldest son and the marriage
          of a daughter in western Virginia in 1773-1774
          before she and Daniel move on to Kentucky.

470   Seton, Anya. MY THEODOSIA.   Houghton, 1941.
          Story of Aaron Burr's daughter, of her rela-
          tions with her father and his schemes, and of
          her love for Meriwether Lewis.

471   Skinner, Constance. BECKY LANDERS, FRONTIER
          WARRIOR.   Macmillan, 1926.   Story of a pio-
          neer girl on the Kentucky frontier.   Daniel
          Boone and George Rogers Clark appear.

472   Slaughter, Frank. THE WARRIOR.   Doubleday,
          1956.   The Seminole War of 1835 describing
          contemporary feeling and the Indian fighting
          culminating in the capture of Osceola.

473   Stanley, Edward. THE ROCK CRIED OUT.   Duell,
          1949.   The Blennerhassetts develop a home-
          stead on an island in the Ohio River and be-
          come involved in Aaron Burr's plot.

474   Sterne, Emma Gelders. SOME PLANT OLIVE
          TREES.   Dodd, 1937.   Napoleonic exiles form
          the Vine and Olive colony at Demopolis, Ala-
          bama in the early 1800's.

475   Street, James. OH, PROMISED LAND.   Dial Press,
          1940.   Frontier life in the Mississippi Terri-
          tory (Alabama and Mississippi) from the founding
          of Natchez to the War of 1812.

476   Sublette, Clifford and Harry Harrison Kroll. PERI-
          LOUS JOURNEY.   Bobbs, 1943.   A tale of the
          Mississippi River and the Natchez Trace; 1821.

477   Taylor, Robert Lewis. TWO ROADS TO GUADA-
          LUPE.   Doubleday, 1964.   The journals of a
          teen-age drummer and his older brother tell
          of their adventures in the Mexican War,
          1845-48.

478   Van Every, Dale. WESTWARD THE RIVER.   Put-

nam, 1945. Trip by flatboat down the Ohio
River from Pittsburgh to Louisville in 1794.

479   -- CAPTIVE WITCH. Messner, 1951. Scout for
George Rogers Clark escorts prisoners from
Vincennes to Virginia, then strikes out for new
land in Kentucky.

480   -- THE VOYAGERS. Holt, 1957. Life on the
frontier in the 1780's; centers around the
Ohio River valley below Pittsburgh, and the
Mississippi River to New Orleans.

481   -- SCARLET FEATHER. Holt, 1959. Story of a
Virginia family who make their way down the
Ohio River and settle in the Kentucky wilder-
ness near Louisville in 1785.

482   Vaughan, Carter. THE RIVER DEVILS. Doubleday, 1968. An adventure tale centering on the
politics leading up to the Louisiana Purchase;
New Orleans under Spanish and French rule;
Thomas Jefferson; James Madison.

483   Ward, Christopher. STRANGE ADVENTURES OF
JONATHAN DREW. Simon and Schuster,
1932. Itinerant peddler wanders through the
New England and Middle Western frontier;
1821-1824. See author's "Yankee Rover"
(Expanding Frontiers--Southwest).

484   Warren, Robert Penn. WORLD ENOUGH AND TIME.
Random, 1950. Story of a Kentucky murder
trial of the 1820's showing the social and
political life of the period.

485   Welty, Eudora. THE ROBBER BRIDEGROOM.
Doubleday, 1942. Fanciful tale of a bandit
who steals his bride. Set in the Natchez country on the Mississippi River in the early 1800's.

486   Wilder, Robert. BRIGHT FEATHER. Putnam,
1948. Fictional history of the Seminole Wars,
1835-1842. The Seminole leader, Osceola, is
one of the characters.

487   Wylie, I. A. R. HO, THE FAIR WIND. Random,

1945.   Narrow-minded religion versus personal
integrity.   Setting is Martha's Vineyard at the
end of the Civil War.

488   Young, Stanley.   YOUNG HICKORY.   Farrar, 1940.
The early years of Andrew Jackson from his
boyhood in Waxhaw, North Carolina to his days
as a circuit lawyer on the Tennessee frontier.

The Middle West

489   Aldrich, Bess Streeter.   SONG OF YEARS.   Appleton, 1939.   Details of home life in pioneer
Iowa; 1854-1865.

490   Allee, Marjorie.   JUDITH LANKESTER.   Houghton,
1930.   Story of a Quaker settlement in Indiana;
1840.

491   -- A HOUSE OF HER OWN.   Houghton, 1934.
Frontier life in Indiana; 1850's and 1860's.

492   Allis, Marguerite.   NOW WE ARE FREE.   Putnam,
1952.   Story of the westward migration from
Connecticut to Ohio just after the Revolution.

493   -- TO KEEP US FREE.   Putnam, 1953.   Development of the Ohio country from 1797 to 1815;
settlement at Marietta; founding of Cleveland;
the first census; the Burr-Blennerhassett conspiracy; and the War of 1812.

494   -- BRAVE PURSUIT.   Putnam, 1954.   Story of the
difficulties of acquiring an education on the
frontier; set in Southern Ohio.   Followed by
"The Rising Storm" (The Civil War--Abolition).

495   Altrocchi, Julia.   WOLVES AGAINST THE MOON.
Macmillan, 1940.   Fur trading in the Great
Lakes region; 1794-1834.

496   Atkinson, Eleanor.   HEARTS UNDAUNTED.   Harper,
1917.   Story of pioneer hardships in the Middle
West, life among the Iroquois Indians, and the
founding of Chicago.

497   Atkinson, Oriana. THE GOLDEN SEASON. Bobb,
      1953. New England sea-faring life and the
      rush to Ohio in the 1790's.

498   Auslander, Joseph. MY UNCLE JAN. Longmans,
      1948. Old World customs and festivals among
      an ebullient family of Czech immigrants in
      Wisconsin in the 1800's.

499   Babcock, Bernie. THE SOUL OF ANN RUTLEDGE.
      Lippincott, 1919. Romance of Abe Lincoln
      and Ann Rutledge; Illinois from 1831 to 1835.

500   Bacheller, Irving. EBEN HOLDEN. Lothrop,
      1900. Story of simple life in the Adirondack
      Mountain region of New York in the 1850's;
      introduces Abraham Lincoln and Horace Greeley.

501   -- A MAN FOR THE AGES. Bobbs, 1919. Pioneer
      days and the formative years of Abraham Lin-
      coln; 1831-1847.

502   Baldwin, Leland. THE DELECTABLE COUNTRY.
      Lee Furman, 1939. Story of the Ohio River
      keelboat age, the Whiskey Rebellion, and
      Pittsburgh in the 1790's.

503   Barney, Helen Corse. FRUIT IN HIS SEASON.
      Crown, 1951. Story of a Quaker boy who
      goes to the Ohio wilderness a few years after
      the Revolution.

504   Benson, Ramsey. HILL COUNTRY. Stokes, 1928.
      Story of James J. Hill and the settling of the
      Northwest Minnesota country.

505   Brigham, Johnson. THE SINCLAIRS OF OLD FORT
      DES MOINES. Torch Press, 1927. Pioneer
      life around Fort Des Moines, Iowa in the early
      1840's; Sioux Indians, bootleggers, and squatters.

506   Brink, Carol. CADDIE WOODLAWN. Macmillan,
      1935. Pioneer Wisconsin in the 1860's.

507   Carnahan, Walter. HOFFMAN'S ROW. Bobbs,
      1963. Account of an incident in the courtship
      of Abraham Lincoln and Mary Todd, when he

was challenged to duel by a rival for her
affections.

508   Colby, Merle. ALL YE PEOPLE. Viking, 1931.
       Social history of a group of migrants from Ver-
       mont to Ohio in 1810.

509   -- THE NEW ROAD. Viking, 1933. Traces the
       development of a settlement on the Maumee
       River in Ohio from about 1820 to 1840.

510   Cook, Roberta St. Clair. THE THING ABOUT
       CLARISSA. Bobbs, 1958. Contrasts life in a
       ladies' seminary in Philadelphia with the man-
       ners and customs on the Ohio frontier in 1837.

511   Cooper, James Fenimore. THE PRAIRIE. Dodd,
       1827. Story of life on the prairies beyond the
       Mississippi River at the time of Jefferson's
       administration. Sequel to "The Pioneers"
       (Colonial America).

512   Cooper, Jamie Lee. THE HORN AND THE FOREST.
       Bobbs, 1963. A tale of frontier life in the
       Indiana Territory and of the events leading to
       General Benjamin Harrison's campaign against
       the Indians at the Battle of Tippicanoe in 1811.

513   Daviess, Maria. THE MATRIX. Century, 1920.
       The love story of Nancy Hanks and Thomas
       Lincoln.

514   Derleth, August. WIND OVER WISCONSIN. Scrib-
       ner, 1938. The Black Hawk Wars and the
       transition from fur trading to farming in Wis-
       consin in the 1830's.

515   -- STILL IS THE SUMMER NIGHT. Scribner,
       1937. Sac Prairie, Wisconsin in the 1880's
       when lumber rafts were floated down the Wis-
       consin River.

516   -- RESTLESS IS THE RIVER. Scribner, 1939.
       Story of the early settlement of Wisconsin;
       1839-1850.

517   -- BRIGHT JOURNEY. Scribner, 1940. Adventures

of Hercules Dousman, an agent of John Jacob
Astor in the Northwest Territory; 1812-1843.

518   -- THE HOUSE ON THE MOUND. Duell, 1958.
Continues the story of Hercules Dousman,
fur trader and railroad builder, begun in
"Bright Journey" (above).

519   -- THE HILLS STAND WATCH. Duell, 1960.
Pioneer life in a small lead-mining town in
Wisconsin in the 1840's; local politics and
the movement toward statehood, trouble with
the Indians, and details of lead mining.

520   -- THE SHADOW IN THE GRASS. Duell, 1963.
Biographical novel of Nelson Dewey, first
governor of Wisconsin, who came to Wisconsin
Territory from New York in 1836.

521   Duncan, Thomas W. BIG RIVER, BIG MAN.
Lippincott, 1959. Story of the Wisconsin
logging industry with many characters and
with settings in the North woods, New Mexico,
New England, and the Civil War South.

522   -- THE LABYRINTH. Doubleday, 1967. Family
and farm life in Iowa in the 1800's.

523   Eggleston, Edward. THE HOOSIER SCHOOL-MAS-
TER. Scribner, 1871. Tale of Indiana back-
woods life and education in the 1850's.

524   -- THE CIRCUIT RIDER. Scribner, 1874. Daily
life and customs and frontier religion in Ohio;
1800-1825.

525   -- THE HOOSIER SCHOOL-BOY. Scribner, 1883.
Life in Indiana and Ohio about 1840, showing
the difficulties of acquiring an education on
the frontier.

526   -- THE GRAYSONS. Scribner, 1887. Picture of
daily life and customs in rural Illinois about
1850.

527   Ellis, William D. THE BOUNTY LANDS. World,
1952. Story of conflict between speculators

and settlers in Ohio after the Revolution involving lands granted to the veterans for their
war service.

528   -- JONATHAN BLAIR, BOUNTY LANDS LAWYER.
World, 1954.   Story of a lawyer on the Ohio
frontier; picture of daily life and customs;
sequel to "The Bounty Lands. "

529   -- THE BROOKS LEGEND. Crowell, 1958. Story
of medical practice and daily life on the Ohio
frontier in the years following the War of
1812; continues the story of some of the characters of "The Bounty Lands. "

530   Faralla, Dana. CIRCLE OF TREES. Lippincott,
1955.   Story of the prairies of Minnesota in
1880, and of the Danes who settle there.

531   Finney, Gertrude E.   THE PLUMS HANG HIGH.
Longmans, 1955.   Story of family life on a
pioneer farm in the American Midwest; 1868 to
1890.

532   Fuller, Iola. THE LOON FEATHER. Harcourt,
1940.   Fictionized autobiography of Tecumseh's
daughter.   Setting is the Mackinac region in
the early 1800's.

533   -- THE SHINING TRAIL. Duell, 1943. Centers
around the life of the Sauk Indians and their
struggles leading up to the Black Hawk Wars;
1820's to the 1830's.

534   Furnas, Joseph C.   THE DEVIL'S RAINBOW.
Harper, 1962.   Biographical novel centering
around Joseph Smith and the Mormons from
his arrival in Kirtland, Ohio in 1831, through
the exodus to Nauvoo, Illinois, and to his
death in 1844.

535   Garth, David. FIRE ON THE WIND. Putnam,
1951.   Story of the Upper Michigan peninsula
in the 1860's; logging, mining, and railroading.

536   Gay, Margaret Cooper. HATCHET IN THE SKY.
Simon and Schuster, 1954.   Life with the

Ojibway Indians under Chief Pontiac in the Northwest Territory; scenes in early Detroit.

537   Hallet, Richard. MICHAEL BEAM. Houghton, 1939.
       Story of the Black Hawk War and life on the Illinois
       and Wisconsin frontier; 1820's and 1830's.

538   Harris, Laura B. BRIDE OF THE RIVER. Crowell,
       1956. Story of the adjustment of a Louisiana
       plantation belle to life in a small Ohio River town
       in the late 1830's, including slave traffic on the
       Underground Railroad.

539   Havill, Edward. BIG EMBER. Harper, 1947. Nor-
       wegian immigrants and the uprising of the Sioux in
       Southern Minnesota in 1862.

540   Havighurst, Walter. QUIET SHORE. Macmillan,
       1937. Homesteading on Lake Erie just after the
       Civil War, and the growth of industry in Ohio.

541   -- WINDS OF SPRING. Macmillan, 1940. The settling
       of Wisconsin; 1840's to 1870's.

542   Kantor, MacKinlay. SPIRIT LAKE. World, 1961.
       Story of the settlers and the Indians involved in the
       Spirit Lake massacre in Iowa in 1857; picture of
       social and economic life on the frontier in the 1850's.

543   Krause, Herbert. THE OXCART TRAIL. Bobbs,
       1954. Story of settlers and traders pushing into the
       Minnesota Territory in the 1850's.

544   Lancaster, Bruce. FOR US THE LIVING. Stokes,
       1940. Abraham Lincoln in Indiana and Illinois.

545   Lockwood, Sarah. FISTFUL OF STARS. Appleton,
       1947. Northern Wisconsin in the 1880's.

546   Lovelace, Maud Hart. THE BLACK ANGELS. Day,
       1926. Story of a musical family touring small
       towns of the Minnesota Territory; local color and
       social history.

547   -- EARLY CANDLELIGHT. Day, 1929. Frontier life
       along the Minnesota and the Mississippi Rivers;
       Fort Snelling (St. Paul), Minnesota in the 1830's

548   -- ONE STAYED AT WELCOME.   Day, 1934.
       Pioneering in Minnesota in the 1850's.

549   -- and D. W. Lovelace.   GENTLEMEN FROM
       ENGLAND.   Macmillan, 1937.   Picture of life
       in Minnesota; 1860's-1870's.

550   Lutes, Della.   GABRIEL'S SEARCH.   Little, 1940.
       Details of daily life in Michigan in the early
       1800's.

551   McLean, Sydney.   MOMENT OF TIME.   Putnam,
       1945.   Seventy years in the life of a pioneer
       woman from girlhood before the Revolution to the
       1840's.

552   McLeod, LeRoy.   THE YEARS OF PEACE.   Apple-
       ton, 1932.   Story of daily life in the Wabash
       River valley of Indiana after the Civil War.

553   McNeil, Everett.   DANIEL DULUTH.   Dutton, 1926.
       Story of the exploration of the Great Lakes from
       Montreal to Lake Superior by Daniel DuLuth.

554   Masters, Edgar Lee.   CHILDREN OF THE MARKET
       PLACE.   Macmillan, 1922.   Story of an English
       immigrant in Illinois; 1833-1861.

555   Matshat, Cecile Hulse.   PREACHER ON HORSEBACK.
       Farrar, 1940.   Story of a circuit-riding preacher
       in Michigan and Northern New York in the 1870's.

556   Mayer, Albert L   FOLLOW THE RIVER.   Doubleday,
       1969.   A long tale of frontier settlement and
       Indian fighting in the Ohio country in the 1790's.
       The hero journeys down the Ohio River to Cincin-
       nati to teach; later joins General Josiah Harmar's
       expedition against the Indians along the Maumee
       River.

557   Meader, Stephen.   BOY WITH A PACK.   Harcourt,
       1939.   Tale of a young itinerant peddler wandering
       from New Hampshire to the Ohio frontier, 1837.

558   Means, Florence.   CANDLE IN THE MIST.   Houghton,
       1931.   Minnesota in the 1870's.

559   Meigs, Cornelia. SWIFT RIVERS. Little, 1932.
        Minnesota in the early 1800's. Floating logs
        down the Mississippi River to St. Louis.

560   Miller, Helen Topping. BORN STRANGERS. Bobbs,
        1949. Picture of life in Michigan from pioneer
        days to the Civil War.

561   Moberg, Vilhelm. UNTO A GOOD LAND. Simon
        and Schuster, 1954. Story of Swedish immigrants
        pioneering in the Minnesota Territory in the
        1850's.

562   -- LAST LETTER HOME. Simon and Schuster,
        1961. Picture of the growth of frontier communi-
        ties in the Minnesota Territory, the Sioux uprising
        and the Civil War, and details of family life up to
        1890. Sequel to "Unto a Good Land" (above).

563   Orr, Myron David. MISSION TO MACKINAC. Dodd,
        1956. Story of English-French conflict in the
        area of Mackinac Island prior to the War of 1812.

564   Oskison, John. BROTHERS THREE. Macmillan,
        1935. Farm life in the Indian Territory after
        1873.

565   Ostenso, Martha. O RIVER, REMEMBER. Dodd,
        1943. Irish and Norwegian pioneers in the Red
        River valley of the Minnesota country; 1870-1941.

566   Peattie, Donald Culross. A PRAIRIE GROVE.
        Simon and Schuster, 1938. Saga of missionaries,
        traders, Indians, settlers, and the founding of
        Chicago.

567   Quick, Herbert. VANDEMARK'S FOLLY. Bobbs,
        1922. Pioneering in Iowa, 1840's to 1860's;
        claim jumping, frontier law, and the Underground
        Railroad.

568   -- THE HAWKEYE. Bobbs, 1923. Political, social,
        and farm life in Iowa, 1857-1878. Sequel to
        "Vandemark's Folly."

569   Reed, Warren. SHE RODE A YELLOW STALLION.
        Bobbs, 1950. Farming and horse raising in

Southeastern Wisconsin, 1840's-1890's; picture
of German, Irish, and Scottish settlers and the
development of the cheese industry.

570   Richter, Conrad. THE TREES. Knopf, 1940.
       First of a series on the development of the
       Ohio wilderness.

571   -- THE FIELDS. Knopf, 1946. Story of the
       development of a community in the Ohio wilder-
       ness. Sequel to "The Trees. "

572   -- THE TOWN. Knopf, 1950. Emergence of a
       frontier town and the trappings of civilization in
       the Ohio wilderness. Sequel to "The Fields. "

573   Seifert, Shirley. THE WAYFARER. M. S. Mill,
       1938. Fictional biography of John Cotter;
       whaling, trading in the West, fighting in the
       Civil War, and stock farming in Missouri.

574   Selby, John. ELEGANT JOURNEY. Rinehart,
       1944. Southerner frees slaves and starts out
       anew in Wisconsin; 1840's.

575   Sinclair, Harold. AMERICAN YEARS. Doubleday,
       1938. History of a small Illinois town; 1830 to
       the Civil War.

576   Skelton, Jess. MARTIN'S LAND. Chilton, 1961.
       Life among the Osage Indians and on a Spanish
       land grant on the Missouri frontier in 1785.

577   Snedeker, Caroline. SETH WAY. Houghton, 1917.
       Life in the New Harmony settlement in Indiana
       in the 1840's.

578   -- BECKONING ROAD. Doubleday, 1929. Story of
       the New Harmony settlement in Indiana in the
       1840's.

579   -- THE TOWN OF THE FEARLESS. Doubleday,
       1931. European background and the founding of
       the New Harmony community in Indiana. Robert
       Owen, Pestalozzi, and others appear.

580   Spicer, Bart. THE WILD OHIO. Dodd, 1953.

Settlement of French emigres at Gallipolis, Ohio.

581   Strong, Philip. BUCKSKIN BREECHES. Farrar,
       1937. Westward migration from Ohio to Iowa,
       1037.

582   Suchow, Ruth. COUNTRY PEOPLE. Knopf, 1924.
       Family chronicle of pioneer hardships of a group
       of German-Americans who settled in Iowa in the
       1850's.

583   Swanson, Neil. THE PHANTOM EMPEROR. Put-
       nam, 1934. Based on an attempt to form a
       separate empire in the Northwest Territory in
       1836.

584   Teilhet, Darwin. STEAMBOAT ON THE RIVER.
       Sloane, 1952. Story of the first steamboat on
       the Sangamon River in Illinois in the 1830's;
       introduces Abe Lincoln, who pilots the boat to
       safety around New Salem.

585   Titus, Harold. BLACK FEATHER. Macrae, 1936.
       Story of the Astor fur trading enterprise around
       Mackinac Island.

586   Todd, Helen. SO FREE WE SEEM. Reynal, 1936.
       Story of a pioneer woman on the Missouri frontier.

587   Troyer, Howard. THE SALT AND THE SAVOR.
       Wyn, 1950. Chronicles the development of
       Indiana from pioneer days to the Civil War;
       development of the Grange movement, daily
       life and customs.

588   Van Every, Dale. THE TREMBLING EARTH.
       Messner, 1953. Lead mining in Southeast
       Missouri at the time of the New Madrid earth-
       quake of 1811.

589   Voelker, John Donaldson. LAUGHING WHITEFISH.
       McGraw, 1965. Follows the course of a law
       suit of an Indian girl against a powerful mining
       company; Marquette, Michigan in 1873.

590   West, Jessamyn. THE FRIENDLY PERSUASION.
       Harcourt, 1945. Episodes in the life of a

Quaker family in Indiana, including a minor Civil
War encounter.

591   -- LEAFY RIVERS. Harcourt, 1967. Life on a
         midwestern homestead and in Cincinnati around
         1818.

592   -- EXCEPT FOR ME AND THEE. Harcourt, 1969.
         Earlier episodes in the courtship and marriage of
         the Birdwell's of "Friendly Persuasion," as they
         settle a farm on the Indiana frontier, cooperate
         with the Underground Railroad, and raise their
         family in good Quaker tradition.

593   Whitlock, Brand. THE STRANGERS ON THE ISLAND.
         Appleton, 1933. Story of the exiled group of
         Mormons on Beaver Island in Lake Michigan in
         1850.

594   Wilson, Margaret. ABLE McLAUGHLINS. Harper,
         1923. Midwestern Scotch community in the 1860's.

595   Wyckoff, Nicholas. THE CORINTHIANS. Macmillan,
         1960. Story of small town life in Illinois and
         Missouri in the 1850's; pictures the effect of the
         Mormons on the places and people they meet on
         their westward movement.

596   Zara, Louis. THIS LAND IS OURS. Houghton,
         1940. Story of American frontier life from the
         Susquehanna to the Mississippi River, 1755 to
         1835; Chief Pontiac, George Rogers Clark, and
         General Anthony Wayne appear.

The Southwest

597   Adams, Andy. LOG OF A COWBOY. Houghton,
         1903. Picture of western ranch life; daily journal
         of a cattle drive from Texas to Wyoming.

598   Allen, Henry. MACKINNA'S GOLD. Random, 1963.
         Dramatic story of a young prospector leading a
         group of outlaws to a hidden treasure in Arizona
         in 1897.

599   -- ONE MORE RIVER TO CROSS. Random, 1967.

An Arkansas Negro escapes to freedom in Texas;
after a career of rustling, he settles on an
Oklahoma cotton farm.

600   Arnold, Elliot. BLOOD BROTHER. Duell, 1947.
        Account of the Apache wars in New Mexico and
        Arizona; sympathetic with the Indians.

601   -- TIME OF THE GRINGO. Knopf, 1953. Story of
        New Mexico under the Mexican governor, Don
        Manuel Armijo, just before the Mexican War.

602   Aydelotte, Dora. TRUMPETS CALLING. Appleton,
        1938. Story of the Cherokee Strip and the
        settling of Oklahoma in the 1890's.

603   -- RUN OF THE STARS. Appleton, 1940. Picture
        of life in the Oklahoma Territory at the time of
        its settlement in the 1890's.

604   Baker, Karle. STAR OF THE WILDERNESS.
        Coward, 1942. Story of the struggle for Texas
        independence; set chiefly in Nacagdoches.

605   Barrett, Monte. THE TEMPERED BLADE. Bobbs,
        1946. Fictional biography of James Bowie from
        1815 to his death at the Alamo in 1836.

606   Barry, Jane. A TIME IN THE SUN. Doubleday,
        1962. Story of two women, captured by the
        Apaches, who witness the Indians' struggle
        against the encroachment of the Americans and
        Mexicans in Arizona Territory in the 1870's;
        introduces the Indian leaders, Cochise, Victorio,
        and Nane.

607   -- A SHADOW OF EAGLES. Doubleday, 1964.
        Life on a cattle ranch in south western Texas
        and on a cattle drive to Montana in the 1870's.

608   -- MAXIMILIAN'S GOLD. Doubleday, 1966. A band
        of Southerners search for a cache of gold,
        supposedly hidden by Emperor Maximilian; set in
        Missouri, Texas, and Mexico in post-Civil War
        days.

609   Bean, Amelia. THE FEUD. Doubleday, 1960.

Violent story of sheep and cattle ranching, based
on the Graham-Tewksbury feud in Arizona in the
1880's.

610   -- TIME FOR OUTRAGE. Doubleday, 1967. Tale
of the Lincoln County War in New Mexico in
1878; hero is a boyhood friend of William Bonney
(Billy the Kid).

611   Bennett, Dwight. CHEROKEE OUTLET. Doubleday,
1961. Opening of the Cherokee Strip in Northern
Oklahoma in 1893; shows the change from open
prairie to farm land and the development of
towns.

612   Blacker, Irwin R. TAOS. World, 1959. Revolt of
the Pueblo Indians against the Spaniards in
New Mexico in 1680; climaxed by the bloody
massacre at Santa Fé.

613   Blake, Forrester. JOHNNY CHRISTMAS. Morrow,
1948. American Southwest from 1836 to 1846,
when Mexicans opposed the incoming Americans.

614   -- THE FRANCISCAN. Doubleday, 1963. A Franciscan priest works to protect the Pueblo Indians
from the Spaniards in early New Mexico in 1675.

615   Bosworth, Allan Bernard. THE LONG WAY NORTH.
Doubleday, 1959. Story of character played out
during a cattle drive from Texas to Montana
Territory.

616   Boyd, James. BITTER CREEK. Scribner, 1939.
Incidents of ranch life and Indian warfare in the
story of a young boy making his way to the
West in the 1870's.

617   Brackett, Leigh. FOLLOW THE FREE WIND.
Doubleday, 1963. Based on the life of James
Beckwourth, son of a slave, who went West as
a blacksmith, was adopted by the Crow Indians
and lived and fought with them against the whites.

618   Brand, Max. THE LONG CHANCE. Dodd, 1941.
The Old West in the days before the Civil War.

619   Bristow, Gwen. JUBILEE TRAIL. Crowell, 1950.
        Story of a trading and honeymoon trip over the
        Santa Fé Trail from New York to California in
        1845.

620   Brown, Dee. WAVE HIGH THE BANNER. Macrae,
        1942. The life of Davy Crockett, from boyhood
        to death at the Alamo.

621   Bryan, Jack Y. COME TO THE BOWER. A New
        Orleans lawyer becomes involved in the war for
        Texas independence in 1835-36; Santa Ana, the
        Battle of the Alamo, the Battle of San Jacinto.

622   Burnett, William Riley. SAINT JOHNSON. Long-
        mans, 1930. Story of lawless Tombstone,
        Arizona and the Earp-Clanton feud.

623   -- ADOBE WALLS. Knopf, 1953. Story of the
        last Apache uprising in the 1880's and of the
        tactics used by Generals Crook and Miles in
        defeating the Indians.

624   -- MI, AMIGO. Knopf, 1959. Based on the Lincoln
        County wars in New Mexico in 1878 and the story
        of Billy the Kid (William Bonney).

625   Busch, Niven. DUEL IN THE SUN. Morrow, 1944.
        Texas in the 1880's with wide-open towns and
        cattlemen fighting the railroad and the homesteaders.

626   Campbell, Walter Stanley. DOBE WALLS. Houghton,
        1929. Life on the Santa Fe Trail in the days of
        Kit Carson.

627   Capps, Benjamin. THE TRAIL TO OGALLALA.
        Duell, 1964. Story of the rough life on a cattle
        drive from Texas to Nebraska.

628   -- SAM CHANCE. Duell, 1965. A Civil War veteran
        becomes a Texas cattle rancher and creates an
        empire before his death in 1922.

629   -- A WOMAN OF THE PEOPLE. Duell, 1966. A
        white girl captured by the Indians in 1854 witnesses
        the daily life and customs of the Comanche Indians
        and their struggle against the encroachment and

raids by the white man; Texas from the 1850's
to the 1870's.

630   -- WHITE MAN'S ROAD. Harper, 1969. Indian
life in the 1890's in the story of a young Comanche
searching for identity in a society taken over by
the white man.

631   Cather, Willa. DEATH COMES FOR THE ARCH-
BISHOP. Knopf, 1927. Story of two French
priests in New Mexico soon after the Mexican
War.

632   Comfort, Will. APACHE. Dutton, 1931. Story of
Mangus Colorado, famous Apache chieftain, and
of his efforts to unite the Indians.

633   Constant, Alberta. OKLAHOMA RUN. Crowell,
1955. Pioneer life and homesteading in the
Oklahoma Territory in the 1890's.

634   Cook, Will. ELIZABETH BY NAME. Dodd, 1958.
Life on a frontier trading post on the Texas
prairie in the post-Civil War period.

635   Cooke, David Coxe. THE POST OF HONOR. Putnam, 1958. Authentic picture of Indian-white
relations and details of Apache Indian fighting on
an isolated outpost in the Arizona Territory.

636   Cooper, Courtney Ryley. OKLAHOMA. Little,
1926. Epic tale of the opening of the Oklahoma
Territory to homesteading, the rush of settlers,
and the development of the state.

637   Cooper, Jamie Lee. SHADOW OF A STAR. Bobbs,
1965. Three brothers from the Basque country
come to Spanish New Mexico in the 1680's; one
becomes a trader, another turns to renegade fur
trapping, the other becomes a priest among the
Indians.

638   Corle, Edwin. BILLY THE KID. Duell, 1953.
Fictional biography of the famous outlaw, William
Bonney.

639   Culp, John H. BORN OF THE SUN. Sloane, 1959.

Life on a Texas cattle ranch in the 1870's; picture of the cattle drives to Kansas. Followed by
"The Restless Land. "

640   -- THE MEN OF GONZALES. Sloane, 1960. Story
of the hurried march of 32 men from Gonzales to
San Antonio in 1836 to reinforce the besieged
garrison at the Alamo.

641   -- THE RESTLESS LAND. Sloane, 1962. Life in
a frontier community in northwest Texas in the
1870's depicting range wars, cattle drives, and
conflicts with the Comanche Indians. Sequel to
"Born of the Sun. "

642   -- A WHISTLE IN THE WIND. Holt, 1968. Story
of the lives of white captives of the Comanche
Indians as the Indians are dispersed and the
land is settled; Texas in the 1870's.

643   -- TIMOTHY BAINES. Holt, 1969. Outlaws,
Indians, and medicine on the Texas frontier in
the 1870's.

644   Davis, James F. THE ROAD TO SAN JACINTO.
Bobbs, 1936. Sam Houston and the struggle for
Texas independence; 1835-1836. Bowie, Crockett,
and Travis appear.

645   Dodge, Louis. THE AMERICAN. Messner, 1934.
Saga of the American West in the 1850's; the
gold rush, homesteading, fur trading, fighting
the Indians, and life on the Santa Fe Trail.

646   Duffus, Robert L. JORNADA. Covici, 1935. A
romance of the Southwest; wagon trains to Santa
Fe; Indian raids; and the Mexican War.

647   Erdman, Loula. THE EDGE OF TIME. Dodd,
1950. Story of a wagon journey to the Texas
panhandle and life on an isolated farm on the
prairie in 1885.

648   -- THE FAR JOURNEY. Dodd, 1955. Overland
trip from Missouri to Texas in the 1890's.

649   Evarts, Hal. TUMBLEWEEDS. Little, 1923. The

Cherokee Strip and the Oklahoma frontier in the
1890's.

650   Ferber, Edna. CIMARRON. Doubleday, 1930.
       Oklahoma from the opening of the Cherokee
       Strip in the 1890's to the striking of oil; picture
       of the development of the state.

651   Fergusson, Harvey. THE CONQUEST OF DON
       PEDRO. Morrow, 1954. Social history of a
       frontier town in New Mexico soon after the Civil
       War.

652   -- IN THOSE DAYS. Knopf, 1929. Story of the
       development of a small town on the Rio Grande
       River from the days of wagon trains and Indian
       raids to the 1920's.

653   Flynn, Robert. NORTH TO YESTERDAY. Knopf,
       1967. Life on a Texas cattle drive after the
       Civil War.

654   Foreman, Leonard. THE ROAD TO SAN JACINTO.
       Dutton, 1943. Story of Davy Crockett on the way
       to join the Texans in defense of the Alamo.

655   Gerson, Noel B. THE GOLDEN EAGLE. Double-
       day, 1953. The Mexican War, 1845-1848; secret
       agent draws maps of Vera Cruz for General
       Winfield Scott.

656   -- SAM HOUSTON. Doubleday, 1968. Fictional
       biography of Sam Houston from his childhood in
       Tennessee, service under Andrew Jackson,
       leading the war for Texas independence, action
       at the Battles of the Alamo and San Jacinto,
       to Governor of Texas and U. S. Senator.

657   Giles, Janice Holt. JOHNNY OSAGE. Houghton,
       1960. Story of a young trader living among the
       Osage Indians in Arkansas Territory in the 1820's.

658   -- SAVANNA. Houghton, 1961. Story of a woman
       facing life alone in Arkansas Territory in the
       1830's; plot involves competition between trading
       posts around Fort Gibson and the activities of
       Sam Houston.

659   -- VOYAGE TO SANTA FE. Houghton, 1962.
       Johnny Fowler and his young wife leave the
       Arkansas Territory in 1823 bound for Santa Fe
       with a 20 man mule train carrying trading
       supplies. Sequel to "Johnny Osage."

660   Gipson, Fred. OLD YELLER. Harper, 1956.
       Boy life on a prairie farm in Texas in the
       1860's.

661   Glidden, Frederick. AND THE WIND BLOWS FREE.
       Macmillan, 1945. Story of the cattlemen evicted
       from the Indian grasslands, later a part of Okla-
       homa, by order of President Cleveland in the
       1880's.

662   Gorman, Herbert. THE WINE OF SAN LORENZO.
       Farrar, 1945. Presents the Mexican viewpoint
       of the Mexican War; an American boy, captured
       at the Alamo, fights with Santa Anna in the war.

663   Grant, Blanch. DONA LONA. Funk, 1941. Santa
       Fe and Taos, New Mexico in the 1830's and
       1840's.

664   Grey, Zane. THE HERITAGE OF THE DESERT.
       Harper, 1910. Mormons, Indians, and cowboys
       in a story of life on the Arizona desert during
       the early days of the settlement of the Southwest.

665   -- FIGHTING CARAVANS. Harper, 1929. The
       West at the time of the Civil War.

666   Hall, Oakley. WARLOCK. Viking, 1958. Story
       of the violent life in a frontier mining town in the
       Southwest Territory in the 1880's.

667   Hogan, Pendleton. THE DARK COMES EARLY.
       Washburn, 1934. Events leading up to the fight
       for Texas independence and to the Mexican War.

668   Hooker, Forrestine. WHEN GERONIMO RODE.
       Doubleday, 1924. Life in a frontier army post
       during the last campaign against the Apache
       Indians in Arizona.

669   Horgan, Paul. A DISTANT TRUMPET. Farrar,

1960. Life on a remote army post, Fort Delivery, in the Arizona Territory in the 1880's in the face of constant threat of attack by the Apaches.

670   Hough, Emerson. NORTH OF 36. Appleton, 1923. Story of the beginnings of the great cattle drives from Texas north to the railroad markets in Kansas.

671   Houston, Margaret Bell. COTTONWOODS GROW TALL. Crown, 1958. Family life and tragedy on a Texas ranch in the 1890's.

672   Irving, Clifford. THE VALLEY. McGraw, 1961. A story of father-son conflict and life on a cattle ranch in New Mexico in post-Civil War years.

673   James, Will. THE AMERICAN COWBOY. Scribner, 1942. Picture of cattle ranching in the Southwest, through three generations of cowhands.

674   Jennings, John. SHADOWS IN THE DUSK. Little, 1955. A tale of Apache revenge for the plot of unscrupulous whites to collect the government bounty on Indian scalps; picture of copper mining in the Southwest.

675   Kelland, Clarence Buddington. VALLEY OF THE SUN. Harper, 1940. Tale of Arizona and the beginnings of Phoenix in the 1870's.

676   Kirkland, Elithe. DIVINE AVERAGE. Little, 1952. Theme of racial tolerance and the conflict between Americans, Indians, and Mexicans in Texas in 1838.

677   -- LOVE IS A WILD ASSAULT. Doubleday, 1959. Daily life, politics, and brutality in early Texas; a biographical novel based on the life of Harriet Ann Moore, a Texas pioneer.

678   Krey, Laura. ON THE LONG TIDE. Houghton, 1940. Story of the American settlement of Texas, 1812-1836; Sam Houston, Stephen Austin, Bill Travis, Andrew Jackson, and others appear.

679   Lanham, Edwin. THE WIND BLEW WEST. Long-

mans, 1935. Political, economic, and social
development of a small Texas town from 1875
to 1885.

680   Laughlin, Ruth. THE WIND LEAVES NO SHADOW.
Whittlesey, 1948. Santa Fe in the years before
the Mexican War.

681   Lea, Tom. THE WONDERFUL COUNTRY. Little,
1952. Story of the people who helped build
Puerto, Texas in the 1880's; includes Texas Rangers, railroad promoters, Mexicans, and Indians.

682   LeMay, Alan. THE SEARCHERS. Harper, 1954.
Life on the Texas frontier just after the Civil
War when the Comanches were opposing en-
croachment by white settlers.

683   -- THE UNFORGIVEN. Harper, 1957. Pioneer
life under the threat of a Kiowa Indian attack
in Texas in the 1870's.

684   Loomis, Noel. A TIME FOR VIOLENCE. Macmillan, 1960. Story of the struggles between
ranchers and outlaws in the Texas panhandle in
the 1880's.

685   Lott, Milton. BACKTRACK. Houghton, 1965.
Story of a cattle drive from Texas to Montana.

686   McCague, James. FORTUNE ROAD. Harper,
1965. An itinerant newspaperman and two children share adventures as they travel west in the
1860's.

687   McCarter, Margaret. VANGUARDS OF THE PLAINS.
Harper, 1917. Story of an expedition from Kansas
City to Santa Fe in the 1840's.

688   McMurtry, Larry. LEAVING CHEYENNE. Harper
& Row, 1963. A woman and two men share life
on a Texas ranch for 50 years.

689   Mulford, Clarence E. BRING ME HIS EARS.
McClurg, 1922. Adventures on the Missouri
River and the Santa Fe Trail in the 1840's.

690   Myers, John. I, JACK SWILLING. Hastings House,
        1961. Story of the founding of Phoenix, Arizona
        following the discovery of a prehistoric waterway
        in the middle of the desert.

691   Newsom, Ed. WAGONS TO TUCSON. Little, 1954.
        Story of a wagon train crossing the plains to
        Arizona at the close of the Civil War. picture of
        Apache raids and life at Fort Reno in Oklahoma
        Territory.

692   Ogden, George Washington. THE LAND OF LAST
        CHANCE. McClurg, 1919. Story of the land
        run and the settling of the Oklahoma Territory
        in the 1890's.

693   -- SOONER LAND. Dodd, 1929. Story of pioneering
        and homesteading in Oklahoma Territory in the
        1890's.

694   O'Meary, Walter. SPANISH BRIDE. Putnam, 1954.
        The Spanish struggling to maintain control in the
        Southwest; story of the mistress of the Spanish
        governor in Santa Fe.

695   O'Rourke, Frank. FAR MOUNTAINS. Morrow,
        1959. An orphan Irish-American boy grows up
        as a Spanish-Mexican in Taos, New Mexico;
        story of the decline of Spanish influence, cul-
        minating in the U. S. annexation of Texas and
        the invasion of Mexico during the Mexican War;
        1801-1848.

696   Oskison, John Milton. BLACK JACK DAVY. Apple-
        ton, 1926. Story of life among pioneer settlers
        who move from Arkansas to the Indian territory
        of the Southwest in the 1800's.

697   Owens, William A. LOOK TO THE RIVER. Athe-
        neum, 1963. Adventures of a young runaway in
        the Texas Red River plains in 1910.

698   Pearce, Richard. THE IMPUDENT RIFLE. Lippin-
        cott, 1951. Life in a frontier fort in the Arkansas
        Territory during the Jackson administration; pic-
        tures the migration of the Choctaws, and war with
        the Comanches.

699   -- THE RESTLESS BORDER. Lippincott, 1953.
       Comanche warfare and fights with Santa Anna
       at an army outpost on the Red River in the
       1840's.

700   Portis, Charles. TRUE GRIT. Simon & Schuster,
       1968. A girl and a U. S. Marshall set out to
       revenge her father's death; Arkansas to the
       Indian Territory in the 1880's.

701   Prebble, John. SPANISH STIRRUP. Harcourt,
       1958. Story of one of the first great cattle
       drives from Texas to market in Kansas,
       depicting hardships of the drive and the savage
       attack of the Comanches.

702   -- THE BUFFALO SOLDIERS. Harcourt, 1959.
       Story of a patrol of Negro recruits accompanying
       a group of Comanches on their last buffalo hunt.

703   Putnam, George Palmer. HICKORY SHIRT. Duell,
       1949. Story of the Hazards encountered by a
       wagon train struggling through Death Valley.

704   Richter, Conrad. TACEY CROMWELL. Knopf,
       1942. Daily life and society in a frontier
       mining town in Arizona in the 1890's; pictures
       the importance of miners and bankers in the
       life of the mining towns of the period.

705   -- THE LADY. Knopf, 1957. Tale of violence and
       revenge in the Mexican-American society of
       Northern New Mexico in the 1880's; rivalry be-
       tween cattlemen and sheepmen.

706   Roark, Garland. BUGLES AND BRASS. Doubleday,
       1964. Story of the U. S. Cavalry fighting Apaches
       in Arizona in the 1870's.

707   Rushing, Jane. WALNUT GROVE. Doubleday, 1964.
       Life in a West Texas frontier community in the
       early 1900's as the young hero matures and leaves
       home for college and a teaching career.

708   Schaefer, Jack. COMPANY OF COWARDS. Hough-
       ton, 1957. Eight Union soldiers, assigned to a
       punishment battalion, redeem themselves in a

frontier battle.

709   -- MONTE WALSH. Houghton, 1963. Accurate
        picture of life in the Western cattle country in
        a story of a cowboy working and enjoying life on
        the open range.

710   Seifert, Shirley. THE TURQUOISE TRAIL. Lippin-
        cott, 1950. Overland from Independence, Missouri
        to Santa Fe in 1846.

711   -- DESTINY IN DALLAS. Lippincott, 1958. Story
        of Alexander and Sarah Cockrell, centering around
        their part in the early development of Dallas,
        Texas; 1858.

712   -- BY THE KING'S COMMAND. Lippincott, 1962.
        A Spanish rancher leads a group of villagers on
        a long trek to San Antonio, and eventually on to
        the founding of Nacogdoches; picture of Texas
        under Spanish rule in the 1770's.

713   Shelton, Jess. HANGMAN'S SONG. Chilton, 1960.
        Story of family pride and revenge set in frontier
        Missouri, Arkansas, and Indian Territory in the
        1850's.

714   Smith, William Fielding. DIAMOND SIX. Double-
        day, 1958. Fictional biography of Wesley Smith,
        Texas Ranger, Southern soldier in the Civil War,
        Indian fighter, sheriff, and owner of the Diamond
        Six ranch.

715   Taylor, Ross. THE SADDLE AND THE PLOW.
        Bobbs, 1942. Conflict between cattlemen and
        farmers in Texas in the 1880's.

716   Thomason, John. GONE TO TEXAS. Scribner,
        1937. Danger and excitement in a fort on the
        Rio Grande River after the Civil War.

717   Venable, Clarke. ALL THE BRAVE RIFLES.
        Reilly and Lee, 1929. Life in Tennessee, in
        Washington, and in Texas and the events leading
        up to the war for Texas independence; fall of
        the Alamo; Santa Anna, Sam Houston, David
        Crockett, and others appear.

718   Ward, Christopher. YANKEE ROVER. Simon &
       Schuster, 1932. Itinerant New England peddler
       wanders through the Southwest; 1824-1829. See
       also "The Strange Adventures of Jonathan Drew"
       (Expanding Frontiers--Eastern and Southern).

719   Ward, John. DON'T YOU CRY FOR ME. Scribner,
       1940. Story of the American West; 1846-1847.

720   Wellman, Paul. BRONCHO APACHE. Macmillan,
       1936. Story of Massai, one of Geronimo's war-
       riors, captured and sent to a Florida prison
       after Geronimo's surrender, and of his escape
       and revenge.

721   -- THE IRON MISTRESS. Doubleday, 1951. Fic-
       tionalized biography of James Bowie.

722   -- THE COMANCHEROS. Doubleday, 1952. A New
       Orleans gambler becomes Texas Ranger and
       tracks down Comancheros leading Indians in
       attacks against settlers on the Texas border.

723   -- RIDE THE RED EARTH. Doubleday, 1958.
       Set in the Southwest and Mexico in the early
       1700's at the time of the struggle between
       France and Spain for the Texas territory; pic-
       tures Louis Juchereau de St. Denis' role in the
       struggle.

724   -- MAGNIFICENT DESTINY. Doubleday, 1962.
       Sweeping story of friendship that led to the
       annexation of Texas; follows the career of
       Andrew Jackson and Sam Houston from 1813 to
       1843; includes descriptions of the Battle of New
       Orleans in the War of 1812, the Battle of San
       Jacinto, and the death of Rachel Jackson.

725   Western Writers of America. RAWHIDE MEN.
       Doubleday, 1965. A collection of stories about
       frontier scouts, cattle drives, and settlers on
       the open ranges of the Old West.

726   Wormser, Richard Edward. BATTALION OF
       SAINTS. McKay, 1960. Story of a battalion of
       Mormons from Council Bluffs, Iowa who march
       to New Mexico to join the U. S. troops in the

Mexican War in 1846.

California and the Pacific Northwest

727   Ainsworth, Edward. EAGLES FLY WEST. Mac-
         millan, 1946. Picture of New York and Cali-
         fornia in the 1840's and 1850's; story of a news-
         paperman who takes part in the fighting between
         U. S. troops and Spanish Californians; the dis-
         covery of gold, and the struggle for statehood.

728   Allen, Henry. THE GATES OF THE MOUNTAINS.
         Random, 1963. Story based on the disappearance
         of Francois Rivet, a young boatman with the
         Lewis and Clark expedition.

729   Allen, T. D. (pseud). DOCTOR IN BUCKSKIN.
         Harper, 1951. Story of Marcus and Narcissa
         Whitman among the Indians in Oregon and the
         Northwest.

730   Ballard, Todhunter. GOLD IN CALIFORNIA.
         Doubleday, 1965. Experiences of a boy in a
         wagon train from Wilmington, Ohio to California,
         and life in the mining camps around Sutter's
         Mill during the gold rush of 1848.

731   Bartlett, Lanier. ADIOS! Morrow, 1929. Cali-
         fornia just after the American acquisition in
         1846, when a band of desperados refuse to re-
         cognize U. S. control and harass the settlers.

732   Beach, Rex. THE WORLD IN HIS ARMS. Putnam,
         1946. Competition between Russian and American
         sealers off Alaska; scenes in Russian Alaska and
         in San Francisco.

733   Bedford, Donald (pseud). JOHN BARRY. Creative
         Age, 1947. Hero rises from clerk to financier
         and prominent citizen; the gold rush starts,
         and Yerba Buena becomes San Francisco.

734   Berry, Don. TRASK. Viking, 1960. Story of the
         first homesteaders in the Oregon Territory in
         the 1840's, and of their troubles with the
         Indians. Based on the life of Elbridge Trask,

an early settler.

735   -- MOONTRAP. Viking, 1962. Picture of the
       conflict between the trappers and the settlers
       who want to establish law and order in the Ore-
       gon Territory in the 1840's.

736   -- TO BUILD A SHIP. Viking, 1963. Homesteading
       hardships in the Oregon Territory in the 1850's.

737   Binns, Archie. MIGHTY MOUNTAIN. Scribner,
       1940. Story of pioneer hardships in Washington
       in the 1850's and of the campaigns against the
       Indians.

738   -- YOU ROLLING RIVER. Scribner, 1947. Life
       in the port town of Astoria at the mouth of the
       Columbia River about 1865.

739   -- THE HEADWATERS. Duell, 1957. Story of a
       young couple struggling against the hardships of
       pioneering in the wilderness of the Northwest in
       the 1890's.

740   Blacker, Irwin R. DAYS OF GOLD. World, 1961.
       Adventures of an ex-teacher who joins the gold
       prospectors in the rush to the Yukon territory
       during the Alaska Gold Rush days of the 1890's.

741   Bretherton, Vivien. ROCK AND THE WIND. Dutton,
       1942. Frontier life of the early settlers in the
       Pacific Northwest, and the development of the
       area with the coming of the railroad.

742   Cameron, Margaret. JOHNDOVER. Harper, 1924.
       Picturesque details of life in California at the
       time of the gold rush.

743   Campbell, Patricia. THE ROYAL ANNE TREE.
       Macmillan, 1956. Romantic novel set on an
       isolated homestead in Washington Territory in
       the 1850's.

744   -- CEDARHAVEN. Macmillan, 1965. Life in
       Washington Territory during and after the Civil
       War.

745   Case, Victoria. THE QUIET LIFE OF MRS.
        GENERAL LANE. Doubleday, 1952. Fictionized
        biography of Polly and Joseph Lane. Contrasts
        Polly's life at home raising ten children with
        that of General Lane in the legislature, the
        Mexican War, and fighting for statehood for
        Oregon.

746   -- A FINGER IN EVERY PIE. Doubleday, 1963.
        Pioneering in Oregon Territory in the 1840's
        and 1850's.

747   Cheshire, Giff. STRONGHOLD. Doubleday, 1963.
        Sad tale of the efforts of the U.S. Army to dis-
        place the Modoc Indian tribe in California.

748   Coolidge, Dane. GRINGO GOLD. Dutton, 1939.
        Life of the Mexican bandit. Joaquin Murrietta;
        a story of California in the gold rush days of
        1849.

749   Cranston, Paul. TO HEAVEN ON HORSEBACK.
        Messner, 1952. Based on the lives of Narcissa
        and Marcus Whitman, missionaries and pioneers
        in Oregon in the 1830's.

750   Davis, Harold Lenoir. THE DISTANT MUSIC.
        Morrow, 1957. Poetic story of the development
        of the Columbia River country in Washington
        Territory from wilderness to settled country,
        and the founding of towns.

751   Downes, Anne Miller. NATALIA. Lippincott, 1960.
        Picture of Russian-American relations in Alaska
        through the story of a Civil War veteran sent to
        study the country at the time of the purchase of
        Alaska in 1867.

752   Elwood, Muriel. AGAINST THE TIDE. Bobbs,
        1950. Los Angeles in 1879. Conflict between
        the old Spanish heritage and the new American
        ways.

753   Emmons, Della. SACAJAWEA OF THE SHOSHONES.
        Binfords and Mort, 1943. Fictional account of
        the life of the Shoshone woman who guided Lewis
        and Clark, from her childhood to later years in

St. Louis and her return to the reservation.

754   Evansen, Virginia B. NANCY KELSEY. McKay,
      1965. Fictional account of the life of Nancy
      Kelsey, one of the first women to travel by
      wagon train from Missouri to California in 1841.

755   Evarts, Hal. FUR BRIGADE. Little, 1928. Story
      of fur trading in the Northwest; 1815-1835.

756   Fisher, Vardis. TALE OF VALOR. Doubleday,
      1958. Story of the Lewis and Clark expedition.

757   Footner, Hulbert. THE FURBRINGERS. McCann,
      1920. Fur trading in the Northwest.

758   Frazier, Neta Lohnes. ONE LONG PICNIC. McKay,
      1962. Pioneer story based on the diary of an
      eleven year old boy who made the covered wagon
      journey from Wisconsin to Oregon in 1851.

759   Gabriel, Gilbert Wolf. I, JAMES LEWIS. Double-
      day, 1932. Story of John Jacob Astor's trading
      post expedition to the Pacific Northwest in 1810-
      1811; founding of Astoria; massacre of the crew
      of the "Tonquin. "

760   Giles, Janice Holt. THE GREAT ADVENTURE.
      Houghton, 1966. Based on the journals of
      Captain Benjamin Bonneville, the story follows
      the grandson of Hannah Fowler leading a trapping
      party from Santa Fe to Oregon where Captain
      Bonneville is assigned to spy on the British in
      the Pacific Northwest.

761   Gulick, Bill. THE LAND BEYOND. Houghton,
      1958. Settlement of the Oregon country, the
      explorations of Captain Bonneville, the English-
      American boundary dispute, and the plight of
      the Nez Perce Indians.

762   Hargreaves, Sheba. THE CABIN AT THE TRAIL'S
      END. Harper, 1928. Indian customs and pio-
      neer life during a family's first year in Oregon;
      1843-1844.

763   Haycox, Ernest. THE EARTHBREAKERS. Little,

1952. Story of settlers in the Oregon Territory, 1845.

764   -- THE ADVENTURERS. Little, 1954. Picture of colonization of the Northwest; Oregon in the mid-1860's; development of the lumber industry.

765   Horan, James David. THE SHADOW CATCHER. Crown, 1961. Story of life on the trail to the Oregon Territory in the 1830's and of the American effort to break the British monopoly of the ful trade; based on first-hand contemporary accounts.

766   Hough, Emerson. 54-40 OR FIGHT. Bobbs, 1909. Story of the political and personal conflicts behind the Northwest boundary treaty and the annexation of Texas; introduces the English minister, Pakenham, John C. Calhoun, and the Russian Baroness von Ritz in major roles.

767   Hueston, Ethel. STAR OF THE WEST. Bobbs, 1935. Story of the Lewis and Clark expedition of 1803-1806.

768   Huffman, Laurie. A HOUSE BEHIND THE MINT. Doubleday, 1969. A tale based on the exploits of Black Bart, outlaw and stage coach robber; San Francisco, 1875-1883.

769   Jackson, Helen Hunt. RAMONA. Little, 1884. Story of relations between Indians and Spanish-Mexicans in California at the time of the American conquest.

770   Jennings, John. RIVER TO THE WEST. Doubleday, 1948. Dangers of frontier exploration contrasted with the picture of New York society in the days of John Jacob Astor and his friend Washington Irving; centers around the Astor fur trading scheme in the Northwest; 1808-1811.

771   Jones, Edwal. VERMILLION. Prentice, 1947. A hundred years of California history centered in the story of the Five Apostles mine started in 1846.

772   Jones, Nard. SWIFT FLOWS THE RIVER. Dodd,
        1940. Oregon and the Columbia River region,
        1856.

773   Kesey, Ken. SOMETIMES A GREAT NATION.
        Viking, 1964. Lusty novel of three generations
        of loggers in the Wakonda River region of
        Oregon.

774   Kyne, Peter B. TIDE OF EMPIRE. Cosmopolitan,
        1928. California during the gold rush.

775   Lauritzen, Jonreed. CAPTAIN SUTTER'S GOLD.
        Doubleday, 1964. Fictional biography of John
        Augustus Sutter, Swiss immigrant to California
        in the 1830's who developed a flourishing
        trading post and precipitated the gold rush in
        the 1840's.

776   -- THE CROSS AND THE SWORD. Doubleday,
        1965. Story of the military and the missionary
        settlement of Spanish California in the 1700's,
        contrasting the careers of Father Junipero
        Serra, who established a chain of missions in
        his conquest for the Church, and General Juan
        de Anza, who was dedicated to military con-
        quest for Spain.

777   Lee, C. Y. LAND OF THE GOLDEN MOUNTAIN.
        Meredith, 1967. Picture of life among the
        Chinese laborers in the gold fields and in
        San Francisco's Chinatown in the 1850's.

778   Lee, Virginia Chin-lan. THE HOUSE THAT TAI
        MING BUILT. Macmillan, 1963. Story of
        four generations of a Chinese-American family
        who divide their time between China and San
        Francisco, building the family fortune during
        the gold rush and the growth of a thriving import
        business.

779   MacDonald, William. CALIFORNIA CABALLERO.
        Covici, 1936. California in the late 1860's when
        the Americans were supplanting the old Spanish
        families.

780   McKay, Allis. THE WOMEN AT PINE CREEK.

Macmillan, 1966. Story of two sisters who settle in the apple-growing region of the Columbia
River valley in Washington state in 1910.

781   McKee, Ruth Eleanor. CHRISTOPHER STRANGE.
       Doubleday, 1941. Growth of San Francisco,
       1853-1901; young lawyer involved in the social
       and business life and the development of the
       railroads; state politics, vigilantes, and life on
       an old Spanish ranch.

782   McNeilly, Mildred. HEAVEN IS TOO HIGH.
       Morrow, 1944. Russian America in the days
       when Aleksandr Baranov was seeking to open
       the Pacific Northwest to the Russian fur trade
       and to establish colonies there; 1780-90's.

783   -- EACH BRIGHT RIVER. Morrow, 1950. Oregon
       in 1845. South Carolina girl goes to Oregon,
       finds her sweetheart dead, and adjusts to frontier
       life.

784   Marshall, Edison. SEWARD'S FOLLY. Little,
       1924. Romance built around the purchase of
       Alaska by the U. S. in 1867.

785   Miller, May. FIRST THE BLADE. Knopf, 1938.
       First part set in Missouri during the Civil War;
       second part deals with settling in the San Joaquin
       Valley in California. Coming of the railroad and
       digging irrigation ditches.

786   Morrow, Honoré. WE MUST MARCH. Stokes,
       1925. Marcus Whitman crosses the Rockies.

787   -- BEYOND THE BLUE SIERRA. Morrow, 1932.
       Story of Juan de Anza and the first overland
       route from Mexico to the Spanish colony at the
       site of San Francisco.

788   Norris, Kathleen. CERTAIN PEOPLE OF IMPOR-
       TANCE. Doubleday, 1922. Fictional history of
       the life and times of San Francisco; the days of
       the gold rush, Spanish ranch life, growth of the
       tea and spice business, and the development of
       the city.

789   O'Dell, Scott. HILL OF THE HAWK. Bobbs, 1947.
       Story of California under Spanish rule about the
       time Captain Fremont led the Americans in the
       conquest of the territory.

790   Older, Cora. SAVAGES AND SAINTS. Dutton,
       1936. Story of Spanish California after the
       American conquest.

791   Paul, Charlotte. GOLD MOUNTAIN. Random,
       1953. Story of hop ranching, teaching in a
       small town, and the effects of smallpox on the
       Indians; set in a small farming community near
       Seattle in the late 1800's.

792   -- THE CUP OF STRENGTH. Random, 1958.
       Logging operations and life in the lumber camps
       of the Northwest in the 1890's.

793   Peattie, Donald Culross. FORWARD THE NATION.
       Putnam, 1942. The Lewis and Clark expedition,
       1805.

794   Peeples, Samuel Anthony. THE DREAM ENDS IN
       FURY. Harper, 1949. Based on the life of
       Joaquin Murrietta, Mexican bandit in California
       in gold rush days.

795   Pendexter, Hugh. OLD MISERY. Bobbs, 1924.
       California in 1853 with its mining camps,
       gambling houses, robber bands, and hostile
       Indians.

796   Pettibone, Anita. JOHNNY PAINTER. Farrar,
       1944. Story of the settling of the Washington
       Territory in the years after the Civil War.

797   Ripley, Clements. GOLD IS WHERE YOU FIND IT.
       Appleton, 1936. California in the 1870's during
       the second gold boom. Conflict between miners
       and ranchers.

798   Roark, Garland. RAINBOW IN THE ROYALS.
       Doubleday, 1950. Story of a race in 1850 from
       Boston around the Horn to San Francisco.

799   Ross, Lillian. THE STRANGER. Morrow, 1942.

Pioneering in the Big Sur country of California
in the 1870's.

800   Scott, Reva. SAMUEL BRANNAN AND THE GOLDEN
       FLEECE. Macmillan, 1944. Fictional biography
       of the Mormon leader, Samuel Brannan, who first
       reported California's gold discovery to the world.

801   Shaftel, George. GOLDEN SHORE. Coward, 1943.
       Rivalry between the United States, Russia, and
       Mexico over the colonizing of California in the
       1840's.

802   Small, Sidney. THE SPLENDID CALIFORNIANS.
       Bobbs, 1928. California in the early 19th cen-
       tury; details of the life of Spanish rancheros in
       a new country.

803   Spearman, Frank. CARMEN OF THE RANCHO.
       Doubleday, 1937. Romance of Spanish California;
       a Texas scout rescues the daughter of a Spanish
       don from the Indians.

804   Sperry, Armstrong. NO BRIGHTER GLORY. Mac-
       millan, 1942. John Jacob Astor's fur trading
       expedition into the Northwest, 1810.

805   Steinbeck, John. EAST OF EDEN. Viking, 1952.
       Chronicle of a family who moves from Connecti-
       cut to California. Details of country and small
       town life; Civil War to World War I.

806   Stewart, George Rippey. EAST OF THE GIANTS.
       Holt, 1938. Chronicle of the development of
       California from 1837 to 1861. Indian fighting,
       the American conquest, the gold rush, the rise
       of San Francisco and the beginnings of big busi-
       ness.

807   Stone, Irving. IMMORTAL WIFE. Doubleday,
       1944. Fictional biography of Jessie Benton
       Fremont, wife of John Fremont, covering his
       part in the conquest and development of Califor-
       nia, politics in Washington, and action in the
       Western campaigns in the Civil War.

808   Stong, Philip. FORTY POUNDS OF GOLD. Double-

day, 1951. Panorama of frontier life from Iowa
to California during the gold rush, by way of
St. Louis, New Orleans, the Isthmus of Panama,
and the sea voyage to San Francisco.

809   -- THE ADVENTURE OF "HORSE" BARNSBY.
Doubleday, 1956. Romanticized story of a teenager's adventures in the California gold fields
in the 1850's.

810   Teilhet, Darwin. THE ROAD TO GLORY. Funk
and Wagnall, 1956. Story of the Spanish missions
in California in 1783; and of the work of Father
Junipero Serra among the Indians; set in and
near San Jose.

811   Terrell, John. PLUME ROUGE. Viking, 1942.
Trek of a fur trading expedition from St. Louis
to the Pacific Northwest.

812   Van Every, Dale. THE SHINING MOUNTAINS.
Messner, 1948. Scout for Lewis and Clark
crosses the Rockies and is captured by the
Indians.

813   Wells, Evelyn. A CITY FOR ST. FRANCIS.
Doubleday, 1967. Background of General Juan
de Anza's expedition in 1775 to found San Francisco; trials of the journey through Apache
country; building of the Mission Dolores; and
Anza's dismissal by Governor Rivera. Includes
an episode with Father Junipero Serra.

814   Wetherell, June. THE GLORIOUS THREE. Dutton,
1951. Pioneering in the Puget Sound region at
the time of the boundary dispute between England
and the United States.

815   White, Helen. DUST ON THE KING'S HIGHWAY.
Macmillan, 1947. Story of early Spanish mis-
sionaries in Mexico and California in 1771.

816   White, Leslie Turner. WAGONS WEST. Doubleday, 1964. Story of a young doctor who joins a
family on their journey from Boston to Mississippi
and on to San Bernardino, California in a Cones-
toga wagon.

817   White, Stewart Edward. ROSE DAWN. Doubleday,
          1920.   Story of California's development from the
          land boom of the 1880's to 1910.   Sequel to "Gold"
          (1913) and "The Gray Dawn" (1915).

818   -- LONG RIFLE.   Doubleday, 1932.   Exploring in
          the Rockies in the 1820's.   First in author's
          second series on California history.

819   -- RANCHERO.   Doubleday, 1933.   Hero of "The
          Long Rifle" crosses the Sierras to Southern
          California.

820   -- FOLDED HILLS.   Doubleday, 1934.   Continues
          the history of California through the American
          conquest; ranch life, and conflict with the Mexi-
          cans.

821   -- STAMPEDE.   Doubleday, 1942.   Conflict between
          landowners and squatters after California became
          a state in 1850; sequel to "The Folded Hills."

822   -- WILD GEESE CALLING.   Doubleday, 1940.
          Lumbering in the Pacific Northwest in 1895;
          scenes in Seattle and Alaska.

823   Young, Gordon.   DAYS OF '49.   Doran, 1925.
          Graphic picture of the color and excitement of
          the California gold rush.

The Plains States and the Far West

824   Aldrich, Bess Streeter.   A LANTERN IN HER HAND.
          Appleton, 1928.   Trek of a pioneer family from
          Iowa to Nebraska.

825   -- A WHITE BIRD FLYING.   Appleton, 1931.
          Second and third generation of a pioneer family
          in Nebraska.   Sequel to "Lantern in Her Hand."

826   -- SPRING CAME ON FOREVER.   Appleton, 1935.
          Chronicle of pioneering on the Nebraska prairie
          from 1866 to the Depression in 1933.

827   -- LIEUTENANT'S LADY.   Appleton, 1942.   Omaha,
          Nebraska just after the Civil War.

828   Allen, Henry. NO SURVIVORS. Random, 1950.
       Background of General Custer's campaign against
       the Sioux in the 1870's, sympathetic toward the
       Indians; white man adopted by Chief Crazy Horse
       rejoins Custer at the Battle of Little Big Horn.

829   -- THE LAST WARPATH. Random, 1966. Story
       of forty years struggles of the Cheyenne Indians
       against the white man; pictures events leading
       to the Sand Creek Massacre, the Battles of the
       Washita, Rosebud, Little Big Horn, and Powder
       Rivers, and the final tragedy at the Battle of
       Wounded Knee.

830   Ames, Francis H. THAT CALLAHAN SPUNK.
       Doubleday, 1965. A Massachusetts family
       settle in Montana in 1908; picture of life in a
       sod house on the prairie.

831   Aydelotte, Dora. ACROSS THE PRAIRIE. Apple-
       ton, 1941. Story of frontier settlers in Kansas
       in the 1890's.

832   Babson, Naomi. I AM LIDIAN. Harcourt, 1951.
       Theatrical troupe, heading west from Massachu-
       setts in 1856 settle down in Montana two years
       later.

833   Bailey, Paul Dayton. FOR TIME AND ALL ETER-
       NITY. Doubleday, 1964. Mormon life in Utah
       in the 1870's and 1880's, centers around the
       government's struggle to abolish the principle of
       polygamy.

834   Bean, Amelia. THE FANCHER TRAIN. Doubleday,
       1958. Based on the massacre of a California-
       bound wagon train at Mountain Meadows, Utah by
       Mormon Danites and Indians in 1857.

835   Berger, Thomas. LITTLE BIG MAN. Dial, 1964.
       Story of frontier and Indian life among the
       Cheyennes at the time of the Washita Massacre,
       and events leading up to the Battle of the Little
       Big Horn; characters include General Custer,
       Wild Bill Hickok, Calamity Jane, and Wyatt Earp.

836   Binns, Archie. THE LAND IS BRIGHT. Scribner,

1939.   Adventures along the Oregon Trail in the
1850's.

837   Birney, Hoffman. GRIM JOURNEY. Minton, 1934.
Story of the Ill-fated trek of the Donner party on
the way to California in 1846.

838   -- THE DICE OF GOD. Holt, 1956. Fictional
biography of General Custer and events leading
up to the Battle of Little Big Horn.

839   Blackburn, Thomas W. A GOOD DAY TO DIE.
McKay, 1967. Story of the Massacre of the
Sioux Indians by the U. S. Cavalry at the Battle
of Wounded Knee in 1890; characters include
Chief Sitting Bull, Buffalo Bill Cody, John J.
Pershing, and Frederick Remington, the artist.

840   -- THEY OPENED THE WEST. Doubleday, 1967.
A collection of stories dealing with the development of transportation and communications in the
opening of the West.

841   Blake, Forrester. WILDERNESS PASSAGE. Random, 1953. Pioneering, hunting, and trapping in
the Utah Territory and along the Oregon Trail.
Conflict between whites and Indians, and between
the Mormons and the United States government.

842   Bojer, Johan. THE EMIGRANTS. Appleton, 1925.
Story of the Norwegian colony who settled the Red
River valley of North Dakota, and their fight
with drought, frost, poverty, and isolation.

843   Borland, Hal. THE SEVENTH WINTER. Lippincott,
1959. Authentic picture of cattle ranching in
Colorado in the 1870's.

844   -- WHEN THE LEGENDS DIE. Lippincott, 1963.
Story of the life and customs of a Ute family in
Wyoming at the turn of the century; when his
parents die a young Indian boy faces conflict at
a reservation school and later as a bronc rider
on the rodeo circuit; he eventually finds himself
by accepting his Indian heritage.

845   Breneman, Mary Worthy. THE LAND THEY

POSSESSED. Macmillan, 1956. Story of farm
and small town life in the Dakota Territory
during the late 1800's.

846   Brink, Carol. BUFFALO COAT. Macmillan, 1944.
Story of small town life in Opportunity, Idaho
in the 1890's.

847   -- SNOW IN THE RIVER. Macmillan, 1964. Life
of Scottish immigrants settling in Idaho at the
turn of the century.

848   Burgess, Jackson. PILLAR OF CLOUD. Putnam,
1957. Story of an expedition of six men from
Kansas to the Rockies to break a new trail to
the West in 1858.

849   Cather, Willa. O PIONEERS! Houghton, 1913.
Pioneer farming on the Nebraska prairie in the
1800's.

850   -- MY ANTONIA. Houghton, 1918. Life on the
Nebraska prairie.

851   Chapman, Arthur. JOHN CREWS. Houghton,
1926. Story of life on the frontier around old
Fort Laramie, Wyoming involving a rescue from
a group of Mormon Danites, fights with the
Indians, and Indian ceremonial life and customs.

852   Chay, Marie. PILGRIMS PRIDE. Dodd, 1961.
Family life of an Italian immigrant family in a
Colorado mining town in the 1890's.

853   Clark, Walter Van Tilburg. THE OX-BOW INCI-
DENT. Random, 1940. A frontier Nevada town
in 1885 is the scene of the lynching of three men
accused of murder and cattle rustling.

854   Cockrell, Marian. THE REVOLT OF SARAH PER-
KINS. McKay, 1965. Story of a school teacher
in a frontier Colorado Territory community;
1869-70.

855   Cooper, Courtney Ryley. THE LAST FRONTIER.
Little, 1923. Opening of the Kansas Indian
lands after the Civil War; Buffalo Bill, General

Custer and others appear.

856   -- THE GOLDEN BUBBLE. Little, 1928. Dis-
       covery of gold in the Pike's Peak region in 1859,
       organization of a People's Court in Denver, and
       life in the lawless frontier towns.

857   -- THE PIONEERS. Little, 1938. Kit Carson and
       the Oregon Trail; 1842.

858   Cooper, Jamie Lee. RAPAHO. Bobbs, 1967.
       Reminiscences of an old trapper reliving his
       past as a preacher's son, buffalo hunter, and
       Indian fighter.

859   Corcoran, William. GOLDEN HORIZONS. Macrae,
       1937.   Traces the agricultural development of
       Kansas from frontier days to the introduction of
       winter wheat.

860   Culp, John H. THE BRIGHT FEATHERS. Holt,
       1965.   Three young cattle drovers take their
       first train ride, their first steamboat ride, and
       see their first "civilized" Indians on a vacation
       trip through Kansas in 1871.

861   Cunningham, John. WARHORSE. Macmillan, 1956.
       Story of ranch life in Montana in 1882.

862   Cushman, Dan. THE SILVER MOUNTAIN. Apple-
       ton, 1957.   Story of a man's rise to wealth and
       power by way of the mining industry in Montana
       in the 1880's and 1890's.

863   Davis, Clyde Brion. NEBRASKA COAST. Farrar,
       1939.   Journey to Nebraska from the Erie Canal
       in 1861.

864   Davis, Harold Lenoir. BEULAH LAND. Morrow,
       1949.   Westward journey of a small group from
       North Carolina in 1851.   Their journey carries
       them into the Southwest, to Kansas, and on to
       Oregon.

865   -- WINDS OF MORNING. Morrow, 1952. An old
       timer tells the story of his early life as a settler
       in the American Northwest, looking back from the

1920's.

866   Downing, J. Hyatt. HOPE OF LIVING. Putnam,
      1939. Tribulations of homesteading in the Dako-
      tas.

867   Drago, Harry Sinclair. MONTANA ROAD. Morrow,
      1935. Early days in the opening of the Dakota
      Territory; General Custer's campaigns against
      the Indians and the Battle of the Little Big Horn.

368   -- SINGING LARIAT. Morrow, 1939. Life in
      Nebraska just before and after admission of the
      Territory to statehood in 1867. Deals with
      problem of whiskey runners to the Indians, and
      the conflicts over statehood.

869   -- BOSS OF THE PLAINS. Morrow, 1940. Open-
      ing of the West, 1840's to 1860's; Mormons,
      General Fremont, and the Pony Express.

870   Ertz, Susan. THE PROSELYTE. Appleton, 1933.
      Story of the hardships endured by Brigham
      Young's Mormon colony in Utah.

871   Evarts, Hal. THE SHAGGY LEGION. Little,
      1930. Story of the passing of the Buffalo;
      Generals Sheridan and Custer, Wild Bill Hickok,
      and Buffalo Bill appear.

872   Fast, Howard. THE LAST FRONTIER. Duell,
      1941. Flight of 300 Cheyennes from Oklahoma to
      Montana in 1878; picture of the hardships of the
      Indians' life on the reservation.

873   Fish, Rachel Ann. THE RUNNING IRON. Coward,
      1957. Story of frontier life in Wyoming in the
      years after the Civil War.

874   Fisher, Richard. JUDGMENT IN JULY. Double-
      day, 1962. Story of conflict between gold miners
      and Indians in the Dakotas, and life in Deadwood,
      S. D. in the period following Custer's defeat
      at the Battle of the Little Big Horn in 1876.

875   Fisher, Vardis. CHILDREN OF GOD. Harper,
      1939. An account of the background of the Mor-

mon movement, persecution in Illinois and
Missouri, and the heroic migration to Utah and
the founding of an empire in the desert; Joseph
Smith and Brigham Young are major characters.

876   -- CITY OF ILLUSION.   Harper, 1941.   The Com-
stock Lode gold boom; picture of life in Virginia
City, Nevada in 1859.

877   -- THE MOTHERS.   Vanguard, 1943.   Story of
the Donner party trapped in the Sierras in 1846.

878   -- MOUNTAIN MAN.   Morrow, 1965.   Trapping,
fishing, and fighting Crow Indians in the
Rocky Mountains in the 1850's.

879   Foreman, Leonard.   THE RENEGADE.   Dutton,
1942.   A white man adopted by the Sioux Indians
faces a decision at the Battle of the Little Big
Horn.

880   Frazee, Steve.   SHINING MOUNTAINS.   Rinehart,
1951.   Story of a mixed group of Civil War
veterans thrown together in a gold rush at the
close of the war; picture of life in a mining
boom-town.

881   Furnas, Marthedith.   THE FAR COUNTRY.   Harper, 1947.   Follows a group on the long journey
from Kentucky to California in 1845.

882   Gardiner, Dorothy.   GOLDEN LADY.   Doubleday,
1936.   Gold mining in a Colorado town from the
1880's to the Depression.

883   -- SNOW-WATER.   Doubleday, 1939.   Saga of a
small Colorado town and its founder from 1868
to 1934; pictures the irrigation projects neces-
sary for life on the plains, and the growth of a
town from prairie land to city.

884   -- THE GREAT BETRAYAL.   Doubleday, 1949.
Based on the treacherous Sand Creek Massacre
of Chief Black Kettle's Cheyenne tribe near
Fort Lyon, Colorado Territory in 1864 under
the leadership of Col. Chivington.

885   Giles, Janice Holt. RUN ME A RIVER. Houghton,
        1964. A Kentucky steamboat captain faces the
        tribulations of riverboating on the Green River
        in the West at the time of the Civil War.

886   -- SIX-HORSE HITCH. Houghton, 1969. More
        about the Fowler clan in this story of the over-
        land stage routes in Utah, Colorado, and the
        Northwest in the 1850's; includes descriptions
        of the stage line business, and life as a captive
        of the Indians.

887   Gold, Douglas. A SCHOOLMASTER WITH THE
        BLACKFEET INDIANS. Caxton, 1963. Stories
        and anecdotes based on the author's experiences
        with the Siksika Indians on the Blackfoot Reser-
        vation in Montana from 1914 to 1934.

888   Grey, Zane. RIDERS OF THE PURPLE SAGE.
        Harper, 1913. Story of Mormon vengeance in
        Southwestern Utah in 1871.

889   -- THE U. P. TRAIL. Harper, 1918. The building
        of the Union Pacific Railroad in the 1860's.

890   -- WESTERN UNION. Harper, 1939. Romance of
        the West and the construction of the first tele-
        graph lines across the plains.

891   Gulick, Bill. THE HALLELUJAH TRAIL. Double-
        day, 1965. The temperance league, hijackers,
        and Indians attempt to stop a wagon train loaded
        with whiskey and champagne; based on the actual
        incident of the Walsingham train near Denver in
        the 1860's. First published in 1963.

892   Guthrie, A. B. THE BIG SKY. Sloane, 1947.
        Fur trapping in the Upper Mississippi River
        country in the 1830's.

893   -- THE WAY WEST. Sloane, 1949. Follows a
        wagon train from Independence, Missouri through
        the wilderness to Oregon on the Oregon Trail in
        the 1840's. Follows "The Big Sky" (above).

894   -- THESE THOUSAND HILLS.   Houghton, 1956.
        Story of cattle ranching in Montana in the 1880's.
        Follows "The Way West" (above).

895   Haines, William Wister.   THE WINTER WAR.
        Little, 1961.   A superior novel of the campaign
        against Chief Sitting Bull and the Sioux Indians in
        Montana during the blizzards of 1876.

896   Haldeman-Julius, Emanuel.   DUST.   Brentano, 1921.
        A story of pioneer life in Kansas.

897   Hanes, Frank Borden.   THE FLEET RABBLE.
        Page, 1961.   Story of Chief Joseph and the Nez
        Perce Indians in their epic flight in 1877 when
        the U. S. Army attempted to force them onto an
        Idaho reservation.

898   Hargreaves, Sheba.   HEROINE OF THE PRAIRIES.
        Harper, 1930.   Picture of life along the Oregon
        Trail in 1848.

899   Harris, Margaret and John Harris.   MEDICINE
        WHIP.   Morrow, 1953.   Wyoming in post Civil
        War days; wagon trains out of Fort Laramie, and
        battles with the Indians.

900   Haycox, Ernest.   TROUBLE SHOOTER.   Doubleday,
        1937.   Construction of the Union Pacific Railroad
        out of Cheyenne, Wyoming in the spring of 1868.

901   -- BUGLES IN THE AFTERNOON.   Little, 1944.
        The Dakota frontier and Indian-white relations
        preceding the campaigns of Custer against the
        Sioux in the 1870's.

902   Heinzman, George.   ONLY THE EARTH AND THE
        MOUNTAINS.   Macmillan, 1964.   Story of the
        destruction of the Cheyenne Indians in the 1860's
        and 70's from the massacres at Sand Creek and
        Washita to the final blow at the Battle of Wounded
        Knee, witnessed by an army scout married to an
        Indian woman.

903   Hough, Emerson.   THE COVERED WAGON.   Apple-

ton, 1922. Wagon train from Missouri to Oregon
along the Oregon Trail in 1848.

904   Hueston, Ethel. THE MAN OF THE STORM. Bobbs,
      1936. Story of John Colter, member of the Lewis
      and Clark expedition, who discovered Yellowstone;
      scenes in old St. Louis under Spanish, French and
      American flags.

905   -- CALAMITY JANE OF DEADWOOD GULCH.
      Bobbs, 1937. Story of early days in Deadwood,
      South Dakota in the 1870's; based on the life of
      Martha Jane Burke (Calamity Jane).

906   Kjelgaard, Jim. THE LOST WAGON. Dodd, 1955.
      A lone family with six children make their way
      along the Oregon Trail from Missouri to Oregon.

907   Laird, Charlton. WEST OF THE RIVER. Little,
      1953. Story of the fur trade in a town on the
      Upper Mississippi in the late 1830's.

908   Lane, Rose Wilder. LET THE HURRICANE ROAR.
      Longmans, 1933. Story of the pioneering days on
      the North Dakota prairie.

909   -- FREE LAND. Longmans, 1938. Homesteading
      in South Dakota in the 1880's.

910   Lathrop, West. KEEP THE WAGONS MOVING.
      Random, 1949. Two young boys join a wagon
      train on the Oregon Trail; pictures life of the
      Indians and of the adventurous pioneers.

911   Lauritzen, Jonreed. THE EVERLASTING FIRE.
      Doubleday, 1962. Story of the persecution of the
      Mormons in Nauvoo, Illinois; the murder of
      Joseph Smith, the leadership of Brigham Young,
      and the beginning of the exodus to Utah.

912   Lavender, David B. RED MOUNTAIN. Doubleday,
      1963. Story of road building during the Colorado
      silver boom in the 1880's.

913   Laxness, Hall d'or. PARADISE RECLAIMED.
      Crowell, 1962. An Icelandic farmer, persuaded
      to make a pilgrimage to Utah by a Mormon

missionary, settles in the new country and brings
his family to join him.

914   Lockwood, Sarah.   ELBOW OF THE SNAKE.
        Doubleday, 1958.   Story of homesteading in the
        Snake River valley of Idaho in the 1890's.

915   Lofts, Norah.   WINTER HARVEST.   Doubleday,
        1955.   California-bound group trapped by snow
        in the Sierras; based on the story of the Donner
        party.

916   Lott, Milton.   THE LAST HUNT.   Houghton, 1954.
        Story of a big hunt for the last of the buffalo
        herds in the 1880's.

917   -- DANCE BACK THE BUFFALO.   Houghton, 1959.
        Based on the rise of the Ghost Dance of the
        Plains Indians in 1889 and the incidents leading
        up to the Battle of Wounded Knee in 1890.

918   Lund, Robert.   THE ODYSSEY OF THADDEUS
        BAXTER.   Day, 1957.   An amusing story of
        the adventures of a young Texan drifting in
        Wyoming in the 1870's.

919   Lutz, Giles A.   THE LONG COLD WIND.   Double-
        day, 1962.   Story of cattle ranching and a family
        feud in Montana in the 1880's.

920   Mabie, Mary Louise.   LONG KNIVES WALKED.
        Bobbs, 1932.   Hardships of a California-bound
        wagon train over the plains and the mountains.

921   McKeown, Martha.   MOUNTAINS AHEAD.   Putnam,
        1961.   Hardships of life on an overland wagon
        train on the Oregon Trail from Independence,
        Missouri to Oregon in 1847.

922   McNames, James.   MY UNCLE JOE.   Viking,
        1963.   Recollections by a 12 year old boy of a
        scouting trip with his uncle into Montana in 1884.

923   Manfred, Frederick F.   LORD GRIZZLY.   McGraw,
        1954.   Story of frontier revenge in the Upper
        Missouri River country in the 1820's.

924   -- CONQUERING HORSE. McDowell, 1959. Story
       of a Sioux boy's search for a vision for his
       initiation into manhood; picture of Indian life,
       customs, lore, and religion.

925   Meigs, Cornelia. RAILROAD WEST. Little, 1937.
       Story of the difficulties encountered in the laying
       of the Northern Pacific Railroad from Minnesota
       to Yellowstone.

926   Morrow, Honoré. ON TO OREGON. Morrow, 1926.
       Life on the Oregon Trail in early pioneer days
       as a wagon train makes its way from Missouri
       to Oregon.

927   Parkhill, Forbes. TROOPERS WEST. Farrar,
       1945. Story of a Ute Indian rebellion in Wyoming
       in 1879; sympathetic to the Indians' grievances.

928   Patten, Lewis B. PROUDLY THEY DIE. Double-
       day, 1964. A white French half-breed joins the
       Sioux Indians and participates in the struggle
       against Custer's troops culminating in the Battle
       of the Little Big Horn.

929   -- THE RED SABBATH. Doubleday, 1968. A ci-
       vilian Army scout, sympathetic to the Indians,
       describes events leading up to the Battle of the
       Little Big Horn.

930   Payne, Robert. THE CHIEFTAIN. Prentice, 1953.
       Sympathetic account of the resistance of the Nez
       Perce Indians under Chief Joseph and of their
       valiant effort to escape to Canada in 1877.

931   Pendexter, Hugh. KINGS OF THE MISSOURI.
       Bobbs, 1921. Northwest from St. Louis to the
       Yellowstone country in the days of the fur trap-
       pers.

932   -- HARRY IDAHO. Bobbs, 1926. Discovery of gold
       in Idaho and the activities of the "avenging angels, "
       the Danite sect of the Mormons; 1860's.

933   Prescott, John. JOURNEY BY THE RIVER. Ran-
       dom, 1954. Journey of a wagon train through
       Missouri and Kansas to Fort Laramie, Wyoming

in 1848.

934   Pryor, Elinor. AND NEVER YIELD. Macmillan,
          1942. Mormons in Illinois and Missouri; Joseph
          Smith's death.

935   Rolvaag, Ole. GIANTS IN THE EARTH. Harper,
          1927. Picture of the Norwegian immigrant as
          a pioneer on the Dakota prairie.

936   Roripaugh, Robert A. HONOR THY FATHER.
          Morrow, 1963. Story of conflict between
          ranchers and homesteaders in the Sweetwater
          Valley of Wyoming in the 1880's.

937   Rush, William. RED FOX OF THE KINAPOO.
          Longmans, 1949. Story of Chief Joseph and the
          Nez Perce Indians from 1872 to 1877.

938   Sandoz, Mari. MISS MORISSA, DOCTOR OF THE
          GOLD TRAIL. McGraw, 1955. Life on the
          Nebraska frontier in the 1870's; historical
          background of a frontier settlement in the
          North Platte River country as seen by a woman
          doctor.

939   -- SON OF THE GAMBLIN' MAN. Potter, 1960.
          Pioneer days in Nebraska centered around the
          lives of a family who go west to found a town,
          enduring hardships of climate, financial difficul-
          ties, and conflicts with cattlemen and fellow
          townsmen.

940   Schaefer, Jack. SHANE. Houghton, 1949. Life on
          a homestead farm in Wyoming; picture of the
          conflict between farmer and rancher.

941   Seifert, Shirley. THOSE WHO GO AGAINST THE
          CURRENT. Lippincott, 1943. Set against the
          background of the founding of St. Louis, the
          Louisiana Purchase, and the exploration of the
          Upper Mississippi and Missouri River country in
          the early 1800's.

942   Sinclair, Harold. THE CAVALRYMAN. Harper,
          1958. Based on the campaign against the
          Sioux in 1864, follows an army of Civil War

veterans through the Dakota Bad Lands in pursuit of the Indians. Sequel to "The Horse Soldiers" (Civil War).

943   Snow, Donald. THE JUSTICER. Rinehart, 1960.
Story of a young lawyer's defense of an Indian
on trial under a tyrannical Federal District
Court judge in Kansas in Indian Territory in
1889.

944   Sorensen, Virginia. A LITTLE LOWER THAN THE
ANGELS. Knopf, 1942. Story of the Mormons
in Nauvoo, Illinois.

945   -- THE EVENING AND THE MORNING. Harcourt,
1949. Scotch-Irish immigrants move out across
the Western plains to Utah.

946   Stark, Joshua. BREAK THE YOUNG LAND.
Doubleday, 1964. Story of conflict between
wheat farming and cattle ranching in post-Civil
War Kansas.

947   Steele, Wilbur. DIAMOND WEDDING. Doubleday,
1950. Chronicle of a typical mountain man and
frontier scout in Colorado and the founding of
Denver; 1835 to 1919.

948   Stewart, Ramona. THE STARS ABIDE. Morrow,
1961. Two generations of family life in the
Nevada ranching and mining country.

949   Straight, Michael. CARRINGTON. Knopf, 1960.
Based on the Fetterman Massacre in Northern
Wyoming in 1866 when the Sioux ambushed and
killed Col. Fetterman and his men who were
marching against the orders of Col. Carrington;
story of Carrington's life and of the events
leading up to the massacre.

950   -- A VERY SMALL REMNANT. Knopf, 1963.
Accurate account of Col. Chivington's massacre
of the Cheyennes under Chief Black Kettle at
Sand Creek near Fort Lyon, Colorado Territory,
in 1864.

951   Swain, Virginia. THE DOLLAR GOLD PIECE.

Farrar, 1942. Background of the livestock industry in Kansas City in the boom years, 1887
to 1888.

952   Taylor, Robert Lewis. THE TRAVELS OF JAMIE
       McPHEETERS. Doubleday, 1958. Hair-raising
       adventures are encountered by an adolescent boy
       and his father as they make their way from
       Louisville to the California gold fields in 1849;
       capture by bandits, torture by Indians, a short
       stay with the Mormons, and settling on a ranch
       in California.

953   Ulyatt, Kenneth. NORTH AGAINST THE SIOUX.
       Prentice, 1965. Based on the building of Fort
       Phil Kearny and of its eventual destruction under
       siege by the Sioux, Cheyenne, and Arapaho under
       Chief Red Cloud.

954   Waters, Frank. THE WILD EARTH'S NOBILITY.
       Liveright, 1935. Settling of Colorado after the
       Civil War; the mining boom; the development of
       Colorado Springs.

955   Wellman, Manly Wade. CANDLE OF THE WICKED.
       Putnam, 1960. Story of a Civil War veteran and
       his search for land in Kansas in 1873; action
       centers around a wilderness tavern on the road
       from Fort Scott to Independence.

956   Wellman, Paul. THE BOWL OF BRASS. Lippin-
       cott, 1944. Settling of the range country of
       Western Kansas in 1889, and the growth of
       county politics and land promotion.

957   Whipple, Maurine. GIANT JOSHUA. Houghton,
       1941. Story of the settlement of the Dixie Mis-
       sion in the desert of Utah by a band of Mormons
       in the 1860's.

958   Winsor, Kathleen. WANDERERS EASTWARD,
       WANDERERS WEST. Random, 1965. Epic story
       of the development of Montana Territory in post-
       Civil War days.

THE CIVIL WAR--BEFORE AND AFTER

The Old South

959 Bontemps, Arna. BLACK THUNDER. Macmillan, 1936. Story of Gabriel's Insurrection in 1810, when 1,100 slaves plotted to seize Richmond.

960 Brown, Joe David. THE FREEHOLDER. Morrow, 1949. Follows the fortunes of a Carolina plantation overseer through immigration to Alabama and on to the time when his slavery hating sons leave to join the Union army in 1861.

961 Campbell, Thomas. OLD MISS. Houghton, 1929. A chronicle of Virginia life in the days of the great plantations, loyal slaves, and leisurely social life to the days of poverty brought on by war and Reconstruction.

962 Cather, Willa. SAPPHIRA AND THE SLAVE GIRL. Knopf, 1940. Relations of the mistress of a Virginia plantation and an intelligent slave girl; 1850's.

963 Courlander, Harold. THE AFRICAN. Crown, 1967. Story of a young African sold into slavery in Georgia in 1802; pictures the effect of the African cultural heritage on the American Negro in his relation with the white man.

964 Gaither, Frances. FOLLOW THE DRINKING GOURD. Macmillan, 1940. Plantation life in Georgia and Alabama; the drinking gourd is the Big Dipper which guides the Negroes on their way north on the Underground Railroad.

965 -- THE RED COCK CROWS. Macmillan, 1944. A young Northerner sympathetic to the slaves is forced to take part in suppressing a slave rebel-

lion in Mississippi in the 1830's.

966   -- DOUBLE MUSCADINE. Macmillan, 1949.
       Plantation life in Mississippi in the 1850's
       exposed in the trial of a young kitchen slave
       accused of poisoning the plantation owner's
       family.

967   Gordon, Caroline. PENHALLY. Scribner, 1931.
       Family chronicle of plantation life from 1826
       through the Civil War and on into the "new South"
       of this century.

968   Graham, Alice Walworth. CIBOLA. Doubleday,
       1961. Picture of life on a Louisiana plantation
       on the Mississippi River near Natchez in 1839.

969   Gray, Elizabeth. JANE HOPE. Viking, 1934.
       Picture of home life in the South just before the
       Civil War; Chapel Hill, North Carolina.

970   Griswold, Francis. TIDES OF MALVERN. Morrow,
       1930. Chronicle showing scenes from each gen-
       eration from Colonial times through World War I,
       set at a plantation house on the river above
       Charleston, South Carolina.

971   -- SEA ISLAND LADY. Morrow, 1939. Long
       chronicle of a Southern family near Beaufort,
       South Carolina from the Civil War to the 1920's.

972   Henkle, Henrietta. DEEP RIVER. Harcourt, 1944.
       Pictures differences between land owning aristo-
       crats in the lowlands and the mountaineers in
       Georgia in 1859.

973   -- FIRE IN THE HEART. Harcourt, 1948. The
       heroine's debut in Covent Garden is followed by
       her unsuccessful marriage to the slave-holding
       owner of a Sea Island, Georgia plantation; pic-
       ture of the temper of the times in England and
       America in the years preceding the Civil War.
       Based on the life of Fanny Kemble.

974   Kane, Harnett T. PATHWAY TO THE STARS.
       Doubleday, 1950. Fictional biography of John
       McDonough, who made a fortune in New Orleans

in the 1840's and left it all to his pet projects,
a plan for the slaves to earn their freedom and
a public school system for the children of
Louisiana.

975   -- THE GALLANT MRS. STONEWALL. Doubleday,
1957. Life of Anna Morrison, Southern belle who
later married Stonewall Jackson.

976   Kantor, MacKinlay. BEAUTY BEAST. Putnam,
1968. Long novel of slave and plantation life
in the Mississippi Gulf Coast in the 1850's.

977   McMeekin, Clark (pseud.) SHOW ME A LAND.
Appleton, 1940. Horse racing, gypsies, tobacco
raising, and politics in Virginia and Kentucky from
1816 to 1875.

978   -- RED RASKALL. Appleton, 1943. Romance of
tidewater Virginia, beginning in 1816; plantation
life and horse racing. Introduces some characters from "Show Me a Land. "

979   Miller, Caroline. LAMB IN HIS BOSOM. Harper,
1933. Pioneer life on a Georgia farm from
1810 through the Civil War.

980   Price, Eugenia. NEW MOON RISING. Lippincott,
1969. Southern white and Negro life on St.
Simeon's Island, Georgia, from the 1830's
through the Civil War. The hero returns from
Yale, spends seven years on a Mississippi river
boat, marries his childhood sweetheart on the
island plantation, and suffers hardships during the
war.

981   Roberts, Walter. ROYAL STREET. Bobbs, 1944.
Sectionalism and conflicting ideals leading to the
Civil War are indicated in the conflict between
Creoles and encroaching Northern business men
in New Orleans in the 1840's.

982   Seifert, Shirley. PROUD WAY. Lippincott, 1948.
Natchez plantation life during the years 1843-1844;
story of the courtship of Varina Howell and
Jefferson Davis.

983   Settle, Mary Lee. KNOW NOTHING. Viking, 1960.
        Story of plantation family life and politics in the
        twenty years before the Civil War in the area
        which became West Virginia; authentic picture of
        the South in that period.

984   Stevenson, Janet. THE ARDENT YEARS. Viking,
        1960. Based on the life of Fanny Kemble,
        English actress who married a wealthy American
        planter; picture of Southern social life and con-
        flicting views about slavery in the years before
        the war.

985   Styron, William. THE CONFESSIONS OF NAT TUR-
        NER. Random, 1967. An account of the slave
        insurrection led by Nat Turner in Virginia in
        1831.

986   Upchurch, Boyd. THE SLAVE STEALER. Wey-
        bright and Talley, 1968. Story of a Jewish mer-
        chant in a Southern city who becomes involved
        in the efforts of a young Negro slave girl to
        escape the horrors of slavery.

987   Walker, Margaret. JUBILEE. Houghton, 1966.
        Story of Negro life on a Georgia plantation
        from the early days of slavery through the
        Civil War and Reconstruction, told from the
        viewpoint of a slave woman.

988   Warren, Lella. FOUNDATION STONE. Knopf,
        1940. Chronicle of the South from 1823 through
        the Civil War; pictures the migration to Alabama
        from worn out land in South Carolina, and the
        planters' economic struggles and relations with
        the Negroes.

989   Young, Stark. HEAVEN TREES. Scribner, 1926.
        Picture of lavish hospitality, genial conversation,
        and light hearted romance on a Mississippi plan-
        tation in the years before the Civil War.

        Abolition

990   Allis, Marguerite. THE RISING STORM. Putnam,
        1955. Operations of the Underground Railroad

in Cincinnati.   Fourth in the author's series on
Ohio history (see Expanding Frontiers--the Middle West).

991   -- FREE SOIL.   Putnam, 1958.   Continues the
        story of the Cincinnati Fields, one of whom
        marries a Southern belle, moves to Kansas Ter-
        ritory and becomes involved in the struggle over
        the slavery versus free-soil issue in the 1840's.

992   Barney, Helen Corse.   GREEN ROSE OF FURLEY.
        Crown, 1953.   A Quaker girl on a farm near
        Baltimore helps runaway slaves on the Under-
        ground Railroad.

993   Brown, Katharine.   THE FATHER.   Day, 1928.
        A New England Abolitionist settles in Illinois and
        publishes an anti-slavery newspaper which
        attracts the attention of Abraham Lincoln.

994   Burnett, William Riley.   THE DARK COMMAND.
        Knopf, 1938.   Picture of the warfare between
        free-soil Kansans and Quantrill's guerrillas and
        the burning of Lawrence, Kansas.

995   Buster, Greene B.   BRIGHTER SUN.   Pageant,
        1954.   Story of slavery on a Kentucky plantation,
        and of the escape to freedom with the help of the
        Underground Railroad.

996   Cannon, LeGrand.   A MIGHTY FORTRESS.   Farrar,
        1937.   Growth of the Abolitionist movement in
        New England; set in Boston and New Hampshire
        in the 1850's.

997   Carrighar, Sally.   THE GLASS DOVE.   Doubleday,
        1962.   Vivid and authentic picture of life on an
        Ohio farm, station on the Underground Railroad;
        1860 through the Civil War.

998   Davis, Julia.   BRIDLE THE WIND.   Rinehart, 1953.
        Struggle of a plantation owner's wife to regain
        acceptance in her home after helping a slave
        escape to freedom in the 1840's.   Followed by
        "Eagle on the Sun" (Expanding Frontiers--South-
        west).

999   Dell, Floyd. DIANA STAIR. Farrar, 1932. Her-
        oine takes part in the Feminist, Socialist, and
        Abolitionist movements; Boston in the 1840's.

1000   Ehrlich, Leonard. GOD'S ANGRY MAN. Simon and
        Schuster, 1932. Biographical novel of the turbu-
        lent life of John Brown.

1001   Fuller, Edmund. STAR POINTED NORTH. Harper,
        1946. Fictional biography of Frederick Douglass,
        escaped slave who became an outstanding Negro
        leader in the Abolitionist movement.

1002   Gruber, Frank. THE BUSHWACKERS. Rinehart,
        1959. Story of the aftermath of the raid and
        massacre of Abolitionists at Lawrence, Kansas
        by Quantrill's raiders in 1863.

1003   Howard, Elizabeth. NORTH WIND BLOWS FREE.
        Morrow, 1949. Story of a Michigan girl in the
        days of the Underground Railroad, and the
        founding of a community in Ontario for the
        fugitives.

1004   Lewis, Sinclair. THE GOD-SEEKER. Random,
        1949. A carpenter doing missionary work among
        the Sioux Indians later becomes a builder in St.
        Paul, organizes a union, and fights for the
        rights of Negroes to join; Minnesota in the 1840's.

1005   Longstreth, Thomas. TWO RIVERS MEET IN CON-
        CORD. Westminster, 1946. Abolitionist senti-
        ment in Massachusetts; 1840's-1850's. Thoreau
        and Emerson appear.

1006   Lynn, Margaret. FREE SOIL. Macmillan, 1920.
        History of the free-soil struggle in Kansas.

1007   -- LAND OF PROMISE. Little, 1927. Settling of
        Kansas and the conflict between free and slave
        state supporters.

1008   Nelson, Truman. THE SIN OF THE PROPHET.
        Little, 1952. The trial of an escaped slave
        under the Fugitive Slave Law in Boston in 1854;
        introduces many notable Abolitionists of the day
        including Theodore Parker and Wendell Philips.

1009   -- THE SURVEYOR. Doubleday, 1960. Story of
        John Brown and the development of the free-soil
        movement in Kansas in the years following the
        Kansas-Nebraska Act of 1854.

1010   Niles, Blair. EAST BY DAY. Farrar, 1941.
        Story of the mutiny of the crew of a slave ship
        captured off Long Island in 1839. Heroine with
        Abolitionist sympathies discovers her grand-
        father's fortune was made in the slave trade.

1011   Parrish, Anne. CLOUDED STAR. Harper, 1948.
        Story of a small slave boy sold away from his
        parents who joined others on the journey to the
        North by way of the Underground Railroad under
        the guidance of Harriet Tubman.

1012   Robertson, Constance. FIRE BELL IN THE NIGHT.
        Holt, 1944. Abolition and the Underground Rail-
        road in Syracuse, New York in the 1850's.

1013   Seifert, Shirley. THE SENATOR'S LADY. Lippin-
        cott, 1967. Five years in the marriage of Addie
        and Stephen A. Douglas, with scenes in Kansas
        and Washington and events leading to the Lincoln-
        Douglas debates.

1014   Stern, Philip Van Doren. THE DRUMS OF MORN-
        ING. Doubleday, 1942. Panoramic picture of
        the Abolitionist movement from the 1830's to
        the 1860's; John Brown, the Underground Rail-
        road, the free-soil struggle in Kansas, and
        scenes of life in Andersonville Prison.

1015   Stevenson, Janet. SISTERS AND BROTHERS.
        Crown, 1966. Fictionalized biography of the
        Abolitionists Angelina and Sara Grimke and their
        Negro nephew Archibald Grimke, who became an
        author and crusader for Negro advancement.

1016   Strachey, Rachel. MARCHIN' ON. Harcourt, 1923.
        The Feminist and Abolitionist movements in
        Michigan in the 1840's and later in Kansas.

1017   Swift, Hildegarde. RAILROAD TO FREEDOM. Har-
        court, 1932. Story of Harriet Tubman, Negro
        slave who escaped in Maryland about 1821 and

became a leader in the Underground Railroad.

1018   Wills, Grace.   MURPHY'S BEND.   Westminster,
       1946.   Frontier settlement on the Susquehanna
       River becomes a station on the Underground Rail-
       road.

The War Years

1019   Allen, Henry.   JOURNEY TO SHILOH.   Random,
       1960.   Seven young Texans who set out in 1862
       for Richmond are recruited into the Army of the
       Mississippi and see action under General Bragg
       at the Battles of Corinth and Shiloh.

1020   Allen, Hervey.   ACTION AT AQUILA.   Farrar,
       1938.   Picture of the war in the Shenandoah
       Valley in 1864.

1021   Andrews, Robert.   GREAT DAY IN THE MORNING.
       Coward, 1950.   Southern conspirators working
       for the South in Colorado in the 1850's; growing
       bitterness between Northern and Southern sym-
       pathizers in the West.

1022   Babcock, Bernie.   SOUL OF ABE LINCOLN.
       Lippincott, 1923.   Story of Lincoln's influence on
       the lives of a Union soldier and his Southern
       fiance.

1023   Bacheller, Irving.   FATHER ABRAHAM.   Bobbs,
       1925.   Story of conflicting ideals in the North;
       Lincoln does not appear, but his influence is
       felt.

1024   Basso, Hamilton.   THE LIGHT INFANTRY BALL.
       Doubleday, 1959.   Southern traditions and Con-
       federate politics seen through the experiences of
       a South Carolina rice planter from his college
       days at Princeton, service through the war as
       assistant in the Confederate cabinet at Richmond,
       and after the war when everything is lost.

1025   Becker, Stephen D.   WHEN THE WAR IS OVER.
       Random, 1969.   A Union officer, wounded by a
       teenaged Kentucky soldier, tries unsuccessfully

to save him from being shot as a spy.

1026   Beebe, Elswyth Thane. YANKEE STRANGER.
       Duell, 1944. Williamsburg, Virginia in the
       1860's. Sequel to "Dawn's Early Light"
       (American Revolution); followed by "Ever After"
       (The Nation Grows Up).

1027   Bellah, James. THE VALIANT VIRGINIANS.
       Ballantine, 1953. Story of the Virginia cavalry
       in the Army of the Shenandoah under Jubal
       Early and of their defeat by Sheridan.

1028   Borland, Hal. THE AMULET. Lippincott, 1957.
       Confederate sympathizers making their way from
       Denver to join the Confederacy in 1861 becoming
       involved in the Battle of Wilson's Creek, Missouri.

1029   Boyd, James. MARCHING ON. Scribner, 1927.
       The war as seen by a Southern soldier on the
       march, in battle against Sherman's march to the
       sea through Georgia, and in a Federal prison
       camp. Hero is a descendant of the characters
       in "Drums" (American Revolution).

1030   Boyd, Thomas Alexander. SAMUEL DRUMMOND.
       Scribner, 1925. Life on an Ohio farm before
       and after the Civil War.

1031   Bradford, Roark. KINGDOM COMING. Harper,
       1933. Negro life on a Louisiana plantation during
       the war.

1032   -- THREE-HEADED ANGEL. Harper, 1937. Fami-
       ly sketches of different types living in Western
       Tennessee during the war.

1033   Branson, Henry C. SALISBURY PLAIN. Dutton,
       1965. Written in the form of a legend, this
       relates the experiences of a young Union officer
       in the war.

1034   Brick, John. TROUBLED SPRING. Farrar, 1950.
       A Union soldier returns to his Hudson Valley
       home to find it a growing commercial center.

1035   -- JUBILEE. Doubleday, 1956. Follows a regiment

of New York volunteers through the campaigns
and battles at Gettysburg, Lookout Mountain and
the siege of Chattanooga, the capture and burning of Atlanta, and Sherman's march to the sea.

1036   -- THE RICHMOND RAID. Doubleday, 1963.
        Story of the Kilpatrick-Dahlgren raid on Richmond
        in February, 1864.

1037   -- ROGUES' KINGDOM. Doubleday, 1965. Story of
        an outlaw family in upstate New York, who vin-
        dicated themselves in the Civil War.

1038   Brier, Royce. BOY IN BLUE. Appleton, 1937.
        The war in the Cumberland Valley and the
        Battle of Chickamauga as it appeared to a Union
        soldier.

1039   Bristow, Gwen. THE HANDSOME ROAD. Crowell,
        1938. Life in a small river town in Louisiana
        before, during, and after the war; 1859-1885.
        Sequel to "Deep Summer" (Expanding Frontiers--
        Southern).

1040   Bromfield, Louis. WILD IS THE RIVER. Harper,
        1941. Story of life in New Orleans during the
        occupation by Union troops under General Butler.

1041   Burress, John. BUGLE IN THE WILDERNESS.
        Vanguard, 1958. Life on a farm in the Missouri
        wilderness during the Civil War.

1042   Castor, Henry. THE SPANGLERS. Doubleday,
        1948. Details of soldiering in the Union army
        and of life in Andersonville prison.

1043   Catton, Bruce. BANNERS AT SHENANDOAH.
        Doubleday, 1955. Story of General Phil Sheri-
        dan's Union cavalry operations in the Shenandoah
        Valley; the Battles of Boonville, Missionary
        Ridge, and Cedar Creek.

1044   Chambers, Robert W. THE WHISTLING CAT.
        Appleton, 1932. Experiences of two young
        Texans serving as telegraph operators in the
        Union army.

1045   -- SECRET SERVICE OPERATOR 13. Appleton,
       1934. Adventures of a woman spy for the Union
       who falls in love with her opponent.

1046   Churchill, Winston. THE CRISIS. Macmillan, 1901.
       Story peopled by carpetbaggers, abolitionists,
       and Southern gentlemen, including a Confederate
       spy; hero is an anti-slavery New Englander,
       heroine is a descendant of the hero of "Richard
       Carvell" (American Revolution).

1047   Cochran, Hamilton. THE DRAM TREE. Bobbs,
       1961. Efforts of a sea captain to run the Con-
       federate blockade to get to the cotton exports in
       Wilmington, North Carolina.

1048   Cocker, Elizabeth. INDIA ALLAN. Dutton, 1953.
       Charleston, South Carolina during the war and
       Reconstruction.

1049   Colver, Anne. MR. LINCOLN'S WIFE. Holt, 1964.
       Biographical novel of Mary Todd Lincoln from the
       days of courtship in Springfield, Illinois through
       the trying years in the White House to the assas-
       sination of Lincoln. First published by Farrar,
       1943.

1050   Corbett, Elizabeth. FAYE'S FOLLY. Appleton,
       1941. Romance of the Civil War and politics on
       an Illinois farm.

1051   Crabb, Alfred Leland. DINNER AT BELMONT.
       Bobbs, 1942. Nashville, Tennessee before and
       during the war; action takes place in and near the
       city under siege.

1052   -- LODGING AT THE SAINT CLOUD. Bobbs, 1946.
       Three Southern spies elude the Yankees in Nash-
       ville in the summer of 1862 when the Union army
       was occupying the city.

1053   -- MOCKINGBIRD SANG AT CHICKAMAUGA.
       Bobbs, 1949. The war around Chattanooga in
       1863; Battles of Chickamauga, Missionary Ridge,
       and Lookout Mountain.

1054   -- HOME TO TENNESSEE. Bobbs, 1952. Effort

of the Confederates, under General Hood and
Nathan Bedford Forest, to recapture Nashville.

1055   -- PEACE AT BOWLING GREEN.   Bobbs, 1955.
        Picture of life in the South and the development
        of Bowling Green, Kentucky, from the early
        1800's through the Civil War.

1056   Crane, Stephen.   THE RED BADGE OF COURAGE.
        Appleton, 1895.   Psychological study of a young
        Union soldier in his first action at the Battle
        of Chancellorsville in 1863.

1057   Davis, Maggie.   THE FARSIDE OF HOME.   Mac-
        millan, 1963.   Moving story of a Georgia sol-
        dier and his young bride facing the hardships of
        the war.

1058   Deland, Margaret.   THE KAYS.   Harper, 1926.
        Experiences of a conscientious objector during
        the Civil War.

1059   Delmar, Viña.   BELOVED.   Harper, 1956.   Life
        of Judah P. Benjamin, Confederate Secretary of
        State, from his boyhood in Charleston to his
        death in Paris in 1884.

1060   Devon, Louis.   AIDE TO GLORY.   Crowell, 1952.
        Fictionized biography of John Rawlins, Grant's
        aide-de-camp and later his Secretary of War.

1061   Dixon, Thomas.   THE MAN IN GRAY.   Appleton,
        1921.   Portrait of Robert E. Lee.

1062   Doneghy, Dagmar.   THE BORDER; A MISSOURI
        SAGA.   Morrow, 1931.   Picture of the ravages
        of war on the Missouri-Kansas border.

1063   Dowdey, Clifford.   BUGLES BLOW NO MORE.
        Little, 1937.   Richmond, Virginia from secession
        to the evacuation of the city in the last year of
        the war.

1064   -- WHERE MY LOVE SLEEPS.   Little, 1945.   Pic-
        ture of the last year of fighting in and around
        Petersburg and Richmond.

1065 -- THE PROUD RETREAT. Doubleday, 1953.
Story of the attempt to save some of the Confederate treasury in a wagon train in the retreat
from Richmond.

1066 -- LAST NIGHT THE NIGHTINGALE. Doubleday,
1962. Vivid picture of the desolation following
the war in a story of family life on a Virginia
plantation in 1865.

1067 Duncan, Harley. WEST OF APPOMATTOX. Appleton, 1961. Story of the Confederate Iron Brigade,
a group of volunteers led by General Joseph Shelby, who march to Mexico to avoid surrender at
the end of the Civil War.

1068 Eberhart, Mignon G. THE CUP, THE BLADE, OR
THE GUN. Random, 1961. The Connecticut
wife of a Confederate officer faces alone the hos-
tility and suspicion of the community at the old
family plantation while her husband is away at
war in 1863.

1069 Edgerton, Lucille. PILLARS OF GOLD. Knopf,
1941. The West in Civil War days; the gold
rush in Arizona, and secessionist activities in
the Southwest.

1070 Edmonds, Walter D. CADMUS HENRY. Dodd,
1949. Soldier on desk detail and scout duty
for Robert E. Lee floats over enemy lines in a
balloon.

1071 Eliot, George Fielding. CALEB PETTINGILL,
U. S. N. Messner, 1956. Story of a Union officer
commanding a ship blockading Southern ports.

1072 Erdman, Loula. MANY A VOYAGE. Dodd, 1960.
Biographical novel of Edmund G. Ross, as anti-
slavery newspaper editor in Kansas during the
free-soil movement, service in the Civil War,
as Senator from Kansas casting the deciding vote
in Andrew Johnson's impeachment trial, as pro-
moter of western railroad expansion, and as
territorial governor of New Mexico; 1848 to 1889.

1073 -- ANOTHER SPRING. Dodd, 1966. Union and

Confederate raiders force rich and poor, black
and white into exile from their burned out homes
in the border region of Missouri in 1863.

1074   Fairbank, Janet Ayer.   THE CORTLANDS OF WASH-
        INGTON SQUARE.   Bobbs, 1922.   New York City
        social life in the early days of the war.

1075   -- BRIGHT LAND.   Houghton, 1932.   Story of life
        in Galena, Illinois, showing the effect of the
        Mississippi River trade, the California gold rush,
        and the Civil War on the town.

1076   Ferrel, Elizabeth and Margaret Ferrel.   FULL OF
        THY RICHES.   M. S. Mill, 1944.   Growth of
        oil companies, politics, and Confederate raids in
        the new state of West Virginia; John D. Rocke-
        feller as a young man appears.

1077   Feuille, Frank.   THE COTTON ROAD.   Morrow,
        1954.   A crippled Southern boy and a young
        Englishman transport cotton by wagon train to
        Brownsville, Texas for shipment to the Glasgow
        cotton mills.

1078   Foote, Shelby.   SHILOH.   Dial, 1952.   Centers
        around the Battle of Shiloh in the spring of
        1862.

1079   Fox, John.   LITTLE SHEPHERD OF KINGDOM
        COME.   Scribner, 1903.   Kentucky mountain
        people before and during the war; description of
        college life, the conflicting feelings about the
        war in Kentucky, and Morgan's raiders.

1080   Frederick, Harold.   THE COPPERHEAD.   1893.
        Story of the problems of an upstate New York
        farmer with pro-Southern sympathies.

1081   Garland, Hamlin.   TRAIL-MAKERS OF THE MIDDLE
        BORDER.   Macmillan, 1926.   Fictional biography
        of the author's father who met Grant as a busi-
        nessman in Galena, Illinois, joined the Union
        army, and participated in Grant's Vicksburg
        campaign.

1082   Garth, David.   GRAY CANAAN.   Putnam, 1947.

Spy story centering around the revelation of
Southern war plans.

1083   Glasgow, Alice.   TWISTED TENDRIL.   Stokes,
       1928.   Biographical novel of John Wilkes Booth.

1084   Glasgow, Ellen.   BATTLE-GROUND.   Doubleday,
       1920.   Picture of Virginia plantation life before
       secession contrasted with the hardships imposed
       by war.

1085   Gordon, Caroline.   NONE SHALL LOOK BACK.
       Scribner, 1937.   The Western campaigns in
       1862-1863; Ft. Donelson and Chickamauga;
       central figure is Nathan Bedford Forest.

1086   Grubb, Davis.   A DREAM OF KINGS.   Scribner,
       1955.   Story of young love in Western Virginia
       from 1855 to 1864.

1087   Haas, Ben.   THE FORAGERS.   Simon & Schuster,
       1962.   An idealistic Confederate officer rounding
       up supplies for his retreating army encounters
       resistance on a Virginia plantation.

1088   Hart, Scott.   EIGHT APRIL DAYS.   Coward, 1949.
       Story of the campaign of Robert E. Lee in the
       days preceding the surrender at Appomattox.

1089   Haycox, Ernest.   THE LONG STORM.   Little, 1946.
       Fight of the Copperheads to take Oregon out of
       the Union.

1090   Heyward, Du Bose.   PETER ASHLEY.   Farrar,
       1932.   Story of a sensitive young Southerner
       witnessing events leading to secession and war
       in Charleston, South Carolina.

1091   Horan, James David.   SEEK OUT AND DESTROY.
       Crown, 1958.   Based on the raiding trip of the
       Confederate ship "Shenandoah" in the last
       months of the war; describes the hardships of
       the voyage and the conflicts leading to mutiny
       during the trip.

1092   Hutchens, Jane.   TIMOTHY LARKIN.   Doubleday,
       1942.   Story of an adventurer who returns from

the California gold fields, settles in Missouri,
and joins the Union army as a scout; 1852
through the war.

1093   Johnston, Mary. THE LONG ROLL. Houghton,
        1911. Military biography of Stonewall Jackson,
        vividly describing his campaigns from the Con-
        federate point of view.

1094   -- MISS DELICIA ALLEN. Little, 1933. Life on a
        Virginia plantation before and during the war.

1095   -- DRURY RANDALL. Little, 1934. Study of a
        Virginia gentleman from 1850 to just after the
        war.

1096   Kane, Harnett T. BRIDE OF FORTUNE. Double-
        day, 1948. Story of Varina Howell Davis from
        the time she first met Jefferson Davis to the
        time he is released from prison after the war.

1097   -- LADY OF ARLINGTON. Doubleday, 1953.
        Based on the life of Mary Custis, wife of
        Robert E. Lee.

1098   -- THE SMILING REBEL. Doubleday, 1955. Story
        of Belle Boyd, Confederate spy.

1099   Kantor, MacKinlay. AROUSE AND BEWARE.
        Coward, 1936. Escape of two Union prisoners
        from Belle Isle, Virginia prison camp.

1100   -- LONG REMEMBER. Coward, 1945. Picture of
        life in Gettysburg, Pennsylvania on the day of
        the great battle.

1101   -- ANDERSONVILLE. World, 1955. Story of the
        Confederacy's largest prison camp at Anderson-
        ville, Georgia.

1102   Kelland, Clarence Buddington. ARIZONA. Harper,
        1939. Arizona in Civil War days; gamblers and
        desperados, robberies, and Indian raids.

1103   Kelly, Eleanor. RICHARD WALDEN'S WIFE. Bobbs,
        1950. Pioneer days in Wisconsin before and
        during the Civil War; Southern wife loyal to her

husband even after his death.

1104 Kennelly, Ardyth. THE SPUR. Messner, 1951.
Story of John Wilkes Booth, of his life in the
theatre, and of the forces that drove him to the
assassination of Lincoln.

1105 Keyes, Frances Parkinson. THE CHESS PLAYERS.
Farrar, 1960. Family affairs and social life in
New Orleans in the mid-1800's; centered around
Paul Charles Morphy, chess expert, and the
activities of the Confederate representatives in
Paris during the Civil War.

1106 -- MADAM CASTEL'S LODGER. Farrar, 1962.
Picture of Louisiana plantation life and Southern
politics leading up to the war in a fictional biography of Pierre Beauregard, Confederate General who ordered the first shot fired at Fort
Sumter.

1107 Knox, Rose Bell. GREY CAPS. Doubleday, 1932.
Story of two children on a Southern plantation
showing the attitude of the South to the war.

1108 Kroll, Harry Harrison. THE KEEPERS OF THE
HOUSE. Bobbs, 1940. Conflict between two
brothers on a Mississippi plantation before and
during the war.

1109 Lancaster, Bruce and Lowell Brentano. BRIDE OF
A THOUSAND CEDARS. Stokes, 1939. Story
of Southern blockade running.

1110 Lancaster, Bruce. THE SCARLET PATCH. Little,
1947. Story of the Rochambeau Rifles, a New
York company, in the fighting during the first
year of war.

1111 -- NO BUGLES TONIGHT. Little, 1948. Campaigns
in the Tennessee Valley from 1862 to the relief
of Nashville; Union spy is among the secret Union
sympathizers in the city.

1112 -- ROLL, SHENANDOAH. Little, 1956. Story of
the Shenandoah Valley campaign of 1864 with
description of General Sheridan's victories at

Opequon and Cedar Creek and the Confederates'
burning of Chambersburg; narrator is a newspaper reporter.

1113   -- NIGHT WATCH. Little, 1958. Based on the
Kilpatrick-Dahlgren raid to free Union prisoners
in Richmond in 1863; two cavalrymen are captured,
imprisoned in Libby Prison, escape and make
their way to Tennessee where they participate
in the Battle of Franklin.

1114   LeMay, Alan. BY DIM AND FLARING LAMPS.
Harper, 1962. Story of violence and conflicting
loyalties on the Missouri frontier at the beginning
of the Civil War.

1115   Lentz, Perry. THE FALLING HILLS. Scribner,
1967. Story of the Battle of Fort Pillow in
Tennessee and the massacre of Negro soldiers
and white Tennessee Union sympathizers in 1864.

1116   Lincoln, Joseph Crosby. STORM SIGNALS. Appleton, 1935. Story of Cape Cod in the early days
of the war.

1117   Longstreet, Stephen. GETTYSBURG. Farrar,
1961. Story of the daily life of the people of
Gettysburg, Pennsylvania as the battle develops
nearby.

1118   Lytle, Andrew. THE LONG NIGHT. Bobbs, 1936.
Story of revenge set in Georgia and Alabama;
protagonist participates in the Battle of Shiloh.

1119   -- THE VELVET HORN. McDowell, 1957. Story
of complex family relationship and of a boy
growing up in the Cumberland Mountains on the
Tennessee wilderness frontier during and after
the Civil War.

1120   McGehee, Thomasine. JOURNEY PROUD. Macmillan, 1939. Pictures the declining fortunes of a
large tobacco plantation in Virginia during the war.

1121   McMeekin, Clark (pseud.) CITY OF TWO FLAGS.
Appleton, 1950. Story of the conflict between
Union and Confederate sympathizers in Louis-

ville who refused to accept Kentucky's neutrality.

1122   McNeilly, Mildred. PRAISE AT MORNING. Morrow,
        1947. International diplomacy when England
        decides not to recognize the Confederacy and the
        Russians stage naval demonstrations at New York
        and San Francisco in 1863.

1123   Mally, Emma Louise. THE MOCKING BIRD IS
        SINGING. Holt, 1944. New Orleans and Texas
        during the war; picture of city and frontier life.

1124   Markey, Morris. THE BAND PLAYS DIXIE. Har-
        court, 1927. Fredericksburg, Richmond, and
        Savannah in the last years of the war.

1125   Mason, F. Van Wyck. PROUD NEW FLAGS.
        Lippincott, 1951. Story of naval warfare; efforts
        of the South to build a navy, the Baltimore riots,
        and the capture of New Orleans.

1126   -- BLUE HURRICANE. Lippincott, 1954. Naval war-
        fare in the West in 1862; the Union drive down
        the Mississippi River.

1127   -- OUR VALIANT FEW. Little, 1956. Story of a
        Southern blockade runner and a newspaperman who
        exposes war profiteers, set in Charleston,
        South Carolina.

1128   Medary, Marjorie. COLLEGE IN CRINOLINE.
        Longmans, 1937. Story of a girl in an Iowa
        college during the Civil War.

1129   Miller, Helen Topping. NO TEARS FOR CHRIST-
        MAS. Longmans, 1954. A tale of Christmas
        at a Tennessee plantation house, used by Union
        troops as headquarters.

1130   -- CHRISTMAS FOR TAD. Longmans, 1956.
        Vignette of Christmas with the Lincolns in the
        White House in 1863.

1131   -- SING ONE SONG. Appleton, 1956. Story of
        persecution, guerrilla raids, and divided loyal-.
        ties in neutral Kentucky during the Civil War.

1132   -- CHRISTMAS WITH ROBERT E. LEE. Longmans,
       1958. Short novel depicting the Lee family's
       first Christmas together after the war at Lexing-
       ton, Virginia where General Lee had accepted the
       presidency of Washington College.

1133   Minnegerode, Meade. CORDELIA CHANTRELL.
       Putnam, 1926. The effects of the war on social
       life in Charleston, South Carolina.

1134   Mitchell, Margaret. GONE WITH THE WIND.
       Macmillan, 1936. Panorama of the war and
       Reconstruction in Georgia; plantation life, hard-
       ships of war at home, Sherman's siege of Atlanta,
       carpetbaggers, Ku Klux Klan, and the rebuilding
       of business after the war.

1135   Montgomery, James Stuart. TALL MEN. Green-
       berg, 1927. Story of Confederate blockade run-
       ning during the war.

1136   Morrison, Gerry. UNVEXED TO THE SEA. St.
       Martins, 1960. Story of the war from both
       sides centering around the siege and capture of
       Vicksburg.

1137   Morrow, Honoré. FOREVER FREE. Morrow,
       1927. Abraham Lincoln from his inauguration
       to the Emancipation Proclamation; 1861-1863.

1138   -- WITH MALICE TOWARD NONE. Morrow, 1928.
       Story of the conflict between Lincoln and Charles
       Sumner over Reconstruction policy during the
       last two years of the war.

1139   -- LAST FULL MEASURE. Morrow, 1930. Pic-
       ture of the last days of the war and of Lincoln's
       plans for Reconstruction; full treatment of John
       Wilkes Booth and the assassination plot.

1140   Noble, Hollister. WOMAN WITH A SWORD.
       Doubleday, 1948. Story of Anna Ella Carroll,
       newspaper woman and writer who is credited
       with planning the Tennessee campaign.

1141   O'Connor, Richard. COMPANY Q. Doubleday,
       1957. Story of the men of one of the punishment

battalions, composed of demoted Union officers, who redeem themselves in heavy fighting; hero undertakes an undercover spying mission into besieged Atlanta.

1142 O'Neal, Cothburn. UNTOLD GLORY. Crown, 1957. Based on the spy activities of Felicia Shover, who made friends with Union officers in occupied Memphis in order to smuggle medical supplies to the Confederacy.

1143 Palmer, Bruce. MANY ARE THE HEARTS. Simon & Schuster, 1961. Four short episodes with various aspects of the war as a background.

1144 Perenyi, Eleanor. THE BRIGHT SWORD. Rinehart, 1955. Picture of Richmond society and the story of General John B. Hood's campaign in Tennessee in 1864; Battles of Franklin and Nashville.

1145 Pulse, Charles. JOHN BONWELL. Farrar, 1952. Ohio and Kentucky frontier before and during the war.

1146 Rhodes, James A. JOHNNY SHILOH. Bobbs, 1959. Story of a nine year old Ohio boy, John Clem, who ran away to join the Union army, won his nickname at the Battle of Shiloh, and after the was became a major in the regular army.

1147 Roberts, Walter. BRAVE MARDI GRAS. Bobbs, 1946. After the Battle of Bull Run a Confederate soldier returns to occupied New Orleans to organize a spy ring; picture of life under the occupation forces of General Benjamin Butler.

1148 Robertson, Constance. THE UNTERRIFIED. Holt, 1946. Copperheads in upstate New York; a Senator's son involved with a group spying for the South.

1149 -- THE GOLDEN CIRCLE. Random, 1951. Story of the Copperhead movement in Ohio under the leadership of Clement Vallandigham; plot to form the Northwest Confederacy; Morgan's raids into Ohio; the Dayton riot; and the Ohio gubernatorial race in 1863.

1150   Robertson, Don. THE THREE DAYS. Prentice,
       1959. Realistic story of the three days of the
       Battle of Gettysburg in June, 1863.

1151   -- BY ANTIETAM CREEK. Prentice, 1960. Story
       of the Battle of Antietam in September, 1862,
       points up the blunders of General McClellan.

1152   -- THE RIVER AND THE WILDERNESS. Double-
       day, 1962. Raw picture of army life and action
       at the Battles of Antietam, Fredericksburg, and
       Chancellorsville.

1153   Sass, Herbert R. LOOK BACK TO GLORY. Bobbs,
       1933. South Carolina in the days preceding the
       Civil War; story of the political events leading to
       the firing on Fort Sumter.

1154   Schachner, Nathan. BY THE DIM LAMPS. Stokes,
       1941. Life in New Orleans and on a Louisiana
       plantation during the war and Reconstruction.

1155   Scott, Evelyn. THE WAVE. Cape and Smith,
       1929. Sweeping picture of the whole war.

1156   Seifert, Shirley. CAPTAIN GRANT. Lippincott,
       1946. Ulysses Grant from his entrance at
       West Point to the beginning of the war; service
       in Mexico and California; his retirement to busi-
       ness in Galena, Illinois; beginning of his Civil
       War service as a Colonel of Illinois volunteers.

1157   -- FAREWELL, MY GENERAL. Lippincott, 1954.
       Fictional account of the life of J. E. B. Stuart
       from his days on the Western frontier in 1855
       to his death while defending Richmond against
       Custer in 1864.

1158   Shuster, George. LOOK AWAY. Macmillan, 1939.
       Kentuckian moves to Wisconsin during a mining
       boom; becomes a Confederate spy during the war.

1159   Sinclair, Harold. THE HORSE SOLDIERS. Harper,
       1956. Story of a Union cavalry mission behind
       Southern lines, based on Grierson's raid. Fol-

lowed by "The Cavalryman" (Expanding Frontiers--
Plains States).

1160 Singmaster, Elsie. BOY AT GETTYSBURG. Houghton, 1924. Story of a young boy who aids the
Union cause at the Battle of Gettysburg.

1161 -- SWORDS OF STEEL. Houghton, 1933. Story of
Gettysburg, Pennsylvania and the events leading
up to the battle, including John Brown's raid on
Harper's Ferry.

1162 -- LOVING HEART. Houghton, 1937. Story of the
Underground Railroad in Gettysburg and of events
moving up to the Battle of Gettysburg.

1163 Slaughter, Frank. IN A DARK GARDEN. Doubleday, 1946. Spies, counter-spies and a medical
student fighting for the Confederacy.

1164 Smith, Chard. ARTILLERY OF TIME. Scribner,
1939. Upstate New York farm and business life
from the 1850's to the end of war.

1165 Stacton, David. THE JUDGES OF THE SECRET
COURT. Pantheon, 1961. Story of the assassination of Abraham Lincoln, showing the effects
of the assassination on the people involved;
unsympathetic portrait of John Wilkes Booth.

1166 Stern, Philip Van Doren. THE MAN WHO KILLED
LINCOLN. Random, 1939. The story of John
Wilkes Booth and his part in the assassination.

1167 Sterne, Emma Gelders. NO SURRENDER. Dodd,
1932. Life on a Alabama plantation during the
war.

1168 Stevenson, Janet. WEEP NO MORE. Viking, 1957.
Based on the life of Elizabeth Van Lew, a
Southern abolitionist in Richmond, who served as
a spy for the North, helped Union soldiers escape
from Libby Prison, and evolved a master plan
for the capture of Richmond.

1169 Steward, Davenport. SAIL THE DARK TIDE.
Tupper and Love, 1954. Blockade running for

the Confederacy between British Nassau and Wil-
mington, Delaware.

1170   Stover, Herbert. COPPERHEAD MOON. Dodd,
        1952. Pennsylvania soldier returning home,
        tangles with Copperheads.

1171   Street, James. TAP ROOTS. Dial, 1942. Story
        of the neutral Dabney clan in Jones County,
        Mississippi; 1858-1865.

1172   -- BY VALOUR AND ARMS. Dial, 1944. Naval
        warfare on the Mississippi River; with the Con-
        federate ironclad "Arkansas"; Natchez and Vicks-
        burg under Union occupation. More about the
        Dabney clan.

1173   -- CAPTAIN LITTLE AX. Lippincott, 1956. Story
        of the actions of a company of teen-age Confed-
        erates from the Battle of Shiloh to Chickamauga.

1174   Stribling, T. S. THE FORGE. Doubleday, 1931.
        Alabama before and during the Civil War and the
        era of Reconstruction. Followed by "The Store"
        (Nation Grows Up).

1175   Sullivan, Walter. SOJOURN OF A STRANGER.
        Holt, 1957. Story of a part-Negro plantation
        owner who finds bitterness in the plantation
        society, but who comes to terms with himself
        after service in the war.

1176   Tate, Allen. THE FATHERS. Putnam, 1938.
        Conflicting ideas in Virginia just across the
        Potomac from Washington; 1850's-1860's.

1177   Toepfer, Ray Grant. THE SCARLET GUIDON.
        Coward, 1958. Follows a group of Confederate
        soldiers from their enlistment in the 43rd Ala-
        bama Infantry through four years of war; action
        in the Shenandoah Valley campaign, and the
        Battles of Gettysburg, Fisher's Hill, and Cold
        Harbor.

1178   -- THE SECOND FACE OF VALOR. Chilton, 1966.
        A young Southern artillery man and guerrilla
        fighter comes of age in the Shenandoah Valley

campaign in 1864.

1179   Toepperwein, Herman. REBEL IN BLUE. Morrow,
        1963. Story of a group of German settlers,
        staunch Union supporters, in Fredericksburg,
        Texas; 1861-64.

1180   Wagner, Constance. ASK MY BROTHER. Harper,
        1959. Civil War background in a story of a
        Southern aristocrat with a Yankee husband.

1181   Waldman, Emerson. BECKONING RIDGE. Holt,
        1940. Story of a neutral Virginia hill farmer
        caught between two armies.

1182   Warren, Robert Penn. BAND OF ANGELS. Ran-
        dom, 1955. Kentucky and Louisiana plantation
        life before, during, and after the Civil War.

1183   -- WILDERNESS. Random, 1961. Story of a
        crippled German Jew who finds his courage and
        his manhood on the battlefield.

1184   Weaver, Ward (pseud.) HANG MY WREATH.
        Funk and Wagnall, 1941. Campaign of Jeb
        Stuart in Maryland and Virginia culminating in
        the Battle of Antietam.

1185   Weber, William. JOSH. A young Southerner
        tracks down his horse, stolen by a band of
        Union soldiers who shot his father. Less about
        the war, more about his growing self-awareness.

1186   Wheelwright, Jere. GENTLEMEN, HUSH! Scribner,
        1948. Story of three young Southern soldiers in
        the war, and of the conditions they find when they
        return home.

1187   -- GRAY CAPTAIN. Scribner, 1954. Story of the
        2nd Maryland Infantry of the Army of Northern
        Virginia in the summer of 1864.

1188   Whitney, Janet. INTRIGUE IN BALTIMORE.
        Little, 1951. Political developments and the
        presidential election of 1860 in Baltimore and
        Illinois.

1189   Whitney, Phyllis. STEP TO THE MUSIC. Crowell,
        1953. Story of a divided family on Staten Island
        during the war.

1190   -- THE QUICKSILVER POOL. Appleton, 1955.
        Story of Copperhead intrigue and rebellion on
        Staten Island; 1862-1863.

1191   Williams, Ben Ames. A HOUSE DIVIDED.
        Houghton, 1947. Saga of an aristocratic Virginia
        family with conflicting loyalties, and of the full
        sweep of the war. Followed by "The Unconquered"
        (Reconstruction).

1192   Willsie, Honoré McCue. BENEFITS FORGOT.
        Stokes, 1917. Story of a young army surgeon
        presumed dead by his neglected mother.

1193   Wilson, William. THE RAIDERS. Rinehart, 1955.
        Story of conflicting loyalties and the efforts to
        defend an Ohio River town under threat of a
        Confederate raid.

1194   Yerby, Frank. THE FOXES OF HARROW. Dial,
        1946. Plantation life and politics in New Orleans;
        1825-1865.

1195   Young, Stark. SO RED THE ROSE. Scribner,
        1934. Plantation life near Natchez, Mississippi
        before and during the war.

1196   Zara, Louis. REBEL RUN. Crown, 1951. Story
        of the daring theft of a railroad engine and the
        race to burn the bridges south of Chattanooga by
        the Union spy, Andrews.

        Reconstruction

1197   Anderson, Alston. ALL GOD'S CHILDREN. Bobbs,
        1965. A Virginia-born slave escapes to Phila-
        delphia on the Underground Railroad, is later
        captured and returned to a Georgia plantation,
        joins the Union army, settles in New Orleans
        during Reconstruction and meets a violent end
        after an affair with a white teacher.

1198   Andrews, Annulet. MELISSA STARKE. Dutton,
        1935. Story of impoverished life on a once-
        prosperous Georgia plantation after the war.

1199   Cain, James M. MIGNON. Dial, 1962. Adven-
        tures of a Union army veteran in postwar New
        Orleans.

1200   Campbell, Marie. A HOUSE WITH STAIRS. Rine-
        hart, 1950. Problems of adjustment faced by
        whites and Negroes on an Alabama plantation
        during Reconstruction; carpetbaggers, occupation
        troops, and the Ku Klux Klan enter the plot.

1201   Cheney, Brainard. LIGHTWOOD. Houghton, 1939.
        Story of the farmers' struggle against a Yankee-
        owned corporation in post-Civil War years in
        Georgia.

1202   Corrington, John William. AND WAIT FOR THE
        NIGHT. Putnam, 1964. Shreveport, Louisiana
        under occupation during the last days of the
        war and the beginning of Reconstruction in 1865.

1203   Crabb, Alfred Leland. SUPPER AT THE MAXWELL
        HOUSE. Bobbs, 1943. Sympathetic portrait of
        impoverished Southern gentry's efforts to rebuild
        a shattered culture; plot centers around a Souther-
        ner's determination to regain his family home;
        set in Nashville.

1204   Dykeman, Wilma. THE TALL WOMAN. Holt, 1962.
        Story of a strong woman whose life was effected
        by the war and its aftermath, through Reconstruc-
        tion and later as she works for tax supported pub-
        lic schools; set in the Smoky Mountains backwoods
        country of North Carolina, 1864 to the 1890's.

1205   Fast, Howard. FREEDOM ROAD. Duell, 1944.
        Story of a freed slave who guides former slaves
        and poor white tenant farmers in founding a
        cooperative community in the face of local opposi-
        tion.

1206   Gersen, Noel B. YANKEE FROM TENNESSEE.
        Doubleday, 1960. Fictionized biography of
        Andrew Johnson centering on the problems he

faced with Reconstruction policies after the
assassination of Abraham Lincoln.

1207   Gordon, Armistead. OMMIRANDY. Scribner,
       1917. Amusing story of a typical old Southern
       Negro sharing privations with her ex-master's
       family.

1208   Harben, William. THE TRIUMPH. Harper, 1917.
       Story of an Abolitionist in a small Georgia town
       and his troubles with the Ku Klux Klan.

1209   Herbst, Josephine. PITY IS NOT ENOUGH. Har-
       court, 1933. Story of easy money and political
       graft in the South in Reconstruction days.
       Followed by "The Executioner Waits" (The Twen-
       ties).

1210   Krey, Laura. AND TELL OF TIME. Houghton,
       1938. Picture of the confusing social, political,
       and economic problems faced by Southerners after
       the war; Ku Klux Klan, relations with Negro
       servants, rebuilding a prosperous plantation, and
       the struggle to establish law and order in Georgia
       and Texas from 1865 to 1888.

1211   McMeekin, Clark (pseud.). TYRONE OF KENTUCKY.
       Appleton, 1954. Story of the conflicting attitudes
       and the problems of Reconstruction in a divided
       Kentucky as they were faced by a Confederate
       veteran and his Alabama bride.

1212   Miller, Helen Topping and John Dewey. REBELLION
       ROAD. Bobbs, 1954. Search for a new way of
       life by a Confederate soldier who returns to find
       his family's plantation in ruins.

1213   Miller, Helen Topping. AFTER THE GLORY.
       Appleton, 1958. Story of the conflicts between
       ex-Confederates and Union sympathizers in
       Eastern Tennessee during the Reconstruction
       period.

1214   Page, Thomas Nelson. RED ROCK. Scribner,
       1898. Social life in the South during Reconstruc-
       tion in the late 1860's, including carpetbaggers
       and the Ku Klux Klan.

1215 Pierce, Ovid William. ON A LONESOME PORCH.
      Doubleday, 1960. A young widow with her small
      son and mother-in-law return to their North
      Carolina plantation in 1865 to begin a new life.

1216 Price, Eugenia. THE BELOVED INVADER. Lip-
      pincott, 1965. Fictional biography of Anson
      Dodge, a Union veteran who devoted himself to
      rebuilding a church on St. Simeon's Island,
      Georgia after the war.

1217 Rhodes, James A. TRIAL OF MARY TODD LIN-
      COLN. Bobbs, 1959. Based on the sanity trials
      of Lincoln's wife in 1875 and 1876.

1218 Sims, Marian. BEYOND SURRENDER. Lippincott,
      1942. An ex-Confederate officer sets out to
      rebuild his ruined plantation with the aid of his
      mother and a few loyal ex-slaves.

1219 Slaughter, Frank. THE STUBBORN HEART.
      Doubleday, 1950. A romance centering around
      the plantation of a young doctor and his wife
      who is a Union spy; has the usual elements of
      Ku Klux Klan, scalawags, carpetbaggers, honest
      Union men, and loyal Southerners.

1220 -- LORENA. Doubleday, 1959. A strongwilled
      Southern belle manages her husband's plantation
      during the war and faces the problems of Recon-
      struction and the Ku Klux Klan after the war.

1221 Stewart, Catherine Pomeroy. THREE ROADS TO
      VALHALLA. Scribner, 1948. A sweeping
      novel of Reconstruction in Jacksonville, Florida;
      carpetbaggers, the Freedmen's Bureau, and the
      social and political turmoil of the times.

1222 Taylor, Robert Lewis. A JOURNEY TO MATE-
      CUMBE. McGraw, 1961. Adventure-packed
      story of the flight of a 14 year old boy, his
      uncle, and a Negro servant from Kentucky after
      a run in with the Ku Klux Klan; includes a stint
      with a quack doctor's medicine show on a Missis-
      sippi River barge en route to New Orleans, a
      harrowing experience at a Tennessee plantation,
      a dangerous crossing of the Everglades with the

guidance of friendly Seminole Indians, and various
economic schemes in Key West; authentic picture
of life in the time and places involved.

1223   Tourgee, Albion W.   A FOOL'S ERRAND.   Harbard,
       1961.   Difficulties faced by a Union officer who
       settles his family in the South; social and political
       life during Reconstruction; first published in
       1879.

1224   Twain, Mark.   THE ADVENTURES OF COLONEL
       SELLERS.   Doubleday, 1965.   Twain's satire
       on the Reconstruction era.   First published in
       1874 as part of "The Golden Age."

1225   Weekley, Robert S.   THE HOUSE IN RUINS.   Ran-
       dom, 1958.   Story of a guerrilla band carrying
       on the war in a small Mississippi community;
       theme is the responsibility one bears to rebuild
       for the future.

1226   Wellman, Paul.   ANGEL WITH SPURS.   Lippincott,
       1942.   Story of General Jo Shelby and the group
       of Confederate volunteers whom he led to Mexico
       to join Maximilian rather than accept surrender
       at the end of the war.

1227   White, Leslie.   LOOK AWAY, LOOK AWAY.   Ran-
       dom, 1943.   Story of the group of Southerners
       who migrated to Brazil after the war rather than
       stay on under Reconstruction, and of their unsuc-
       cessful efforts to pioneer on the Amazon River.

1228   Williams, Ben Ames.   THE UNCONQUERED.
       Houghton, 1953.   Picture of political, social,
       and economic strife in New Orleans during
       Reconstruction, 1865 to 1874; development of
       the cotton-seed oil industry, and the temperate
       attitude promoted by General James Longstreet.

1229   Yerby, Frank.   THE VIXENS.   Dial, 1947.   Story
       of New Orleans plantation life and Reconstruction
       legislation.

1230   -- GRIFFIN'S WAY.   Dial, 1962.   Romantic novel
       of political and social life in Mississippi following
       the Civil War.

1231   Adams, Henry. DEMOCRACY. 1879. Story
of Washington social life, and political corrup-
tion during the second administration of U. S.
Grant.

1232   Adams, Samuel Hopkins. TENDERLOIN. Random,
1959. New York City in the 1890's. A clergy-
man undertakes a crusade against gambling and
prostitution in spite of corrupt police and politicians.

1233   Allen, Henry. SAN JUAN HILL. Random, 1962.
An Arizona cowboy joins Teddy Roosevelt's
Rough Riders and sees action in the Spanish-
American War.

1234   Anderson, Sherwood. WINDY MCPHERSON'S SON.
Cape, 1916. Story of a Midwestern small town
boy who becomes a successful Chicago financier
in the years following the Spanish-American War.

1235   Angoff, Charles. JOURNEY TO THE DAWN.
Yoseloff, 1951. A Russian family migrates to
America and settles in Boston at the turn of the
century. Followed by "In the Morning Light"
(World War I).

1236   Asch, Sholem. EAST RIVER. Putnam, 1946.
Story of conflicts between Jews and Irish-Catho-
lics in New York's East Side at the turn of the
century.

1237   Atherton, Sarah. MARK'S OWN. Bobbs, 1941.
Industrial history of a Pennsylvania coal mine
from 1849 to 1929, through the story of the mine
owner, his descendants, laborers and labor
organizers.

1238   Aydelotte, Dora. LONG FURROWS. Appleton,
        1935. Picture of country social life in the
        1890's; Fourth of July picnics, quilting bees,
        revival meetings, school exercises, and other
        local affairs.

1239   -- MEASURE OF A MAN. Appleton, 1942. Busi-
        ness and social life in a small Illinois town in
        the 1890's; effects of mail order houses on small
        business, the coming of the automobile, and the
        depression of 1893.

1240   Barber, Elsie. HUNT FOR HEAVEN. Macmillan,
        1950. Picture of labor developments in the
        1890's and an experiment in communal living on
        a Pennsylvania farm; Chicago's Haymarket Riots;
        Samuel Gompers.

1241   Barker, Squire Omar. A LITTLE WORLD APART.
        Doubleday, 1966. Story of boyhood life on a
        New Mexico ranch in the years before World War
        I.

1242   Barnes, Margaret Ayer. YEARS OF GRACE.
        Houghton, 1930. Background of changing social
        life from the 1890's to 1930's; setting is Chicago.

1243   -- WITHIN THIS PRESENT. Houghton, 1933. Two
        decades in the life of a wealthy Chicago family
        from 1914 to the 1930's; World War I; Depression;
        flashbacks show the development of Chicago from
        1840.

1244   -- EDNA, HIS WIFE. Houghton, 1935. Social and
        business life in Chicago suburb and in Washington,
        D. C. through the Gibson Girl days and World
        War I to the Depression.

1245   Beebe, Elswyth Thane. EVER AFTER. Duell,
        1945. The Spanish-American War, the Rough
        Riders, and the Battle of San Juan Hill, as seen
        by a Virginia war correspondent. One of the
        author's Williamsburg series.

1246   Beer, Thomas. SANDOVAL. Knopf, 1924. New
        York social scene in the 1870's.

1247   Bell, Thomas. OUT OF THIS FURNACE. Little,
        1941. The steel industry in Homestead, Penn-
        sylvania from 1881 to the 1930's; development of
        the labor movement and the organizing of the
        Committee for Industrial Organization; Hungarian
        immigrant family.

1248   Bellamann, Henry. KING'S ROW. Simon and
        Schuster, 1940. Life in a small Midwestern
        town at the turn of the century.

1249   Benasutti, Marion. NO STEADY JOB FOR PAPA.
        Vanguard, 1967. Nostalgic story of the happy
        life of a poor Italian immigrant family in Phila-
        delphia.

1250   Benson, Sally. MEET ME IN ST. LOUIS. Random,
        1942. Typical Midwestern family at the St.
        Louis Exposition, 1903-1904.

1251   Berlin, Ellin. LACE CURTAIN. Doubleday, 1948.
        Long Island, New York, and Paris society in
        the first decade of the century. Story of preju-
        dice in the marriage of a Protestant and an
        Irish-Catholic.

1252   Betts, Doris. THE SCARLET THREAD. Harper,
        1964. Life in a North Carolina textile mill
        town at the turn of the century.

1253   Bisno, Beatrice. TOMORROW'S BREAD. Liveright,
        1938. Story of the sweatshop conditions in the
        Chicago garment making industry in the 1890's;
        and of the effort to organize labor.

1254   Bissell, Richard. JULIA HARRINGTON. Little,
        1969. A nostalgic, Sears Roebuck catalog of
        life in a small town in Iowa in 1913.

1255   Bjorn, Thyra Ferre. PAPA'S WIFE. Rinehart,
        1955. Large Swedish family migrate to America
        and settle in New England where Papa becomes a
        minister. Story of family life and customs.

1256   -- PAPA'S DAUGHTER. Rinehart, 1958. Story of
        a Swedish immigrant's daughter's ambition and
        struggle to be a writer; set in New England in

the early 1900's.   Sequel to "Papa's Wife."

1257   Blanton, Margaret.   THE WHITE UNICORN.   Vik-
           ing, 1961.   Family life and the story of a girl
           growing up in Nashville at the turn of the century.

1258   Blassingame, Wyatt.   HALO OF SPEARS.   Double-
           day, 1962.   Brutal story of life on a chain gang
           in Georgia and Florida in the early 1900's.

1259   Brace, Gerald Warner.   THE WORLD OF CARRICK'S
           COVE.   Norton, 1957.   Nostalgic view of a young
           boy's life in a Maine seafaring-farming community
           near the turn of the century.

1260   Brinig, Myron.   THE SISTERS.   Farrar, 1937.
           Life in Silver Bow, Montana, San Francisco,
           and New York, as seen by the daughters of a
           small town druggist; 1904-1910.

1261   -- MAY FLAVIN.   Farrar, 1938.   Chicago, New
           York, and Hollywood from the 1890's to the
           1930's.

1262   Brink, Carol Ryrie.   STRANGERS IN THE FOREST.
           Macmillan 1959.   Story of homesteading in
           Idaho in the early 1900's; centers around a
           Forest Service agent sent to find out if the
           settlers were actually farming the land or selling
           the timber.

1263   Bristow, Gwen.   THIS SIDE OF GLORY.   Crowell,
           1940.   Life on a Louisiana plantation from about
           1885 to the period following World War I.
           Sequel to "The Handsome Road" (Civil War).

1264   Bromfield, Louis.   MRS. PARKINGTON.   Harper,
           1943.   Daughter of a Nevada mining-town hotel
           keeper marries a rich robber baron and becomes
           famous on two continents.

1265   Budd, Lillinn.   LAND OF STRANGERS.   Lippincott,
           1953.   Story of the struggles of a young Swedish
           couple to make a life for themselves in their
           new country.

1266   -- APRIL HARVEST.   Duell, 1959.   Story of the

daughter of Swedish immigrant parents in Chicago
from the early 1900's through the outbreak of
World War I as she struggles to support herself
and get an education. Sequel to "Land of Strangers. "

1267   Burke, J. F. NOAH. Sherbourne, 1968. A love
        story with a background of the I. W. W. movement
        in a small town in Illinois and in New York City
        in 1910; brief glimpses of Theodore Dreiser,
        Emma Goldman, small town life, and radical
        politics of the day.

1268   Byron, Gilbert. THE LORD'S OYSTERS. Little,
        1957. Story of a boy's life among the oyster
        men of Chester River in the Eastern shore
        region of Maryland about the turn of the century.

1269   Caldwell, Janet Taylor. THIS SIDE OF INNOCENCE.
        Scribner, 1946. Social novel set in upstate
        New York, 1868-1880's.

1270   -- NEVER VICTORIOUS, NEVER DEFEATED.
        McGraw, 1954. Pictures the rise of American
        capitalism and the exploitation of labor in the
        one hundred years from Jackson's administration
        to 1935.

1271   -- A PROLOGUE TO LOVE. Doubleday, 1961.
        Story of an ambitious woman who rises from
        poverty to great wealth, set in Boston, 1880-
        1914.

1272   -- TESTIMONY OF TWO MEN. Doubleday, 1968.
        Problems of an outspoken medical doctor in a
        small town in Pennsylvania in 1901 following the
        abortion death of his wife.

1273   Carroll, Gladys Hasty. A FEW FOOLISH ONES.
        Macmillan, 1935. Depicts the lives of a few
        Maine farmers from the 1870's to the 1930's.

1274   -- WEST OF THE HILL. Macmillan, 1949. Vil-
        lage life in Maine in the late 1800's.

1275   Carson, Katharine. MRS. PENNINGTON. Putnam,
        1939. Social picture of a small Kansas town

in the 1880's.

1276   Carson, Robert. THE MAGIC LANTERN. Holt,
        1954. Growth of the movie industry from silent
        to sound movies in New York and Hollywood;
        1907-1927.

1277   Carter, Isabel. SHIPMATES. W. R. Scott, 1934.
        Story of a seafaring family in Maine in the 1870's.

1278   Castor, Henry. THE YEAR OF THE SPANIARD.
        Doubleday, 1950. The Spanish-American War
        and its impact on the United States; Cuba, Puerto
        Rico, and the Philippines.

1279   Chase, Mary Ellen. THE LOVELY AMBITION.
        Norton, 1960. Story of the family of an English
        Methodist minister who emigrate to Pepperell,
        Maine around 1900.

1280   Chevalier, Elizabeth Pickett. DRIVIN' WOMAN.
        Macmillan, 1942. Life on a Kentucky plantation
        from the end of the Civil War to 1905; teaching
        school, development of tobacco growing enter-
        prise, and the Kentucky tobacco war of 1905.

1281   Clune, Henry W. THE BIG FELLA. Macmillan,
        1956. Story of machine politics in an Eastern
        state in the early 1900's.

1282   Corbett, Elizabeth. THE LANGWORTHY FAMILY.
        Appleton, 1937. Family life in a Midwestern
        city at the turn of the century.

1283   -- SHE WAS CARRIE EATON. Appleton, 1938.
        Recreates the life of a small Ohio city in the
        1870's. One of the author's Mrs. Meigs series.

1284   -- THE FAR DOWN. Appleton, 1939. Story of
        a large family living on the outskirts of a Mid-
        western city in 1877.

1285   -- MR. AND MRS. MEIGS. Appleton, 1940. Family
        life in a Midwestern city of the 1880's.

1286   -- EARLY SUMMER. Appleton, 1942. Rural
        Illinois in post-Civil War days.

1287   -- THE HEAD OF APOLLO.   Lippincott, 1956.
       Light romance set in a small Illinois town in the
       1890's.

1288   -- HAMILTON TERRACE.   Appleton, 1960.   Story
       of a woman at the turn of the century cut off
       from the social life of her small Wisconsin com-
       munity by her wealth.

1289   Gerdell, Alexander.   THE RACE AND THE TIGER.
       Doubleday, 1963.   Story of labor agitation and
       violence and the Molly Maguire movement in the
       steel industry in Pittsburg when the new Bessemer
       process throws many Irish immigrants out of
       work, in the 1870's.

1290   Corey, Paul.   THREE MILES SQUARE.   Bobbs,
       1939.   Picture of agricultural America through
       the story of an Iowa farm family; 1910-1916.

1291   Crabb, Alfred Leland.   BREAKFAST AT THE HER-
       MITAGE.   Bobbs, 1945.   Story of the development
       of Nashville and the rebuilding of the Hermitage
       in the period following Reconstruction.

1292   -- REUNION AT CHATTANOOGA.   Bobbs, 1950.
       Social and economic developments in post-Recon-
       struction Chattanooga; 1876-1890.

1293   Curry, Peggy.   SO FAR FROM SPRING.   Viking,
       1956.   Story of ranch life in the cattle country
       of the Colorado Rockies in the early 1900's.

1294   Davenport, Marcia.   THE VALLEY OF DECISION.
       Scribner, 1942.   Rise of the steel industry from
       1873 through the story of a Pennsylvania steel
       manufacturer's family.

1295   Davis, Burke.   THE SUMMER LAND.   Random,
       1965.   Story of one summer in the life of an
       adolescent boy in the North Carolina tobacco
       country in 1916, with sidelights on the tobacco
       wars going on at the time.

1296   Davis, Clyde Brion.   JEREMY BELL.   Rinehart,
       1947.   Life in a small Illinois town, in Chicago,
       in an Arkansas lumber camp, in the army, and

in various other places in 1897.

1297 -- SHADOW OF A TIGER. Day, 1963. Story of a
       boy growing up in Denver from the turn of the
       century to World War I.

1298 Davis, Harold Lenoir. HONEY IN THE HORN.
       Harper, 1935. Oregon homesteading in the early
       1900's.

1299 Dawson, Cleo. SHE CAME TO THE VALLEY.
       Morrow, 1943. Saga of a Texas border town
       in the years prior to World War I. Small town
       life, droughts, and Mexican raids.

1300 De Capite, Raymond. A LOST KING. McKay,
       1961. Family life of an Italian immigrant in the
       industrial section of Cleveland, Ohio.

1301 De Forest, J. W. PLAYING THE MISCHIEF.
       Bald Eagle Press, 1961. Washington, D. C. in
       the 1870's. Story of a fraudulent claim for a
       barn destroyed in the War of 1812. Originally
       published, 1875.

1302 Deal, Borden. THE TOBACCO MEN. Holt, 1965.
       Story of the tobacco industry in Kentucky; pic-
       tures the tobacco war of 1905 and the struggle
       to form cooperatives.

1303 Deasy, Mary. O'SHAUGHNESSY'S DAY. Double-
       day, 1957. Story of family relationships of a
       corrupt Irish politician in Corioli, Ohio from the
       turn of the century to 1922.

1304 Dempsey, David. ALL THAT WAS MORTAL.
       Dutton, 1957. Novel of the social and economic
       struggles of a family in a small Illinois town
       from 1889 to 1924; conveys the manners and cus-
       toms of the period.

1305 Dowdey, Clifford. SING FOR A PENNY. Little,
       1941. Unscrupulous financial dealings in Rich-
       mond in the 1880's and 1890's.

1306 Downing, J. Hyatt. SIOUX CITY. Putnam, 1940.
       Picture of the growth of Sioux City, Iowa up to

the year 1884.

1307   Dreiser, Theodore. SISTER CARRIE. 1900.
       Depicts life of the lower middle classes in
       New York and Chicago with insights into the
       business world.

1308   -- JENNIE GERHARDT. Harper, 1911. Pictures
       the materialism of American society at the turn
       of the century, through the lives of two families,
       German and Irish immigrants.

1309   -- THE FINANCIER. Harper, 1912. Story of the
       love affairs and business career of a Philadel-
       phia financier whose enterprises lead finally to
       his arrest and conviction for embezzlement in
       the late 1800's. Followed by "The Titan."

1310   -- THE TITAN. Lane, 1914. Continues the story
       of Frank Cowperwood in the financial world in
       Chicago in the 1870's.

1311   Ducharme, Jacques. THE DELUSSON FAMILY.
       Funk and Wagnall, 1939. Social and industrial
       developments around Holyoke, Massachusetts in
       the years after 1874.

1312   Edmonds, Walter D. THE BOYDS OF BLACK RIVER.
       Dodd, 1953. Upstate New York is the setting of
       a story about a horse loving family who look
       with disdain at the coming of the horseless
       carriage.

1313   Ellsberg, Edward. MID WATCH. Dodd, 1954.
       Story of the pre-World War I navy, based on the
       explosion aboard the cruiser "Manhattan" on its
       trial run in 1909.

1314   Emerson, Elizabeth. THE GARNERED SHEAVES.
       Longmans, 1948. Quaker farmers in Illinois
       at the turn of the century.

1315   Erdman, Loula Grace. THE SHORT SUMMER.
       Dodd, 1958. Life in a Missouri town during the
       summer of 1914, with church socials, the
       Chautauqua, band concerts, family gatherings,
       and a faint echo of the trouble brewing in Europe.

1316   Eyre, Katherine Wigmore. THE CHINESE BOX.
        Appleton, 1959. Life in the upper social circles
        in San Francisco in the 1880's.

1317   Fairbank, Janet Ayer. THE SMITHS. Bobbs, 1925.
        Life in growing Chicago, from early 1860's to the
        1920's.

1318   Falstein, Louis. LAUGHTER ON A WEEKDAY.
        Obelensky, 1965. Story of a Jewish family's
        escape from the Russian pogroms in the early
        twentieth century, and of their difficulties in
        establishing themselves in a small town in the
        American Middle West.

1319   Farralla, Dana. THE MADSTONE. Lippincott,
        1958. Story of character conflict between three
        children and their stern mother during a summer
        vacation at a lake in Minnesota in 1914.

1320   Fast, Howard. THE AMERICAN. Duell, 1946.
        Sympathetic portrait of Peter Altgeld, governor
        of Illinois during the Haymarket Riots, a one-
        sided picture of the struggle between capital and
        labor in the 1890's.

1321   Ferber, Edna. SHOW BOAT. Doubleday, 1926.
        Life on a Mississippi River showboat, in New
        Orleans and St. Louis in the 1870's and after.

1322   -- SARATOGA TRUNK. Doubleday, 1941. Back-
        ground of social and business life in New Orleans
        and Saratoga, New York in the 1880's.

1323   -- GREAT SON. Doubleday, 1945. Chronicle of
        the Melendy clan and the growth of Seattle,
        Washington from early Alaska gold rush days to
        1941.

1324   Field, Rachel. TIME OUT OF MIND. Macmillan,
        1935. Story of the declining fortunes of a New
        England ship building family with the passing of
        the sailing ship, the coming of steam, and the
        beginning of the influx of summer colonists.

1325   Fischer, Marjorie. MRS. SHERMAN'S SUMMER.
        Lippincott, 1960. Story of events in the household

of the matriarch of a large Jewish family on
Long Island in 1911.

1326 Ford, Elizabeth. NO HOUR OF HISTORY. Ives
Washburn, 1940. Politics, theater, fashions,
songs, and books as seen by a girl growing up
in a small town of Iowa from 1859 to World War L

1327 Ford, James. HOT CORN IKE. Dutton, 1923.
Politics and political bosses in New York City;
1880's-1900.

1328 Ford, Paul Leicester. THE HONORABLE PETER
STIRLING. Holt, 1894. A story of politics,
based on the career of Grover Cleveland; set
in New York in the 1870's.

1329 Gabriel, Gilbert Wolf. BROWNSTONE FRONT.
Century, 1924. Social background of New York
City in the 1890's.

1330 Giles, Barbara. THE GENTLE BUSH. Harcourt,
1947. Louisiana plantation life at the turn of the
century showing the conflicts in the transition from
the old society to new customs and economics.

1331 Giles, Janice Holt. THE PLUM THICKET. Houghton, 1954. Farm and village life in Arkansas
at the turn of the century, with religious revivals,
Confederate reunions, and baseball.

1332 Goertz, Arthemise. NEW HEAVEN, NEW EARTH.
McGraw, 1953. Doctor in New Orleans in 1909
faces conflict between his loyalty to the past and
his desire to progress with the times.

1333 Grant, Ozro F. KICK THE DOG GENTLY. Bobbs,
1965. Memories of a young man's boyhood days,
centering on life in the family hotel in a small
Oklahoma town in 1914.

1334 Hagedorn, Hermann. THE ROUGH RIDERS. Harper, 1927. The Spanish-American War and the
United States in the 1890's; emphasizes the dis-
order and mismanagement of our entry into the
war.

1335   Hart, Alan. IN THE LIVES OF MEN. Norton,
        1937. Panorama of national events and life in
        a logging town on Puget Sound from 1890 to 1907.
        The depression of 1893; Spanish-American War;
        the Alaska gold rush, and labor unrest.

1336   Hergesheimer, Joseph. THREE BLACK PENNYS.
        Knopf, 1917. The development of the steel indus-
        try in Pennsylvania through the chronicle of a
        manufacturing family.

1337   Holt, Isabella. RAMPOLE PLACE. Bobbs, 1952.
        A period piece of the American Middle West
        from 1906 to 1912.

1338   Horan, Kenneth. A BASHFUL WOMAN. Doubleday,
        1944. Growth of the automobile industry as a
        background of family life in a Michigan city;
        1890's to World War II.

1339   Horgan, Paul. THINGS AS THEY ARE. Farrar,
        1964. Picture of childhood and growing up in
        a town in New York in the early 1900's.

1340   Howard, Elizabeth. BEFORE THE SUN GOES DOWN.
        Doubleday, 1946. Life in a small Pennsylvania
        town in 1880, from the mansions to the hovels
        seen from the viewpoint of a tolerant, kindly
        doctor.

1341   Howells, William Dean. A HAZARD OF NEW FOR-
        TUNES. Dutton, 1890. Story of the exploitation
        of labor and the unionization of industry set around
        the streetcar strike in New York City in the late
        1800's.

1342   Idell, Albert. CENTENNIAL SUMMER. Holt,
        1943. Political and social issues of the period
        of 1876; Philadelphia family witnesses the open-
        ing of the Centennial Exposition, and visits New
        York City.

1343   -- BRIDGE TO BROOKLYN. Holt, 1944. Picture
        of the period 1877 to 1883 centering around con-
        struction of the Brooklyn Bridge. Sequel to
        "Centennial Summer. "

1344   -- THE GREAT BLIZZARD. Holt, 1948. Brooklyn
       and New York from 1884 to the "Blizzard of
       1888. " Some of the same characters who appear
       in "Centennial Summer. "

1345   -- STEPHEN HAYNE. Sloane, 1951. Picture of
       social and financial dealings in the Pennsylvania
       coal mining region; 1870's-1880's; conflict be-
       tween the native Dutch and immigrant Irish.

1346   James, Henry. THE BOSTONIANS. 1886. Satiri-
       cal view of Boston society in the 1870's.

1347   Johnston, Mary. MICHAEL FORTH. Harper,
       1919. Emergence of the new economic and
       social order in the South at the turn of the cen-
       tury.

1348   Jones, Nard. WHEAT WOMEN. Duffield, 1933.
       Three generations of Oregon wheat growers,
       from the arrival of the pioneers to the crash of
       the market in 1930.

1349   Kapstein, Israel. SOMETHING OF A HERO.
       Knopf, 1941. Life in a small Midwestern indus-
       trial city in the early 1900's; bankers, bootleg-
       gers, iron workers, politicians, and labor
       agitators.

1350   Kaup, Elizabeth. NOT FOR THE MEEK. Macmil-
       lan, 1941. Rise of the Pittsburg steel industry
       through the story of a Danish immigrant who
       rose to the top under Andrew Carnegie.

1351   Kelland, Clarence Buddington. GOLD. Harper,
       1931. High finance and struggle for control of
       the railroads; 1860's to 1870's. Sequel to
       "Hard Money" (The Young Nation).

1352   -- JEALOUS HOUSE. Harper, 1934. Business,
       finance, and politics; 1880's to World War I.
       Sequel to "Gold. "

1353   Kelly, Wallace. DAYS ARE AS GRASS. Knopf,
       1941. Depicts the changes in the social struc-
       ture of a small Kentucky town from the late
       1870's to the early 1900's.

1354   Kennelly, Ardyth. THE PEACEABLE KINGDOM.
       Houghton, 1949. Salt Lake City, Utah in the
       1890's and the difficulties which beset the
       Mormons after the death of Brigham Young.

1355   -- UP HOME. Houghton, 1955. Sequel to the
       "Peaceable Kingdom" presents further events in
       the lives of a Mormon family in Salt Lake City
       in the 1890's.

1356   -- MARRY ME, CARRY ME. Houghton, 1956.
       Story of the nomadic life of a young couple in
       the West in the early 1900's.

1357   Keyes, Frances Parkinson. HONOR BRIGHT.
       Messner, 1936. Story of an aristocratic Boston
       family from 1890 to 1925. Washington politics
       and Boston and Virginia social life.

1358   -- BLUE CAMELLIA. Messner, 1957. Story set
       in the rice growing Cajun country of Louisiana
       from the 1880's to the early 1900's; description
       of life in New Orleans and the customs of the
       Cajuns.

1359   Laman, Russell. MANIFEST DESTINY. Regnery,
       1963. Story of forty years in the life of a
       rural Kansas community from the 1880's to
       1920's; a bankrupt Eastern financier becomes a
       farmer, supporting the Populist Party of
       William Jennings Bryan.

1360   LaPiere, Richard. WHEN THE LIVING STRIVE.
       Harper, 1941. Life in San Francisco's China-
       town; 1875-1929. Tong wars, the earthquake,
       and Chinese and American social customs.

1361   Latham, Edythe. THE SOUNDING BRASS. Little,
       1953. Chronicle of three generations of a
       powerful North Carolina family following the
       Civil War.

1362   Leonard, Jonathan. BACK TO STAY. Viking,
       1929. Portrays the life and spirit of an isolated
       New England village in the 1870's.

1363   Lewisohn, Ludwig. THE ISLAND WITHIN. Harper,

1928. Saga of a family of Polish Jews who mi-
grate to New York City in the 1870's; story of
the son's medical education at Columbia and the
cultural conflicts between his Jewish heritage
and Americanization.

1364   Lion, Hortense. THE GRASS GROWS GREEN.
Houghton, 1935. Changing social scene in
New York from the 1840's to 1918.

1365   Lipsky, Eleazar. THE DEVIL'S DAUGHTER.
Meredith, 1969. Story based on a scandal-trial
in San Francisco in the 1880's; gives a good
feeling of the time and place.

1366   Lord, Eda. CHILDSPLAY. Simon and Schuster,
1961. Story of a girl's childhood in Evanston,
Illinois at the turn of the century.

1367   McDonald, N. C. SONG OF THE AXE. Ballantine, 1957. Adventure tale of lumbering and
smuggling of Chinese workers into the country;
setting is an island in Puget Sound in the early
1900's.

1368   McGehee, Florence. BRIDE OF KING SOLOMON.
Macmillan, 1958. Story of a woman raising her
children in the Ozarks; details of daily life
covering the period from 1871 through the turn
of the century.

1369   McKay, Allis. THEY CAME TO A RIVER. Macmillan, 1941. The development of the apple
growing industry in the Columbia River region
from the early 1900's through World War I.

1370   McMeekin, Clark (pseud.) THE OCTOBER FOX.
Putnam, 1956. Family conflict on an estate in
the Kentucky bluegrass country in the 1890's.

1371   -- THE FAIRBROTHERS. Putnam, 1961. Family
life, horse breeding and racing, in post-Civil
War Kentucky; the first running of the Kentucky
Derby in 1875.

1372   McMillion, Bonner. SO LONG AT THE FAIR.
Doubleday, 1964. An orphan and his older bro-

ther join a touring theatrical company and settle
into the insurance business in Dallas, Texas at
the turn of the century.

1373   McSorley, Edward. OUR OWN KIND. Harper,
        1946.   Picture of life in the Irish section of
        Providence, Rhode Island in the early 1900's.

1374   Marius, Richard. THE COMING OF RAIN. Knopf,
        1969.   A traditional novel of the old South, set
        in Tennessee in 1885, with mystery in the back-
        ground of a genteel white family, violence, and
        murder.

1375   Marshall, Catherine. CHRISTY. McGraw, 1967.
        Story of a Quaker teacher in a mission school
        in Appalachia in 1912; moonshine, feuding, and
        religion among the hill people.

1376   Mathewson, Janet. A MATTER OF PRIDE. Dodd,
        1957.   Romance of post-Civil War South Caro-
        lina and Connecticut dealing with the Yankee wife
        of a Southerner connected with the invention of
        a cotton loom.

1377   Meeker, Arthur. PRAIRIE AVENUE. Knopf, 1949.
        The changing social scene in Chicago's South
        Side from 1885 to 1918.

1378   Mian, Mary Lawrence. YOUNG MEN SEE VISIONS.
        Houghton, 1958.   Social life and customs in a
        New England town at the turn of the century;
        episodes of church bazaars, carriage rides, and
        Decoration Day parades.

1379   Morris, Ira Victor. THE CHICAGO STORY.
        Doubleday, 1952.   Story of a German immigrant
        family in the meat packing industry in Chicago
        from 1905 to the present.

1380   Murphy, Robert William. A CERTAIN ISLAND.
        Lippincott, 1967.   A boy growing up in a small
        Iowa town in the early 1900's joins a scientific
        expedition to a Pacific island to study the birds
        and wild life.   Based on an actual incident.

1381   Norris, Frank. MCTEAGUE. Doubleday, 1899.

Picture of the depressing poverty of the laboring
classes and of the evils of the lust for money;
set in California.

1382   -- THE OCTOPUS. Doubleday, 1901. Story of
the war between California wheat growers and
the railroads they depend upon to reach their
markets.

1383   -- THE PIT. Doubleday, 1903. Novel of protest,
dealing with the Chicago wheat market, an
attack on the financiers' manipulations on the
wheat exchange with no regard for the welfare
of the producers.

1384   Norris, Kathleen. THE VENABLES. Doubleday,
1941. Family life in San Francisco before
and after the great earthquake.

1385   Nyburg, Sidney. THE GATE OF IVORY. Knopf,
1920. A romance with a political background,
laid in Baltimore in the 1890's.

1386   O'Connor, Richard. OFFICERS AND LADIES.
Doubleday, 1958. Story of two brothers serving
in the American occupation forces in the Philippines in the 1890's.

1387   O'Daniel, Janet. THE CLIFF HANGERS. Lippincott, 1961. Story of the early motion picture
industry, set in Ithaca, New York in 1915.

1388   O'Neal, Cothburn. PA. Crown, 1962. Saga of
the rise of a Texas family from poor farmers in
1910 to wealth in the oil boom.

1389   Osterman, Marjorie K. DAMNED IF YOU DO,
DAMNED IF YOU DON'T. Chilton, 1962.
A German-Jewish immigrant family achieves
success as department store owners in New
York in the early 1900's.

1390   Owens, William. FEVER IN THE EARTH. Putnam, 1958. Story of the first oil well and of
the oil boom towns in the Texas Spindletop oil
region in 1901.

1391   Page, Evelyn. THE CHESTNUT TREE. Vanguard,
        1964. Social and business life of a wealthy
        Philadelphia family summering at a resort hotel
        in 1916.

1392   Parmenter, Christine. A GOLDEN AGE. Crowell,
        1942. Life in a small New England town in the
        1880's and 1890's.

1393   Parrish, Anne. PERENNIAL BACHELOR. Harper,
        1925. Panorama of American manners, fads,
        and fashions from 1860 to 1920's.

1394   Pound, Arthur. ONCE A WILDERNESS. Reynal,
        1934. Family life on a Michigan farm from
        1890 to about 1913.

1395   -- SECOND GROWTH. Reynal, 1935. Development
        of the automobile industry, 1913-1930's, through
        the story of the Michigan family of "Once a
        Wilderness. "

1396   Quick, Herbert. THE INVISIBLE WOMAN. Bobbs,
        1924. Politics and the rise of the railroad
        interests in Iowa in the 1890's. Sequel to
        "The Hawkeye" (Expanding Frontiers--Middle
        West).

1397   Reniers, Percival. ROSES FROM THE SOUTH.
        Doubleday, 1959. Social life in and around the
        famous resorts of the 1880's; setting in White
        Sulphur Springs, West Virginia, Saratoga, and
        New York City.

1398   Richter, Conrad. ALWAYS YOUNG AND FAIR.
        Knopf, 1947. Life in a Pennsylvania town from
        the Spanish-American War to World War L

1399   -- A SIMPLE HONORABLE MAN. Knopf, 1962.
        Story of the daily life and activities of a preacher-
        storekeeper in the Dutch Pennsylvania country at
        the turn of the century.

1400   Ritner, Ann Katherine. SUMMER BRINGS GIFTS.
        Lippincott, 1956. Light romance picturing small
        town life in Fidelia, Colorado during the summer
        of 1915.

1401   Roberts, Dorothy James. MISSY. Appleton, 1957.
        Picture of small town life at the turn of the
        century; story of a girl growing up in West Vir-
        ginia.

1402   Robertson, Don. PARADISE FALLS. Putnam,
        1968. Robust tale of business and social life
        and corruption in an Ohio town in the years
        following the Civil War.

1403   Roscoe, Theodore. ONLY IN NEW ENGLAND.
        Scribner, 1959. New England atmosphere and
        folkways pictured in the story of a murder com-
        mitted in 1911.

1404   -- TO LIVE AND DIE IN DIXIE. Scribner, 1961.
        Southern and Victorian mores pictured in the
        story based on an actual murder trial in Amity-
        burg, Virginia in 1902.

1405   Ross, Zola Helen. CASSY SCANDAL. Bobbs,
        1954. Business and social life and the growth
        of Seattle in the 1880's.

1406   Rubins, Harold. DREAM MERCHANTS. Knopf,
        1949. Picture of the movie industry from
        penny arcade to serials and sound, and the
        financial deals behind it.

1407   Sandburg, Helga. THE WIZARD'S CHILD. Dial,
        1967. Poetic picture of harsh life in the
        North Carolina mountain country in 1915.

1408   Selby, John. ISLAND IN THE CORN. Rinehart,
        1941. Period novel of a Wisconsin town on the
        Fox River in the 1880's and 1890's. Sequel to
        "Elegant Journey" (Expanding Frontiers--Middle
        West).

1409   Seton, Anya. THE TURQUOISE. Houghton, 1946.
        Pictures the social climb of the beautiful heroine
        from a Mexican hovel to a Fifth Avenue mansion
        in the 1870's.

1410   Shellabarger, Samuel. TOLBECKEN. Little, 1956.
        Story of American life at the turn of the century

in which old traditional family values are in conflict with rising commercialism.

1411   Sinclair, Harold. YEARS OF GROWTH. Doubleday,
        1940. Life in a small Illinois town from 1861
        to 1893.

1412   Sinclair, Upton. THE JUNGLE. Viking, 1906.
        Pictures the oppressed life of the workingman
        in and around the Chicago stockyards at the turn
        of the century.

1413   Skinkin, Elizabeth. BROWNSTONE GOTHIC. Holt,
        1961. Family story set in a Fifth Avenue man-
        sion in New York City in 1871; shows the cul-
        tural and social background of the period.

1414   Smith, Betty. MAGGIE-NOW. Harper, 1958.
        Story of immigrant Irish and Germans in
        Brooklyn at the turn of the century.

1415   Smith, Chard. LADIES DAY. Scribner, 1941.
        Social conditions in a New York manufacturing
        town in the 1880's-1890's; exploitation of labor
        and the movement for women's rights.

1416   Sorensen, Virginia. MANY HEAVENS. Harcourt,
        1954. Mormon life and customs at the turn of
        the century.

1417   Steegmuller, Francis. THE CHRISTENING PARTY.
        Farrar, 1960. Social life and customs as ob-
        served by a six-year old boy at a christening
        party in Connecticut in 1906.

1418   Steele, Wilbur. THEIR TOWN. Doubleday, 1952.
        Business and social development of a Colorado
        town from 1897 to the 1930's.

1419   Steelman, Robert. CALL OF THE ARCTIC. Coward,
        1960. Adventures of a young Harvard man who
        joined the Arctic expeditions of Charles Francis
        Hall in the years between 1860 and 1873.

1420   Stegner, Wallace. THE PREACHER AND THE
        SLAVE. Houghton, 1950. Fictional biography of
        Joseph Hillstrom, song writer and labor organizer

for the Industrial Workers of the World, 1910-1916.

1421   Stephenson, Howard. GLASS. Claude Kendall, 1933.
        Struggle between agriculture and industry in Ohio
        at the turn of the century and the development of
        gas wells and the glass industry.

1422   Steuber, William. THE LANDLOOKER. Bobbs,
        1957. Adventures of the sons of a Chicago harness
        maker in 1871 on a selling trip in Wisconsin; life in
        the small towns, isolated farms, and lumber camps
        punctuated by a forest fire and the great Chicago fire.

1423   Stevens, James. BIG JIM TURNER. Doubleday,
        1948. Labor agitation and the I. W. W. in the Pacific
        Northwest; 1900 to 1903.

1424   Stone, Irving. ADVERSARY IN THE HOUSE. Double-
        day, 1947. Based on the life of Eugene V. Debs.

1425   Street, James and James Childers. TOMORROW WE
        REAP. Dial, 1949. Lumber industry and political
        corruption in a Mississippi valley in the 1890's.
        Sequel to "By Valour and Arms" (Civil War).

1426   --MINGO DABNEY. Dial, 1950. Member of the
        Mississippi Dabney clan becomes involved in the
        Cuban revolt; 1895. Sequel to "Tomorrow We Reap. "

1427   Stribling, T. S. THE STORE. Doubleday, 1932.
        Picture of Southern life in the 1880's. Traces the
        transformation of the Old South into the new.
        Sequel to "The Forge" (Civil War).

1428   Suchow, Ruth. THE JOHN WOOD CASE. Viking, 1959.
        Story of small town life in Iowa at the turn of the
        century and the effects on a high school senior when
        he learns his father has been embezzling company
        funds.

1429   Sugrue, Thomas. SUCH IS THE KINGDOM. Holt,
        1940. Everyday life in an Irish community in a
        Connecticut factory town in 1909.

1430   Swarthout, Glendon. THEY CAME TO CORDURA.
        Random, 1958. Story of a small band of Ameri-
        cans making their way to a rear base following

action against Mexican revolutionists who
attacked across the border in 1916.

1431   Synon, Mary. GOOD RED BRICKS. Little, 1941.
        Politics, horse racing, and prize-fighting in
        Chicago in the 1890's.

1432   Taber, Gladys. SPRING HARVEST. Putnam,
        1959. Life on the campus of a small college
        in Wisconsin in the spring of 1914.

1433   Tarkington, Booth. THE MAGNIFICENT AMBER-
        SONS. Doubleday, 1918. Rise and decline of a
        typical Midwestern family in the 1870's.

1434   Taylor, R. S. IN RED WEATHER. Holt, 1961.
        Story of the varied political reactions produced
        by a catastrophic fire in a New England city in
        1871.

1435   Telfer, Dariel. THE NIGHT OF THE COMET.
        Doubleday, 1969. A simple family story set in
        a Midwestern city at the time of Halley's Comet.

1436   Thompson, Ariadne. THE OCTAGONAL HEART.
        Bobbs, 1956. Nostalgic memories of a Greek-
        American family living in an octagonal house
        in St. Louis at the turn of the century.

1437   Tippett, Thomas. HORSE SHOE BOTTOMS. Har-
        per, 1935. The early labor movement and the
        problems of Illinois mine workers in the 1870's
        and after.

1438   Towne, Charles H. GOOD OLD YESTERDAYS.
        Appleton, 1935. Picture of a Southern family
        growing up and finding a place in life in New
        York in the 1880's and 1890's.

1439   Train, Arthur Cheney. TASSLES ON HER BOOTS.
        Scribner, 1940. New York society and politics
        in the days of Boss Tweed and the Grant adminis-
        tration.

1440   Turnbull, Agnes Sligh. GOWN OF GLORY. Hough-
        ton, 1952. Life of a minister and his family in
        a small Pennsylvania town at the turn of the

century.

1441   -- THE NIGHTINGALE. Houghton, 1960. Nostalgic,
       romantic picture of life in the United States in
       the early 1900's.

1442   Walker, Mildred. LIGHT FROM ARCTURUS. Har-
       court, 1935. Development of a girl's character
       built around the Philadelphia Centennial Exposi-
       tion, 1876, the Chicago Columbian Exposition,
       1893, and the Chicago World's Fair, 1933.

1443   -- THE QUARRY. Harcourt, 1947. Life in Ver-
       mont from just before the Civil War to the begin-
       ning of World War L

1444   Wall, Roy. THIS WAS MY VALLEY. Naylor,
       1964. Autobiographical story of childhood life
       on a Texas ranch at the turn of the century.

1445   Warren, Lella. WHETSTONE WALLS. Appleton,
       1952. Struggles of a young doctor in Alabama
       at the turn of the century. Sequel to "Founda-
       tion Stone" (Civil War--Old South).

1446   Warren, Robert Penn. NIGHT RIDER. Houghton,
       1939. Story of the Kentucky tobacco war of
       1905 and the development of the tobacco coopera-
       tives.

1447   Watts, Mary. THE NOON-MARK. Macmillan,
       1920. Picture of life in a prosaic American
       city in the 1880's.

1448   Wellman, Manly Wade. NOT AT THESE HANDS.
       Putnam, 1962. Portici, North Carolina in 1916
       is the setting for the story of the personal and
       business fueds, the social and educational insti-
       tutions, and the life of the citizens of the com-
       munity.

1449   Wellman, Paul. THE WALLS OF JERICHO.
       Lippincott, 1947. Story of social and political
       life in a small town in Kansas from 1901 to the
       1940's.

1450   -- JUBAL TROOP. Doubleday, 1953. Story of

the rise and decline of an adventurer in the Southwest and a picture of the oil industry; set in
Texas, Mexico, the Dakotas, and Oklahoma from
1886 to the 1920's.

1451   West, Jessamyn. THE WITCH DIGGERS. Har-
        court, 1951. Picture of life on a farm in
        Southern Indiana in 1899.

1452   -- SOUTH OF THE ANGELS. Harcourt, 1960.
        Pictures the daily life and drama of the families
        who settle in a new farming community near Los
        Angeles in 1916.

1453   Wharton, Edith. AGE OF INNOCENCE. Appleton,
        1920. Study of American manners and of New
        York's original 400 in the 1870's.

1454   -- THE BUCCANEERS. Appleton, 1938. Social
        life in New York and Newport in the 1870's.

1455   White, Leslie Turner. LOG JAM. Doubleday,
        1959. Story of the days of the lumber barons
        of Michigan's lower peninsula in the 1870's, and
        of the conflicts resulting in the first attempts
        to break the monopoly and to introduce new
        methods and machinery to the logging operation.

1456   White, Victor. PETER DOMANIG IN AMERICA:
        STEEL. Bobbs, 1954. Story of a young Austrian
        immigrant and the steel industry in Pittsburg
        about 1919.

1457   White, William Allen. IN THE HEART OF A FOOL.
        Macmillan, 1918. Pictures the growth of a
        Kansas town from the 1870's to World War I;
        story of political corruption and conspicuous con-
        sumption following a mining boom.

1458   Whitlock, Brand. J. HARDIN & SON. Appleton,
        1923. Picture of the political, social, and
        industrial life of a small Ohio town in 1880's.

1459   Whitney, Phyllis A. THE TREMBLING HILLS.
        Appleton, 1956. Light romance set in San
        Francisco at the time of the 1906 earthquake.

1460   -- SKYE CAMERON. Appleton, 1957. Creole
        society in New Orleans in the 1880's.

1461   -- WINDOW ON THE SQUARE. Appleton, 1962.
        Social customs observed in a light romance set
        in the opulent social circles of New York in the
        1870's.

1462   Wilder, Thornton. THE EIGHTH DAY. Harper,
        1967. Introspective picture of life in a small
        Illinois town about 1910.

1463   Wiley, John W. ABBIE WAS A LADY. St. Mar-
        tin, 1962. Pleasant recollections of social life
        and customs in New England and New York, fic-
        tionalized account of the life of the author's
        grandmother.

1464   Williams, Ben Ames. SPLENDOR. Houghton,
        1927. Picture of American family life and
        interests from 1872 to 1916 in the life of a
        newspaper man.

1465   -- OWEN GLEN. Houghton, 1950. The develop-
        ment of the United Mine Workers union and the
        American social and political scene from the
        viewpoint of a boy in a small town in the Southern
        Ohio coal fields in the 1890's.

1466   Williams, Elva. SACRAMENTO WALTZ. McGraw,
        1957. A romance set in Sacramento, San Fran-
        cisco, and Paris from about 1910 to the Prohi-
        bition era.

1467   Williams, Vinnie. GREENBONES. Viking, 1967.
        Story of a mother and her son, a boy evangelist,
        on the revival trail; set in Georgia from 1912 to
        the beginning of World War I.

1468   Winslow, Anne Goodwin. IT WAS LIKE THIS.
        Knopf, 1949. A love story set in Southern Mis-
        sissippi after the Civil War.

1469   -- THE SPRINGS. Knopf, 1949. Gentle story of
        a beautiful girl and her beaux at a resort hotel
        in a Southern town in the late 1800's.

1470   Yellen, Samuel. THE WEDDING BAND. Atheneum,
       1961.   Story of cultural conflict in the marriage
       of a hard-working Jewish immigrant and a sensi-
       tive Gentile woman; Cleveland, Ohio at the turn of
       the century.

1471   Yerby, Frank. PRIDE'S CASTLE.   Dial, 1949.
       New York social and business rivalry in the
       1870's.

1472   -- SERPENT AND THE STAFF.   Dial, 1958.   Pic-
       ture of medical and social life in New Orleans
       at the turn of the century.

1473   Young, Agatha. I SWEAR BY APOLLO.   Simon
       and Schuster, 1968.   Story of the medical pro-
       fession in the 1870's; scenes in Harvard Medical
       School in Boston.

1474   Zara, Louis. DARK RIDER.   World, 1961.   Fic-
       tional biography of Stephen Crane, journalist
       and author of "The Red Badge of Courage. "

1475   Leslie, Aleen. THE SCENT OF ROSES.   Viking,
       1963.   Light romance evoking a nostalgic
       view of life in a German-American family in
       Pittsburg at the turn of the century.

1476   Adams, Samuel Hopkins. COMMON CAUSE.
Houghton, 1919. A newspaper man tries to promote patriotism in a Midwestern city in war
time; conflicts created by large German-American population.

1477   Allen, Hervey. IT WAS LIKE THIS. Farrar, 1940.
Two stories describing what war was actually
like in July and August, 1918.

1478   Andrews, Mary Shipman. HER COUNTRY. Scribner, 1918. Story of a girl singer who gave her
talents to the patriotic cause of singing for the
Liberty Bond drives.

1479   -- HIS SOUL GOES MARCHING ON. Scribner, 1922.
The spirit of Theodore Roosevelt inspires a young
soldier in the Rainbow Division in France.

1480   Angoff, Charles. IN THE MORNING LIGHT. Yoseloff, 1952. Follows a family of Russian Jews in
Boston up through World War I and after; development of the young son in the public school system,
the war years, and some of the bad times after-
ward. Followed by "The Sun at Noon" (1920's).

1481   Anonyomous. CONSCRIPT 2989. Dodd, 1918.
Amusing experiences in training camp related by
a young draftee.

1482   Babson, Naomi. LOOK DOWN FROM HEAVEN.
Reynal, 1942. New England village at the time
of the war.

1483   Bacheller, Irving. THE PRODIGAL VILLAGE.
Bobbs, 1920. Story of the beginning of flapper
society during the inflated days of 1917-1918.

1484   Bailey, Temple. THE TIN SOLDIER. Penn, 1918.
        Story of a young millionaire of draft age whose
        promise to his dying mother prevents his enlist-
        ment. Set in wartime Washington.

1485   Beebe, Elswyth Thane. LIGHT HEART. Duell,
        1947. Williamsburg, New York, and London
        customs and traditions at the time of the war.
        In the author's Williamsburg series (see other
        categories).

1486   -- KISSING KIN. Duell, 1948. Williamsburg,
        Virginia, London and the continent at the time of
        the war. Sequel to "Light Heart."

1487   Binns, Archie. THE LAURELS ARE CUT DOWN.
        Reynal, 1937. The American army in the
        Siberian campaign and the indifference of people
        at home in the Puget Sound area of Washington.

1488   Bonner, Charles. LEGACY. Knopf, 1940. Family
        life and war service of five brothers; 1905-1918.

1489   Boyd, Thomas Alexander. THROUGH THE WHEAT.
        Scribner, 1923. Describes the maturing experi-
        ences of a young Marine in the war.

1490   Bromfield, Louis. GREEN BAY TREE. Stokes,
        1924. Saga of a Midwestern city growing from
        farmland to industrial center at the time of the
        war.

1491   Brown, Alice. BROMLEY NEIGHBORHOOD. Mac-
        millan, 1917. Life in a New England village
        showing the effect of the war on everyone in the
        community.

1492   Caldwell, Janet Taylor. BALANCE WHEEL. Scrib-
        ner, 1951. Story of a munitions family in a
        Pennsylvania town.

1493   Campbell, W. M. COMPANY K. Smith and Haas,
        1933. Experiences of a company from training
        camp to action in France and return.

1494   Cather, Willa. ONE OF OURS. Knopf, 1922.
        A frustrated Nebraska farm boy prefers life

as a soldier in France to farm life.

1495   Corey, PauL THE ROAD RETURNS. Bobbs,
        1940. Farm life through the difficult years of
        the war and after; 1917-1923.

1496   Dawson, William James. THE WAR EAGLE.
        Lane, 1918. Story of the indifference of
        Americans to the war until the sinking of the
        "Lusitania" brings the United States into active
        involvement.

1497   Di Donato, Pietro. THREE CIRCLES OF LIGHT.
        Messner, 1960. Story of family life in the
        Italian community of West Hoboken, New Jersey
        during the war.

1498   Dinneen, Joseph. WARD EIGHT. Harper, 1936.
        Politics in the north end of Boston before and
        during the war.

1499   Dodge, Henry Irving. THE YELLOW DOG. Har-
        per, 1918. Short tale of a plan to hand out a
        "yellow dog" card to complainers who undermine
        morale by finding fault with the war effort.

1500   Dos Passos, John. THREE SOLDIERS. Doran,
        1921. Military history of three men from
        training camp through the war and the disillusion-
        ment following demobilization.

1501   -- 1919. Houghton, 1932. Camera-eye view of the
        United States in 1919; catches the spirit of the
        period.

1502   -- CHOSEN COUNTRY. Houghton, 1951. Chicago
        and its suburbs in wartime.

1503   Downes, Anne Miller. HEARTWOOD. Lippincott,
        1945. Love story of a mountain boy who takes a
        wife to his mountain home after serving in the
        war.

1504   Downey, Fairfax. WAR HORSE. Dodd, 1942.
        Story of a Texas mare attached to American
        artillery regiment in France.

1505   Ellsberg, Edward. PIGBOATS. Dodd, 1931.
       Story of submarine and destroyer warfare in the
       war.

1506   Fee, Mary Helen. PLAIN AMERICANS. McClurg,
       1926. Story of a provincial family at the
       time of World War I. After the death of her
       husband at the end of the war, the heroine joins
       a "Save-America" movement.

1507   Fredenburgh, Theodore. SOLDIERS MARCH!
       Harcourt, 1930. Combat experiences of a young
       American soldier.

1508   Goodrich, Marcus. DELILAH. Rinehart, 1941.
       Story of a destroyer of the U. S. battle fleet in
       the six months before the declaration of war.

1509   Grey, Zane. DESERT OF WHEAT. Harper, 1919.
       Story of German-inspired labor troubles with
       the I. W. W. in the Washington wheat fields,
       life in training camp, and the horrors of the war
       in France.

1510   Harrison, Henry. SAINT TERESA. Houghton,
       1922. Picture of anti-German feeling during the
       war; story of a steel manufacturer who refused
       to make munitions.

1511   Hemingway, Ernest. A FAREWELL TO ARMS.
       Scribner, 1929. Love story of an American
       soldier and a Swiss nurse on the Italian front in
       1917.

1512   Heth, Edward H. TOLD WITH A DRUM. Houghton,
       1937. Effects of anti-German feeling in a Ger-
       man-American community in the Midwest.

1513   Hodson, James. GREY DAWN--RED NIGHT.
       Doubleday, 1930. Picture of army life from
       training camp to battlefield.

1514   -- RETURN TO THE WOOD. Morrow, 1955.
       Story of a veteran who returns to the battlefields
       of his youth and relives his wartime experiences.

1515   Hobson, Laura Keane. FIRST PAPERS. Random,

1964. Russian-Jewish immigrant family become
involved with unpopular causes before and during
World War I.

1516   Hunt, Frazier. BLOWN IN BY THE DRAFT.
        Doubleday, 1918. Character sketches of life in
        an army camp, showing the variety of races and
        nationalities thrown together by the draft.

1517   Knox, James. SUNDAY'S CHILDREN. Houghton,
        1955. Small town parsonage life in the Shenan-
        doah Valley before and during World War I.

1518   Kyne, Peter B. THEY ALSO SERVE. Cosmopoli-
        tan, 1927. Wartime experiences of a U. S. Army
        horse.

1519   Lardner, Ring. TREAT 'EM ROUGH. Bobbs,
        1918. Humorous letters on life in an army
        training camp written by an illiterate Chicago
        baseball player.

1520   Lee, Mary. IT'S A GREAT WAR. Houghton,
        1929. War and its effects on the individuals as
        seen by a New England girl in the hospital, in a
        Y hut, and with the army of occupation in Ger-
        many.

1521   Lewis, Flannery. BROOKS TOO BROAD FOR
        LEAPING. Macmillan, 1938. A young child's
        experiences while his father is serving in France.

1522   Lewis, Herbert C. SPRING OFFENSIVE. Viking,
        1940. Reflections on his life in Indiana by a
        young soldier trapped in the no-man's land of
        the Maginot Line during a German offensive.

1523   Lutes, Della Thompson. MY BOY IN KHAKI.
        Harper, 1918. Emotional story of a mother
        whose son is in the army; shows his life in
        training camp, his war wedding, and his depar-
        ture for France.

1524   Lutz, Grace Livingston Hill. THE SEARCH.
        Lippincott, 1919. Story of the Salvation Army in
        the war.

1525   McClure, Robert E. THE DOMINANT BLOOD.
        Doubleday, 1924. Dilemma of a young German-
        American with conflicting loyalties between his
        German heritage and love for his new country.

1526   -- SOME FOUND ADVENTURE. Doubleday, 1926.
        Story of the life and love of an American soldier
        in France during the war.

1527   McCutcheon, George B. SHOT WITH CRIMSON.
        Dodd, 1918. Story of German agents in the
        U. S. spying and sabotaging the war effort,
        aided by a New York society woman.

1528   McKee, Ruth. THREE DAUGHTERS. Doubleday,
        1938. Story of the civilian role behind the
        front lines; nurse, telephone operator, and Red
        Cross representatives. Shows the waste and
        horror of war.

1529   Martin, Mrs. George. MARCH ON. Appleton,
        1921. Presents the reaction of the South to the
        war.

1530   Montague, Margaret. UNCLE SAM OF FREEDOM
        RIDGE. Doubleday, 1920. Eccentric old man
        leads the patriotic spirit of his small Virginia
        community; loses faith when the United States
        refuses to join the League of Nations.

1531   Murphy, Robert William. THE POND. Dutton,
        1964. Virginia in 1917 is the background for
        the adventures of a 14-year old boy during
        several visits to his soldier-father's hunting and
        fishing camp.

1532   Nason, Leonard. CHEVRONS. Doran, 1926. The
        account of a soldier and his buddies on the front
        lines in France.

1533   -- SERGEANT EADIE. Doubleday, 1928. Humorous
        account of a doughboy's experience in the A. E. F.

1534   -- A CORPORAL ONCE. Doubleday, 1930. Adven-
        tures of a soldier through the ups and downs of
        war life.

1535   North, Sterling. NIGHT OUTLASTS THE WHIPPOOR-
       WILL. Macmillan, 1936. Liberty Bond crusades,
       propaganda, food conservation, in a small Wiscon-
       sin farming community during the war.

1536   Odum, Howard. WINGS ON MY FEET. Bobbs,
       1929. Negro's narrative of his part in the war.

1537   Paul, Charlotte. HEAR MY HEART SPEAK.
       Messner, 1950. Story of the rehabilitation of a
       shell-shocked veteran.

1538   Putnam, Nina Wilcox and Norman Jacobsen.
       ESMERALDA. Lippincott, 1918. Amusing satire
       centering around a down to earth girl from
       California who shocks the New York social set
       into entering war work.

1539   Richmond, Grace Louise. THE WHISTLING MOTHER.
       Garden City, 1917. Tells of the farewell visit
       home of a college boy who is leaving for the war.

1540   Scanlon, William. GOD HAVE MERCY ON US.
       Houghton, 1929. Story of the U. S. Marines at
       Belleau Wood in 1918.

1541   Sheean, Vincent. BIRD OF THE WILDERNESS.
       Random, 1941. Reactions of the people of a
       small town in Illinois to the war, seen by a high
       school boy with German-American relations.

1542   Sherwood, Margaret Pollock. A WORLD TO MEND.
       Little, 1920. Observations of life in a New Eng-
       land village during the war by a philosophical
       shoe mender.

1543   Sinclair, Upton. WORLD'S END. Viking, 1940.
       Story of the world munitions industry, the war,
       and the peace conference as seen by the son of
       an American munitions maker. First in the
       author's Lanny Budd series. Followed by "Be-
       tween Two Worlds" (1920's).

1544   Smith, Betty. A TREE GROWS IN BROOKLYN.
       Harper, 1943. Life of a tenement family in the
       Williamsburg section of Brooklyn before and
       during World War I.

1545   Stallings, Lawrence. PLUMES. Harcourt, 1924.
        Story of the futility of war, expressed in the
        life of a college professor completely broken by
        his war experiences.

1546   Streeter, Edward. DERE MABLE. Stokes, 1918.
        Humorous letters from a rookie to his girl
        friend relating incidents of life in a Southern
        training camp.

1547   Tilden, Freeman. KHAKI. Macmillan, 1918.
        Story of a pacifist community jarred out of its
        complacency and into the war effort by the death,
        in France, of the rich spinster who was the
        town's only patriot.

1548   Tucker, Augusta. MISS SUSIE SLAGLE'S. Harper,
        1939. Life in a boarding house for medical
        students at Johns Hopkins at the time of the war.

1549   Van Doren, Dorothy. DACEY HAMILTON. Harper,
        1942. Picture of life in New York City in 1918.

1550   Walker, Mildred. BREWER'S BIG HORSES. Har-
        court, 1940. Michigan girl flouts conventions by
        working as a newspaperwoman and marrying a
        brewer's son.

1551   Wharton, Edith. THE MARNE. Appleton, 1918.
        An American boy is shocked at the American
        attitude of selfish indifference at the beginning of
        the war; at the second battle of the Marne he
        discovers that other Americans love France as
        he does.

1552   -- SON AT THE FRONT. Scribner, 1923. Novel
        of America's participation in the war showing the
        feeling of neutrality and isolationism felt by some.

1553   Wharton, James. SQUAD. Coward, 1928. Story of
        trench warfare experienced by a variety of Ameri-
        can youths thrown together by the draft.

1554   Whitehouse, Arch. SQUADRON FORTY-FOUR.
        Doubleday, 1965. Story of young Americans with
        the Royal Flying Corps; pictures the hazards and
        excitement of the early days of air warfare.

1555 Wise, Evelyn. AS THE PINES GROW. Appleton,
        1939. Story of farming community from 1910
        to post-war days; centers on the conflict over
        pacificist and anti-German feeling in the family
        and in the community.

1556 Abbe, George. THE WINTER HOUSE. Doubleday,
1957. Son of a small town minister rebels at
a society based on money and social position and
turns to Socialism during his college days.

1557 Adamic, Louis. GRANDSONS. Harper, 1935.
Cross-section of American life in the Twenties;
story centers around a neurotic war veteran, an
Al Capone henchman, and a labor organizer.

1558 Adams, Samuel Hopkins. SIEGE. Boni and Liveright,
1924. Story of the struggles of the labor unions
in conflict with benevolent paternalism.

1559 -- REVELRY. Boni and Liveright, 1926. Social
and political life in Washington based on the
scandals during the Harding administration.

1560 Anderson, Sherwood. DARK LAUGHTER. Boni and
Liveright, 1925. Story of a newspaper man dis-
satisfied with the undemanding society of his day,
who leaves his job and wife to go drifting.

1561 -- KIT BRANDON, A PORTRAIT. Scribner, 1936.
Depicts the confusion of values in American life
in the Twenties; factory working conditions, and
bootlegging.

1562 Angoff, Charles. THE SUN AT NOON. Yoseloff,
1955. Story of the life and customs of a family
of Russian Jews in Boston; 1919-1923. Sequel to
"In the Morning Light" (World War I).

1563 -- BETWEEN DAY AND DARK. Yoseloff, 1959.
Continues the story of family life and customs of
a Russian Jewish family in Boston during the
1920's. Followed by "Summer Storm" (Nineteen-
Thirties).

1564   Arnold, Oren. THE GOLDEN CHAIR. Elsevier,
        1954. Texas family life in the Twenties seen
        through the experiences of two children; centers
        around the family grocery store.

1565   Atherton, Gertrude. BLACK OXEN. Boni and
        Liveright, 1923. Story of life in the sophisti-
        cated social and literary circles of New York
        City of 1922.

1566   Bacheller, Irving. THE SCUDDERS. Macmillan,
        1923. Contemporary novel which pictures the
        insecurity of family life of the period.

1567   -- UNCLE PEEL. Stokes, 1933. Story of the
        financial boom and of its consequences; Florida
        real estate boom.

1568   Backer, George. APPEARANCE OF A MAN. Ran-
        dom, 1966. Story of the career of a Wall Street
        broker culminating in the stock market crash in
        1929.

1569   Bailey, Temple. ENCHANTED GROUND. Penn,
        1933. Story of Florida after the collapse of
        the land boom.

1570   Banning, Margaret Culkin. SPELLBINDERS.
        Doran, 1922. Story of the movement for woman's
        suffrage in a Midwestern city.

1571   Beals, Charleton. BLACK RIVER. Lippincott,
        1934. Story of American oil companies in Mexico;
        closes with the scandal of Teapot Dome.

1572   Becker, Stephen D. A COVENANT WITH DEATH.
        Atheneum, 1965. A judge reviews his life as
        a trial lawyer in the Southwest during the 1920's.

1573   Bellow, Saul. ADVENTURES OF AUGIE MARCH.
        Viking, 1953. Picture of the lower level of
        American society of the Twenties; set in Chicago.

1574   Bethea, Jack. BED ROCK. Houghton, 1924.
        Realistic story of coal mining in Alabama with
        conflict arising from bootlegging and sabotage.

1575   Blassingame, Wyatt. THE GOLDEN GEYSER.
        Doubleday, 1961. Story of the Florida land boom
        in the early 1920's, and of its consequences for
        a young couple getting started with a plant nursery.

1576   Block, Libbie. WILD CALENDAR. Knopf, 1946.
        Story of disillusionment and unrest in Denver in
        the late Twenties.

1577   Brace, Ernest. COMMENCEMENT. Harper, 1924.
        Picture of the problems and conflicts facing
        young people emerging from college to face life
        in the jazz age.

1578   Bradbury, Ray. DANDELION WINE. Doubleday,
        1957. One summer in the life of a 12-year old
        boy in a small town in Illinois in 1928.

1579   Brown, Fredric. THE OFFICE. Dutton, 1958.
        Story of a shy office boy and of the people
        around him in Cincinnati in the 1920's.

1580   Burgan, John. THE LONG DISCOVERY. Farrar,
        1950. Story of the change, from iron-ruled
        company towns to the union strength of the
        workers; set in the Pennsylvania coal fields.

1581   Burnett, William Riley. LITTLE CAESAR. Dial,
        1929. Story of the rise and fall of a Chicago
        gangster, based on the life of Al Capone and
        other gangsters of the Prohibition era.

1582   Burt, Maxwell Struthers. THE DELECTABLE
        MOUNTAINS. Scribner, 1927. Picture of
        American life and manners of the day; set in
        Wyoming.

1583   Carlisle, Helen Grace. MERRY, MERRY MAIDENS.
        Harcourt, 1937. The story of the life of six
        girls as they grow up during the post-war Twen-
        ties.

1584   Carter, John Stewart. FULL FATHOM FIVE.
        Houghton, 1965. Family portrait of a wealthy
        Midwestern surgeon.

1585   Caspary, Vera. EVVIE. Harper, 1960. Story of

the life of a murdered divorcee during the high-
living days of the 1920's in Chicago.

1586   Coker, Elizabeth Boatwright.   THE BEES.   Dutton,
       1968.   Charleston, South Carolina in 1924; story
       centers around the management of the family
       cotton mill.

1587   Colby, Nathalie Sedgwick.   BLACK STREAM.
       Harcourt, 1927.   New York society life in a
       novel of manners, showing the selfishness, greed,
       and meaningless activity of the period.

1588   Coleman, Lonnie.   KING.   McGraw, 1967.   Nostal-
       gic story of boyhood diversions in a small town
       in Georgia in the nineteen-twenties.

1589   Condon, Richard.   MILE HIGH.   Dial, 1969.
       Story of a cold opportunistic Irish-Sicilian-
       American increasing his fortune by promoting the
       18th Amendment and profiting from his gangster-
       controlled prohibition empire.

1590   Cooley, Leland Frederick.   THE RUN FOR HOME.
       Doubleday, 1958.   Story of the squalid conditions
       prevailing in the U. S. Merchant Marine Service
       during the Twenties.

1591   -- THE RICHEST POOR FOLKS.   Doubleday, 1963.
       Folksy picture of family life in the Upper Sacra-
       mento River Valley of California through the
       recollection of a ten-year old boy.

1592   Corbett, Elizabeth.   THE HEART OF THE VILLAGE.
       Appleton, 1963.   Story of family life centering
       around the family book store in Greenwich Village.

1593   Corey, Paul.   COUNTY SEAT.   Bobbs, 1941.   Boot-
       legging; violent stock markets upsets; farm fore-
       closures; picture of everyday life in an Iowa farm-
       ing community.

1594   Cowen, William.   THEY GAVE HIM A GUN.   Smith
       and Haas, 1936.   Story of confused young war
       veteran who turns to crime; an indictment of post-
       war American society.

1595   Cunningham, Sara and William. DANNY. Crown,
         1953. Adventures of a young cub reporter in a
         small Oklahoma town.

1596   Curran, Henry. VAN TASSEL AND BIG BILL.
         Scribner, 1923. Humerous story of New York
         ward politics.

1597   Cushman, Dan. GOODBYE, OLD DRY. Doubleday,
         1959. A quack doctor tries to bolster the econ-
         omy of a village in Montana in the 1920's.

1598   Davis, Elmer. WHITE PANTS WILLIE. Bobbs,
         1932. Story of the Florida boom and Chicago;
         1923-24.

1599   Davis, Wesley Ford. THE TIME OF THE PANTHER.
         Harper, 1958. Story of a boy growing up during
         the summer he was 14 years old; set in a Florida
         lumber camp in the 1920's.

1600   De Capite, Raymond. THE COMING OF FABRIZZE.
         McKay, 1960. Happy story of life in the Italian
         colony of Cleveland, Ohio in the 1920's; the
         stock market crash affects, but does not depress
         the characters.

1601   Doner, Mary Frances. THE GLASS MOUNTAIN.
         Doubleday, 1942. Picture of social and cultural
         life in the Great Lakes region; influence of the
         Chautauqua, and shipping on the Great Lakes.

1602   Dos Passos, John. MANHATTAN TRANSFER.
         Harper, 1925. View of various types of life in
         New York City.

1603   -- THE 42ND PARALLEL. Houghton, 1930. Pic-
         tures the United States during the period of the
         Twenties.

1604   -- THE BIG MONEY. Houghton, 1936. Picture
         of American life in the frenzied boom days from
         1919 to 1929.

1605   -- ADVENTURES OF A YOUNG MAN. Houghton,
         1939. Social and economic problems of American
         society met by a young man growing up in the

Twenties until his death in the Spanish Civil War.
Hero is sympathetic to Communist ideals.

1606   Douglas, Marjory. ROAD TO THE SUN. Rinehart,
        1952. Story of South Florida and the Everglades
        in the days when Miami was growing.

1607   Downes, Anne Miller. UNTIL THE SHEARING.
        Stokes, 1940. Story of the growing up of a
        sensitive boy in upstate New York.

1608   -- THE ANGELS FELL. Stokes, 1941. Greenwich
        Village and Westchester County from the end of
        the war through the Twenties.

1609   -- KATE CAVANAUGH. Lippincott, 1958. Story of
        a shaky marriage which reflects the spirit of the
        restless Twenties.

1610   Dreiser, Theodore. AN AMERICAN TRAGEDY.
        Boni and Liveright, 1925. Graphic picture of
        American society in the Twenties.

1611   Dudley, Frank. KING COBRA. Carrick and Evans,
        1940. The rise of a national terrorist organiza-
        tion in the Twenties.

1612   Eastman, Max. VENTURE. Boni, 1927. Story of
        a young man, expelled from college, who lives it
        up in New York, until he becomes interested in
        the labor movement.

1613   Fairbank, Janet Ayer. RICH MAN: POOR MAN.
        Houghton, 1936. Picture of the American poli-
        tical and social scene from 1912 to 1929;
        Theodore Roosevelt and the reform movement;
        women's suffrage; prohibition; the stock market
        boom; and the financial crash.

1614   Farrar, Rowena Rutherford. A WONDROUS MOMENT
        THEN. Holt, 1968. Story of the struggle for
        women's suffrage in Nashville, Tennessee during
        and after World War I; events leading to the
        state's ratification of the Nineteenth Amendment
        in 1920.

1615   Farrell, James T. JUDGMENT DAY. Vanguard,

1935. Follows the career of Studs Lonigan
growing up in Chicago.

1616   -- FATHER AND SON. Vanguard, 1940. Story of
Danny O'Neill growing up from the seventh
grade through high school; Chicago setting.

1617   -- MY DAYS OF ANGER. Vanguard, 1943. Follows Danny O'Neill through his college years in
the middle Twenties.

1618   -- THE SILENCE OF HISTORY. Doubleday, 1963.
Daily life and struggles of a poor young man
working his way through the University of Chicago. Followed by "What Time Collects. "

1619   -- WHAT TIME COLLECTS. Doubleday, 1964.
Story of the married life of a young couple
showing life on Chicago's South Side. Sequel to
"The Silence of History. "

1620   -- LONELY FOR THE FUTURE. Doubleday, 1966.
Picture of the literary and social life of three
friends, one a struggling writer, on Chicago's
South Side. Sequel to "What Time Collects. "

1621   Fitch, Albert. NONE SO BLIND. Macmillan,
1924. Story of college life set in Harvard and
Boston; shows effect of democratic ideas of the
day clashing with tradition.

1622   Fitzgerald, F. Scott. THE BEAUTIFUL AND
DAMNED. Scribner, 1922. Story of a rich
playboy and of the downward spiral of his marriage during the wild excesses of the jazz age.

1623   -- GREAT GATSBY. Scribner, 1925. Picture of
the jazz-age society on Long Island in the years
after World War I.

1624   Fleming, Berry. TO THE MARKET PLACE. Harcourt, 1938. Picture of New York social and
economic life in the Twenties.

1625   Flint, Margaret. BACK O' THE MOUNTAIN.
Dodd, 1940. Story of Maine life in the Twenties.

1626   Gann, Ernest. BLAZE OF NOON. Holt, 1946.
        Story of aviation in the Twenties when barn-
        storming pilots started carrying the U.S. Mail.

1627   Goodrich, Norma Lorre. THE DOCTOR AND MARIA
        THERESA. St. Martin, 1962. Life of a village
        doctor in rural New England.

1628   Grubb, Davis. THE VOICES OF GLORY. Scribner,
        1962. The townspeople of Glory, West Virginia
        describe their troubles during the early 1920's;
        centers around the efforts of U.S. Public Health
        Service nurse to combat juvenile delinquency and
        the apathy of the town's conservative element.

1629   Grubb, Davis. SHADOW OF MY BROTHER. Holt,
        1966. Story of hate and prejudice in a small
        Southern town, centering around a lynching
        witnessed by two young people.

1630   Halper, Albert. THE FOUNDRY. Viking, 1934.
        Chicago industrial scene, 1928-29; conflict
        between owners, bosses, and laborers.

1631   Hardman, Ric. FIFTEEN FLAGS. Little, 1968.
        Story of the American troops in the Siberian
        Expeditionary Force patrolling the Trans-Siberian
        Railway during the counter-revolution of the
        White Army in Russia in 1920.

1632   Harris, Corra May. FLAPPER ANNE. Houghton,
        1926. Story of a typical flapper in the South in
        the early 1920's.

1633   Hawes, Evelyn. THE HAPPY LAND. Harcourt,
        1965. Diary of a high school girl growing up in
        a politically oriented family near the Canadian
        border in the far West.

1634   Herbst, Josephine. THE EXECUTIONER WAITS.
        Harcourt, 1934. Story of a middle class family
        caught in the changing times, victims of the
        economic process; 1919-1929.

1635   Hobart, Alice Tisdale. THE CLEFT ROCK. Bobbs,
        1948. Picture of power monopolies and irrigation
        projects in a California valley in the Twenties.

1636   Hoffman, William.   THE DARK MOUNTAINS.
       Doubleday, 1963.   Story of a West Virginia coal
       mine owner and his battle against unionism and
       reform.

1637   Hull, Helen Rose.   THE HAWK'S FLIGHT.   Coward,
       1946.   Family life in Connecticut in the Twenties.

1638   Irwin, Inez Hayes.   P. D. F. R.   Harper, 1928.
       Sympathetic view of the self-sufficient life of
       rich sophisticated youth in New York City.

1639   Jackson, Margaret.   FIRST FIDDLE.   Bobbs, 1932.
       Conflict between a war veteran and his career wife.

1640   Keene, Day and Dwight Vincent.   CHAUTAUQUA.
       Putnam, 1960.   Story of the events which occurred
       in an Iowa town in the summer of 1921 during
       the visit of the Chautauqua.

1641   Kelland, Clarence Buddington.   CONTRABAND.
       Harper, 1923.   A girl newspaper editor exposes
       the murderers and bootleggers in control of her
       town.

1642   Kelleam, Joseph.   BLACKJACK.   Sloane, 1948.
       Story of a decaying Oklahoma town brought back
       to life by the discovery of oil.

1643   Kerkbride, Ronald.   WINDS, BLOW GENTLY.   Fell,
       1945.   Family life on a run down plantation in
       South Carolina; conflict with Southern conservatism
       on the issues of fair wages and education for
       Negroes, and diversified crops; activities of the
       Ku Klux Klan.

1644   Kerr, Sophie.   MISS J. LOOKS ON.   Farrar, 1935.
       Picture of a wealthy family hit by the financial
       crash of 1929.

1645   Keyes, Frances Parkinson.   VICTORINE.   Messner,
       1958.   Mystery plot set in the rice growing coun-
       try of Louisiana in the mid-1920's, showing the
       manners and customs of the time.

1646   Killens, John Oliver.   YOUNGBLOOD.   Trident,
       1966.   Story of a Negro family in a small Georgia

town, pictures the oppression of the Negro in the
white man's world, and centers on the rise of a
Negro hotel worker's union. First published in
1954.

1647   Levin, Meyer. OLD BUNCH. Viking, 1937. Reunion in Chicago during the World's Fair in
1934; characters review events in their lives
since 1921.

1648   -- COMPULSION. Simon and Schuster, 1956.
Fictionized account of the Leopold-Loeb murder
case in Chicago in 1925.

1649   Lewis, Sinclair. BABBITT. Harcourt, 1922.
Picture of American middle-class life, through
the story of a conservative Republican real
estate agent.

1650   -- ARROWSMITH. Harcourt, 1925. Picture of
medical education and practice; story of a doctor
through medical school and general practice as
a country doctor to his conflicts with politics in
public health work.

1651   -- ELMER GANTRY. Harcourt, 1927. An attack
on the hypocrisy of the times centering around
the story of the sensational rise of an evange-
list.

1652   Lloyd, Norris. A DREAM OF MANSIONS. Random,
1962. Story of a year in the life of an adolescent
girl; setting is rural Georgia.

1653   Longstreet, Stephen. THE CRIME. Simon &
Schuster, 1959. Story of the murder of a minister and his mistress, based on the Halls-Mills
murder case in New Jersey in 1922.

1654   -- REMEMBER WILLIAM KITE? Simon & Schuster,
1966. In the form of a memoir by a dashing,
wealthy American World War I flying ace; shows
the excitement of life in Europe and America
during the 1920's and 1930's.

1655   McGibeny, Donald. SLAG. Bobbs, 1922. Story
of conflict between management and labor in a

steel mill; characters are an arrogant capitalist,
a labor agitator, and a society girl experimenting
with Communism.

1656   McKenna, Richard. THE SAND PEBBLES. Harper,
        1963.   Story of the crew who manned a U. S.
        gunboat in Hunan Province, China, during the
        Kuomintang rebellion, 1925-1927.

1657   McKenney, Ruth. JAKE HOME. Harcourt, 1943.
        Picture of the proletarian struggle from 1912 to
        the early 1930's; organization of labor, Communist
        activity, and the Sacco-Vanzetti trial.

1658   McMillion, Bonner. THE LOT OF HER NEIGHBORS.
        Lippincott, 1953.   Pictures the spirit of a Texas
        town in the Twenties.

1659   Marks, Percy. PLASTIC AGE. Century, 1924.
        Detailed picture of all sides of college life in
        the post-war years.

1660   Maxwell, William. THE FOLDED LEAF. Harper,
        1945.   Picture of high school life in Chicago in
        the early Twenties.

1661   Meagher, Joseph William. TIPPY LOCKLIN. Little,
        1960.   A story of boyhood and of Catholic family
        life in Brooklyn in the 1920's.

1662   Millar, Margaret. IT'S ALL IN THE FAMILY.
        Random, 1948.   Story of family life during the
        year 1925.

1663   Moll, Elick. MEMOIR OF SPRING. Putnam, 1961.
        Reminiscences of a Jewish boyhood in Brooklyn
        in the post-World War I era; picture of immigrant
        workers in the ladies clothing industry.

1664   Morley, Christopher. PANDORA LIFTS THE LID.
        Doran, 1924.   Adventurous tale of a group of
        school girls who kidnap a financier and a radical
        professor; a story of the flapper age.

1665   -- KITTY FOYLE. Lippincott, 1939.   Story of a
        girl growing up struggling against tradition in an
        industrial section of Philadelphia in the 1920's

and 1930's.

1666   Morris, Wright. THE HUGE SEASON. Viking,
        1954. Pictures the problems of the generation
        of the jazz age, told in flashbacks from the view-
        point of the protagonists in 1952.

1667   Nathan, Robert. ONE MORE SPRING. Knopf, 1933.
        Effect of the financial crash of 1929 on a diverse
        group who spend the winter in a tool shed in
        Central Park.

1668   Neff, Wanda Fraiden. LONE VOYAGERS. Houghton,
        1929. Story of economic hardships faced by the
        faculty of a Midwestern university.

1669   Nichols, Edward. DANGER! KEEP OUT. Houghton,
        1943. Story of the gas and oil industry in Chi-
        cago in the Twenties pictures the growth of the
        automobile industry and conflict between the
        workers and the industrial plant.

1670   Norris, Charles. PIG IRON. Dutton, 1926. Story
        of a Massachusetts farm boy's rise from hard-
        ware store to success as a financier and iron
        manufacturer during the war years; criticism of
        American society and the effect of industrializa-
        tion on human relations.

1671   O'Hara, John. LOVEY CHILDS. Random, 1969.
        A social-sexual whirl through New York and
        Philadelphia society in the nineteen-twenties.

1672   Parks, Gordon. THE LEARNING TREE. Harper,
        1963. A small town in Kansas in the 1920's is
        the setting for the story of a year in the life of
        a teen-age Negro boy.

1673   Pascal, Ernest. CYNTHIA CODENTRY. Brentano,
        1926. Biographical novel of a young woman of
        the jazz age, set in Long Island and Florida;
        a satire on the society of the period.

1674   Paterson, Isabel. GOLDEN VANITY. Morrow,
        1934. New York City before and during the
        crash of 1929.

1675   Perretta, Armando. TAKE A NUMBER. Morrow,
       1957. Happy story of boyhood and family life in
       the Italian section of Hartford, Connecticut.

1676   Powell, Dawn. THE GOLDEN SPUR. Viking,
       1962. Satirical view of Greenwich Village life in
       the 1920's and 1950's as a young man from Ohio
       searches for his father.

1677   Pratt, Theodore. THE BAREFOOT MAILMAN.
       Duell, 1943. Picture of the early Florida land
       booms and politics in and around Palm Beach and
       Miami.

1678   Prouty, Olive Higgins. LISA VALE. Houghton,
       1938. Boston in 1929 is the setting of a story
       about the social and economic problems of a
       middle aged woman and her four grown children.

1679   Puzo, Mario. THE FORTUNATE PILGRIM.
       Atheneum, 1965. Tragic story of an Italian-
       American family living in the Chelsea district of
       New York City from 1928 to World War II.

1680   Rexroth, Kenneth. AN AUTOBIOGRAPHICAL NOVEL.
       Doubleday, 1966. A literary tall tale of the
       author's life up to 1927; covers art, radical
       politics, bootlegging, jazz, Negro life and race
       relations.

1681   Richter, Conrad. THE GRANDFATHERS. Knopf,
       1964. Story of life in the hills of western Mary-
       land in the 1920's.

1682   Riesenberg, Felix. EAST SIDE, WEST SIDE. Har-
       court, 1927. Story of the rise of the main char-
       acter from poverty on the East Side to a position
       of wealth and power, and the growth of New York
       City.

1683   Rogers, Samuel. DUSK AT THE GROVE. Little,
       1934. Scenes in the lives of three young people
       as they grew up in the Twenties.

1684   Rylee, Robert. ST. GEORGE OF WELDON. Farrar,
       1937. Thirty years in the life of a man who is
       drowned in 1929.

1685   Sachs, Emanie N. TALK. Harper, 1924. Story
        of an insecure marriage threatened by sudden
        wealth and a flapper dominated society.

1686   Shenkin, Elizabeth. MIDSUMMER'S NIGHTMARE.
        Rinehart, 1960. Story of family life at a New
        York beach resort in 1923.

1687   Shipley, C. L. THE JADE PICCOLO. Atheneum,
        1969. Small town America seen through the
        eyes of two adolescent boys as they hero-worship
        the mysterious town bootlegger.

1688   Siebel, Julia. FOR THE TIME BEING. Harcourt,
        1961. Family life in a small town in Kansas in
        the Post-World War I years.

1689   Sinclair, Harold. MUSIC OUT OF DIXIE. Rine-
        hart, 1952. Story of the growth of jazz music in
        the Twenties, from New Orleans' Storyville dis-
        trict to the success of Jelly Roll Morton in New
        York.

1690   Sinclair, Upton. OIL. Boni, 1927. Oil industry in
        Southern California, based on the Teapot Dome
        oil scandals during the Harding administration.

1691   -- BOSTON. Boni, 1928. Story of the Sacco-Van-
        zetti trial; condemns the state of mind which
        permitted their conviction and execution.

1692   -- THE WET PARADE. Farrar, 1931. Passionate
        defense of prohibition showing the evil effects of
        alcohol, the ineffective methods of prohibition
        agents, and the efforts of the respectable rich to
        circumvent the law.

1693   -- BETWEEN TWO WORLDS. Viking, 1941. Poli-
        tical and economic developments in post-war
        Europe and America from 1919 to 1929; Treaty of
        Versailles, the rise of Mussolini in Italy, growing
        Nazi power in Germany, and the stock market
        crash in 1929. One of author's Lanny Budd
        series (see other categories).

1694   -- ANOTHER PAMELA; OR, VIRTUE STILL RE-
        WARDED. Viking, 1950. Satire on the social

history of the U. S. in the Twenties.

1695   Smith, Betty. TOMORROW WILL BE BETTER.
        Harper, 1948. Typical family life in Brooklyn
        in the Twenties.

1696   Soles, Gordon H. CORNBREAD AND MILK.
        Doubleday, 1959. Family and boy life on a Kan-
        sas farm during the 1920's.

1697   Sorensen, Virginia. ON THIS STAR. Reynal, 1946.
        Story of Mormon life in Utah in the Twenties.

1698   Sprague, Jesse Rainsford. THE MIDDLEMAN.
        Morrow, 1929. Story of the wholesale merchan-
        dising business and its place in the economic sys-
        tem.

1699   Sterrett, Frances Roberta. THE GOLDEN STREAM.
        Penn, 1931. Story of a wealthy family in con-
        flict with a son's wife until her common sense
        saves them in the financial crash of 1929.

1700   Stone, Alma. THE HARVARD TREE. Houghton,
        1954. Story of a happy family life and amiable
        race relations in a small Texas town.

1701   Stribling, T. S. BACKWATER. Doubleday, 1930.
        Social and business life in an Arkansas rural
        community.

1702   -- THE UNFINISHED CATHEDRAL. Doubleday,
        1934. The real estate boom, and a skyscraper
        cathedral project in a North Alabama town.
        Sequel to "The Store" (Nation Grows Up).

1703   Suchow, Ruth. THE FOLKS. Farrar, 1934.
        Family life in a small Iowa town from World War I
        through the Twenties.

1704   Suhl, Yuri. ONE FOOT IN AMERICA. Macmillan,
        1950. Humorous story of a Jewish boy and his
        father, immigrants from Poland; the son becoming
        Americanized, the father clinging to the old ways.

1705   -- COWBOY ON A WOODEN HORSE. Macmillan,
        1953. Continues the story of a Jewish boy and

his problems, from courtship to labor unions.
Sequel to "One Foot in America. "

1706   Tarkington, Booth. CLAIRE AMBLER. Doubleday,
        1928. Social life and customs in the jazz age
        of the 1920's; picture of contemporary flapper
        society.

1707   -- MIRTHFUL HAVEN. Doubleday, 1930. Life in
        a small village in Maine as seen by the daughter
        of the local rum runner.

1708   Thielen, Benedict. THE LOST MEN. Appleton,
        1946. Story of World War I veterans given the
        job of building a road across the Florida Keys.

1709   Train, Arthur Cheney. THE NEEDLE'S EYE.
        Scribner, 1924. A story of labor union activity
        in the West Virginia coal fields. Minor charac-
        ter is society girl with socialistic ideas.

1710   -- PAPER PROFITS. Liveright, 1930. Plea
        against stock market speculation.

1711   Updegraff, Robert Rawls. CAPTAINS IN CONFLICT.
        Shaw, 1927. Story of the change in business
        methods from the turn of the century to the
        Twenties as two men compete for control of the
        company they founded together.

1712   Walker, Charles Rumford. BREAD AND FIRE.
        Houghton, 1927. A thesis novel dealing with
        the problems of labor in the steel mil and the
        growth of the Socialist movement.

1713   Watts, Mary Stanbery. THE FABRIC OF THE LOOM.
        Macmillan, 1924. A story depicting the superfi-
        cial aspect of materialistic American society in
        contrast with European culture.

1714   Webber, Gordon. YEARS OF EDEN. Little, 1951.
        Story of a boy growing up in Michigan in the
        Twenties.

1715   Webster, Henry Kitchell. AN AMERICAN FAMILY.
        Bobbs, 1923. Story of contemporary family in
        Chicago in the post-war years and the early

Twenties.

1716   Welty, Eudora. DELTA WEDDING. Harcourt,
        1946. Story of the week before the wedding of
        one of the girls of a Mississippi Delta family in
        1923.

1717   Wharton, Edith. TWILIGHT SLEEP. Appleton,
        1927. Novel of social life in the upper levels of
        society; picture of the optimism and self-indulgence
        of the jazz age.

1718   Widdemer, Margaret. GALLANT LADY. Harcourt,
        1926. Story of flippant irresponsibility among the
        young married set in the jazz age.

1719   Wiley, John. THE EDUCATION OF PETER.
        Stokes, 1924. Story of undergraduate life at
        Yale in the Twenties.

1720   -- QUEER STREET. Scribner, 1928. Set in
        New York City, the story of an old family house
        encroached on by night clubs, speakeasies, and
        rooming houses.

1721   Williams, Joan. OLD POWDER MAN. Harcourt,
        1966. Story of the life of Frank Wynn who intro-
        duced the use of dynamite in Mississippi River
        valley flood control projects for the U.S. Corps
        of Engineers.

1722   Williamson, Thames Rose. HUNKY. Coward,
        1929. Slav laborer in a big city, buffeted by a
        system he cannot understand; social study of a
        workingman's life in the Twenties.

1723   Wilson, Mary B. YESTERDAY'S PROMISE. Penn,
        1934. The effect of the 1929 market crash on
        the country club set.

1724   Wilson, Mitchell. MY BROTHER, MY ENEMY.
        Little, 1952. Story of early experiments with
        television.

1725   Zugsmith, Leane. NEVER ENOUGH. Liveright,
        1932. Portrays the extravagance, restlessness,
        and lack of purpose that characterized most of
        American life in the Twenties.

THE NINETEEN-THIRTIES

1726 Algren, Nelson. A WALK ON THE WILD SIDE.
Farrar, 1956. Story of degenerate life in
New Orleans during the Depression.

1727 Angoff, Charles. SUMMER STORM. Yoseloff,
1963. Sixth in a series on Russian-Jewish
family life covers the period 1933-35; shows
effects of Franklin Roosevelt's New Deal policies
to combat the Depression, reaction to Father
Coughlin's broadcasts, and economic life of the
magazine publishing world in Boston. Sequel to
"Between Day and Dark" (Nineteen-Twenties).

1728 Astor, Brooke. THE BLUEBIRD IS AT HOME.
Harper & Row, 1965. New York and Washington
social life and fashions in the 1930's.

1729 Atherton, Gertrude. HOUSE OF LEE. Appleton,
1940. Effect of the Depression on the women of
an upper class San Francisco family.

1730 Atwell, Lester. LOVE IS JUST AROUND THE COR-
NER. Simon & Schuster, 1963. Communist
activity in the fashion and advertising world in
1936.

1731 Auchincloss, Louis. THE EMBEZZLER. Houghton,
1966. Picture of the social and financial world
of New York City, centering around a scandal on
Wall Street during the Depression.

1732 Baker, Elliott. THE PENNY WARS. Putnam, 1968.
Moving story of an adolescent boy experiencing
life in a small town in upstate New York as war
breaks out in Europe.

1733 Banning, Margaret Culken. MESABI. Harper, 1969.
Story of the iron ore mining business of the

Mesabi range; set in and around Duluth, Minnesota in the years before World War II.

1734   Barrett, B. L. LOVE IN ATLANTIS. Houghton,
        1969. Story of a teen-age girl's view of the world
        from a small California town, and of her first
        innocent love; good feeling for the period of the
        nineteen-thirties.

1735   Behrman, S. N. THE BURNING GLASS. Little,
        1968. Picture of the world of the theatre in
        Europe, Hollywood, and New York from 1937 to
        1940, showing the effect of the growing Nazi
        menace on the career of a young Jewish play-
        wright.

1736   Bell, Thomas. ALL BRIDES ARE BEAUTIFUL.
        Little, 1936. Story of a young couple living in
        the Bronx during the Depression on $25 a week,
        who determine to be happy in their marriage,
        and succeed.

1737   Blackwell, Louise. THE MEN AROUND HURLEY.
        Vanguard, 1957. Story of life in a remote small
        town in Alabama from the time of the Depression,
        through the 1930's, to the outbreak of World War
        II.

1738   Blake, Sally M. WHERE MIST CLOTHES DREAM
        AND MYTH RUNS NAKED. McGraw, 1965.
        A Boston slum during the Depression is the set-
        ting for this tragedy of an immigrant family in
        conflict over the old world Jewish culture and
        facing the harsh realities of urban poverty.

1739   Boyd, Thomas Alexander. IN TIME OF PEACE.
        Minton, 1935. Picture of American life in the
        Twenties and Thirties through the story of World
        War I veteran, a newspaper reporter struggling
        against the economic system and the Depression.
        Sequel to "Through the Wheat" (World War I).

1740   Breckenridge, Gerald. THE BESIEGED. Double-
        day, 1937. Effect of the Depression on the char-
        acter of the members of several different families.

1741   Brelis, Dean. MY NEW FOUND LAND. Houghton,

1963. Story of a Greek-American family in Newport, Rhode Island in 1932; the father is a shoe-
maker and part-time bootlegger.

1742   Brody, Catherine. NOBODY STARVES. Longmans,
1932. Story of the Depression among automobile
factory workers in and around Detroit.

1743   Browne, Lewis. SEE WHAT I MEAN? Random,
1943. Rise of a subversive movement in Southern
California in the late thirties; anti-Semitism used
as a tool by Nazi sympathizers.

1744   Brush, Katherine. DON'T EVER LEAVE ME.
Farrar, 1935. Picture of the hard-drinking,
fast living country club set with the fashions,
catch-words, and songs of 1932.

1745   Buckles, Eleanor. VALLEY OF POWER. Creative
Age, 1945. Story of TVA, its value and meaning,
and the reaction of the Tennessee mountain families who must be evicted to make way for it.

1746   Burnett, William Riley. KING COLE. Harper,
1936. Picture of state politics, set around the
last six days in a gubernatorial campaign in
which the honest governor resorts to a planned
riot to help him win re-election.

1747   Burwell, Basil. A FOOL IN THE FOREST. Macmillan, 1964. Story of an actor's first year in
summer stock in Cape Cod in 1930.

1748   Caldwell, Janet Taylor. EAGLES GATHER. Scribner, 1940. Brings the story of a Pennsylvania
munitions family up to 1938. Sequel to "Balance
Wheel" (World War I).

1749   Callaghan, Morley. THEY SHALL INHERIT THE
EARTH. Random, 1935. Effects of the Depres-
sion on a group of people in a moderate sized
American city.

1750   Carousso, Dorothee. OPEN THEN THE DOOR.
Morrow, 1942. Story of a happy marriage in
spite of mothers-in-law and the Depression.

1751   Champagne, Marian Mira. QUIMBY AND SON.
        Bobbs, 1962. A century old family grocery
        company becomes a chain of supermarkets in a
        story set in New York State in the Depression
        years.

1752   Chinn, Lawrence Chambers. BELIEVE MY LOVE.
        Crown, 1962. Chicago during the Depression is
        the setting for this love story of a Nebraska girl
        and a Japanese-American engineering student.

1753   Clarke, Tom E. THE BIG ROAD. Lothrop, 1964.
        Story of a farm boy who leaves home during the
        Depression to become a hobo. Includes a glos-
        sary of hobo terms.

1754   Connell, Evan S. MR. BRIDGE. Knopf, 1969.
        A quiet story of the social problems on the
        American scene from the Depression to the years
        before World War II in Kansas City.

1755   Corbett, Elizabeth. THE CROSSROADS. Appleton,
        1965. Story of a family bookshop in Greenwich
        Village during the Depression. Sequel to "Heart
        of the Village" (Twenties).

1756   Corey, Paul. ACRES OF ANTAEUS. Holt, 1946.
        The plight of the farmers when foreclosures and
        eviction threatened during the hard years of the
        1930's.

1757   Corrigan, Barbara. VOYAGE OF DISCOVERY.
        Scribner, 1945. Sophisticated picture of college
        life in the 1930's.

1758   Covert, Alice. RETURN TO DUST. Kinsey, 1939.
        Dust bowl conditions and the reaction to govern-
        ment relief in a small Oklahoma community.

1759   -- THE MONTHS OF RAIN. Kinsey, 1941. Okla-
        homa farm family fights droughts, storms, and
        the Depression.

1760   Curran, Dale. PIANO IN THE BAND. Reynal,
        1940. Story of the feverish atmosphere of the
        world of jazz music in 1933.

1761   Curry, Peggy. OIL PATCH. McGraw, 1959.
        Story of life in a Western oil town in the 1930's;
        wife rebels against strict company rule.

1762   Davis, Julia. THE SUN CLIMBS SLOW. Dutton,
        1942. America at the time of the Spanish Civil
        War.

1763   Davis, Kenneth. THE YEARS OF THE PILGRIMAGE.
        Doubleday, 1948. Conflicting philosophies in a
        Kansas town in the Thirties.

1764   Deal, Bordon. DUNBAR'S COVE. Scribner, 1957.
        Study of the social and economic life in the
        Tennessee River valley in the Thirties; a family's
        fight with TVA over condemnation of their land
        for a dam.

1765   -- THE LEAST ONE. Doubleday, 1967.
        An ordinary family faces up to the hard times
        of the Depression.

1766   Deasy, Mary. DEVIL'S BRIDGE. Little, 1952.
        Politics in a Southern town; 1929-1933.

1767   -- THE CELEBRATION. Random House, 1963.
        Story of the rise and fall of a proud family in
        a Midwestern city in the 1930's.

1768   Dos Passos, John. NUMBER ONE. Houghton,
        1943. Politics and the gullibility of the masses
        in a story of a Southern demagogue; based on
        the career of Huey Long.

1769   -- GRAND DESIGN. Houghton, 1949. Story of New
        Deal politics in Washington.

1770   Drake, Robert. AMAZING GRACE. Chilton, 1965.
        Eighteen short stories which combine to present
        a picture of rural Tennessee in the 1930's and
        1940's.

1771   Duncan, David. THE LONG WALK HOME FROM
        TOWN. Doubleday, 1964. Nostalgic view of
        boyhood life in a small town in Montana in the
        early nineteen-thirties.

1772   Dutton, Mary. THORPE. World, 1967. Southern
        race relations in Arkansas in the nineteen-thirties.

1773   Ehle, John. LION ON THE HEARTH. Harper,
        1961. Story of a mountain family who move to
        the outskirts of Ashville, North Carolina, and
        face the hardships of the Depression.

1774   Ellison, Earl. THE DAM. Random, 1941. Story
        of the construction of a W. P. A. dam near
        Chicago and its effect on the chief engineer.

1775   Ellison, Ralph. INVISIBLE MAN. Random, 1952.
        Story of a Negro trying to find himself and of
        Negro-white relations during the Depression
        years. Set in a small Southern town and in
        New York's Harlem.

1776   Epstein, Seymour. THE SUCCESSOR. Scribner,
        1961. Portrait of a young Jewish salesman in
        the business world of a small town in New York
        from 1935 to 1947.

1777   Ethridge, Willie Snow. MINGLED YARN. Macmil-
        lan, 1938. Story of a paternalistic Georgia mill
        owner; welfare plan and social clubs offered as
        compensation for starvation wages.

1778   Fast, Howard. POWER. Doubleday, 1962. Story
        of the rise of Benjamin R. Holt as a labor
        leader in the coal miners union in the mine
        fields of West Virginia and Illinois in the Twen-
        ties and Thirties.

1779   Faulkner, John. MEN WORKING. Harcourt, 1941.
        Story of a shiftless family who leave tenant farm-
        ing to go to work for the W. P. A.

1780   Feibleman, Peter S. A PLACE WITHOUT TWI-
        LIGHT. World, 1958. Negro life in New Orleans
        in the 1930's and 1940's.

1781   Fumento, Rocco. TREE OF DARK REFLECTION.
        Knopf, 1961. Troubled life of an Italian immi-
        grant family in a Massachusetts textile mill
        town and in an industrial suburb of Boston in the
        1930's.

1782   Gallagher, Thomas. THE GATHERING DARKNESS.
        Bobbs, 1952. Follows the economic ups and
        downs of a middle class family in New York;
        1929-1942.

1783   Gilbreth, Frank B. LOBLOLLY. Crowell, 1959.
        Warm and funny story of an eccentric family in
        Charleston, South Carolina in 1935, bringing in
        the Depression and the New Deal as background.

1784   Gold, Herbert. THEREFORE BE BOLD. Dial,
        1960. Story of a Jewish boy growing up in a
        non-Jewish suburb of Cleveland, Ohio in the
        1930's.

1785   -- FATHERS. Random, 1967. Story of family life
        and growing up in a Jewish immigrant family in
        Cleveland, Ohio and New York City through the
        Depression and into World War II.

1786   Granit, Arthur. TIME OF THE PEACHES. Abe-
        lard, 1959. Poetic story of Jewish life in the
        Brownsville section of Brooklyn in the 1930's.

1787   Green, Gerald. TO BROOKLYN WITH LOVE. Tri-
        dent, 1967. A nostalgic look back on boyhood
        survival in pre-World War II Brooklyn.

1788   Grubb, Davis. A TREE FULL OF STARS. Scrib-
        ner, 1965. A sentimental tale of Christmas in
        a small Ohio town during the Depression.

1789   -- FOOL'S PARADE. World/NAL., 1969. Adven-
        tures of three ex-convicts in the mining country of
        West Virginia in 1935.

1790   Grumbach, Doris. THE SHORT THROAT, THE
        TENDER MOUTH. Doubleday, 1964. Members
        of the class of 1939 of the Washington Square
        Campus of New York State University look back
        on their student days as rebels and Communists.

1791   Halper, Albert. UNION SQUARE. Viking, 1933.
        Story of a few days in the life of the radicals
        and the destitute in the tenements in the Union
        Square area of New York.

1792   -- THE CHUTE. Viking, 1937. Proletarian novel
        set in the order department of a Chicago mailing
        house; theme is the inhuman activity needed to
        keep the package chute fed.

1793   Hamilton, Harry. RIVER SONG. Bobbs, 1945.
        Story of two Mississippi River bums after a
        radio scout discovers their musical talent.

1794   Harnack, Curtis. LOVE AND BE SILENT. Har-
        court, 1961. Farm and town life in Iowa is the
        setting for a story of two brothers and two sis-
        ters and their emotional entanglements.

1795   Herbst, Josephine. ROPE OF GOLD. Harcourt,
        1939. Continues the story of a middle class
        American family through the Depression; 1933-
        1937. Sequel to "The Executioner Waits"
        (Twenties).

1796   Herrick, William. HERMANOS! Simon and Schus-
        ter, 1969. A tale of social unrest and inter-
        national violence in a review of Communist acti-
        vity in Cuba, the United States, and in the
        Spanish Civil War.

1797   Heyward, Du Bose. STAR SPANGLED VIRGIN.
        Farrar, 1939. Story of the Virgin Islands;
        showing the disintegrating effect of New Deal
        relief measures on the natives.

1798   Hicks, Granville. ONLY ONE STORM. Macmillan,
        1942. World events from 1937 to 1939 as seen
        by a family who retreated from the pressures of
        New York City business life.

1799   Hobart, Alice Tisdale. THE CUP AND THE SWORD.
        Bobbs, 1942. Story of the California grape and
        wine industries from the 1920's to the beginning
        of World War II.

1800   Hubbell, Catherine. FRANCES. Norton, 1950.
        Picture of life in New York City from the 1920's
        to the 40's.

1801   Hudson, Lois Phillips. THE BONES OF PLENTY.
        Little, 1962. A wheat farmer loses his rented

farm as a result of drought, dust storms, wheat
smut, and economic depression in a North Dakota
wheat growing community.

1802   -- REAPERS OF THE DUST. Little, 1965. Episodes based on memories of a farm childhood in
the wheat farming area of North Dakota suffering
from drought and the dust storms of the 1930's.

1803   Hueston, Ethel. A ROOF OVER THEIR HEADS.
Bobbs, 1937. Picture of moral disintegration
brought on by the Depression; theme is that
unemployment forced families together in over-
crowded conditions and going on relief was
inevitable.

1804   Hulbert, James. THE DISPUTED BARRICADE.
Holt, 1966. Story of a young iron worker who
rises to power in the labor movement in Gary,
Indiana during the Depression.

1805   Hull, Morris. CANNERY ANNE. Houghton, 1936.
Picture of life among the migratory workers in
a California cannery.

1806   Humphrey, William. A TIME AND A PLACE.
Knopf, 1968. Collection of stories depicting the
effects of the Depression, oil strikes, and cli-
mate on small town life in Oklahoma and Texas.

1807   Idell, Albert. THE CORNER STORE. Doubleday,
1953. Family life in a run down section of
Philadelphia during the Depression.

1808   Jackson, Margaret. KINDY'S CROSSING. Bobbs,
1934. Story of the rise and fall of an American
industrialist family from wealth and power in
the automobile industry to the loss of everything
during the Depression.

1809   Jackson, Shirley. THE ROAD THROUGH THE WALL.
Farrar, 1948. Picture of American middle class
family life in a California town in 1936.

1810   Janeway, Elizabeth. LEAVING HOME. Doubleday,
1953. Story of the insecurity of three children
growing up in Brooklyn in the 1930's.

1811   Johnson, Josephine. NOW IN NOVEMBER. Simon
        & Schuster, 1934. Story of poor crops, labor
        troubles, drought, and debt on a Midwestern farm
        in the years leading up to the Depression.

1812   -- JORDANSTOWN. Simon and Schuster, 1937.
        Story of the hopelessness of the poor in a small
        town contrasted with the indifference of the finan-
        cially secure.

1813   Johnson, Robert Proctor. LEGACY OF THORNS.
        Morrow, 1965. Realistic and grim picture of
        growing up in small town near Lake Superior
        during the Depression.

1814   Jones, Nard. STILL TO THE WEST. Dodd, 1946.
        Building of the Grand Coulee Dam on the Colum-
        bia River.

1815   Kanin, Garson. BLOW UP A STORM. Random,
        1959. Story centers around the members, white
        and Negro, of a small jazz combo in the days
        of jazz muxic in the early Thirties.

1816   Kaufman, Charles. FIESTA IN MANHATTAN.
        Morrow, 1939. Story of a Mexican couple
        lured to New York; stranded by unemployment in
        the Depression they turn to the marijuana racket.

1817   Keyes, Frances Parkinson. ALL THAT GLITTERS.
        Messner, 1941. Picture of social changes in
        Washington during the period from December
        1927 to June 1940.

1818   Kroll, Harry Harrison. THE USURPER. Bobbs,
        1941. Conflict between the growers and the
        sharecroppers of the South through prosperity
        and the Depression.

1819   Langley, Adria Locke. A LION IS IN THE STREETS.
        Whittlesey, 1945. Rise and fall of a demagogue;
        based on the career of Huey Long.

1820   Lanham, Edwin. THE STRICKLANDS. Little, 1939.
        Story of the conflict centering around organizing
        the tenant farmers of Oklahoma into unions after
        the Depression had changed the system of owner-

operated farms.

1821   -- THUNDER IN THE EARTH.   Harcourt, 1941.
       Story of a Texas oil town in the 1930's; empha-
       sizes that rich natural resources should not be
       exploited.

1822   Lawrence, Josephine.   IF I HAVE FOUR APPLES.
       Stokes, 1935.   Story of a middle-class family
       trying to live beyond their income in spite of
       the Depression and of the inevitable consequences
       of installment buying.

1823   -- SOUND OF RUNNING FEET.   Stokes, 1937.
       Effects of the Depression on the staff of a real
       estate office; picture of home and office life
       during the period.

1824   -- BUT YOU ARE YOUNG.   Little, 1940.   Economic
       struggles of a young girl forced to support her
       family through the Depression years.

1825   -- NO STONE UNTURNED.   Little, 1941.   Picture
       of the moral and economic standing of an ordinary
       American family during the Depression and the
       recovery.

1826   Lee, Harper.   TO KILL A MOCKINGBIRD.   Lippin-
       cott, 1960.   Two children growing up in Alabama
       in the Thirties witness small town life and vio-
       lence when their lawyer father defends a falsely
       accused Negro.

1827   Lewis, Janet.   AGAINST A DARKENING SKY.
       Doubleday, 1943.   Family life in the Santa Clara
       valley near San Francisco during the Depression.

1828   Lewis, Sinclair.   ANN VICKERS.   Doubleday, 1933.
       Social satire of a professional feminist, social
       worker, and prison reformer.

1829   Linn, James Weber.   WINDS OVER THE CAMPUS.
       Bobbs, 1936.   Picture of students and faculty
       life at the University of Chicago.

1830   Littleton, Betty.   IN SAMSON'S EYE.   Atheneum,
       1965.   Life in a small town in Oklahoma through

the Depression into the 1940's.

1831   Litwak, Leo. WAITING FOR THE NEWS. Double-
        day, 1969. Family life of a Jewish labor leader
        in Detroit in 1939; the joys of childhood shadowed
        by violence and the news of Hitler's aggressions
        against the Jews in Germany.

1832   Longo, Lucas. THE FAMILY ON VENDETTA
        STREET. Doubleday, 1968. Life in the Italian
        colony of New York City.

1833   Longstreet, Stephen. DECADE, 1929-1939. Ran-
        dom, 1940. Story of the financial decline of a
        benevolent old capitalist, from the crash of 1929
        to the years preceding World War II.

1834   McCarthy, Cormac. THE ORCHARD KEEPER.
        Random House, 1965. Picture of life in the
        Smoky Mountains of East Tennessee in the Twen-
        ties and Thirties, as the characters resist the
        forces of change.

1835   McIntyre, John Thomas. STEPS GOING DOWN.
        Farrar, 1936. Novel of underworld life in an
        American city of the Thirties.

1836   -- FERMENT. Farrar, 1937. Proletarian novel of
        strike-breaking and labor racketeering in Phila-
        delphia; theme is the futility of the workingman's
        struggle against the evils of industralism and
        fascism.

1837   McKay, Allis. GOODBYE, SUMMER. Macmillan,
        1953. Teenager grows from adolescence on an
        apple ranch in the Columbia River valley near
        Seattle to manhood working on the Grand Coulee
        Dam.

1838   MacLeish, Archibald. CONE OF SILENCE. Hough-
        ton, 1944. Story of the United States in the sum-
        mer of 1933; the growth of fascism in Europe and
        America.

1839   McWhirter, Millie. HUSHED WERE THE HILLS.
        Abingdon, 1969. Bits of family life as a widowed
        school teacher raises her children in the hill

country of Tennessee during the Depression.

1840   Maltz, Albert. THE UNDERGROUND STREAM.
        Little, 1940. Industrial conflict between Com-
        munists and organized labor on the one hand
        and fascists on the other.

1841   Martin, Peter. THE BUILDING. Little, 1960.
        Story of a Russian Jewish family struggling
        through the Depression in Upstate New York,
        with a background of immigration from Russia
        in the early 1900's and family and business life
        to the nineteen-thirties.

1842   Mayhall, Jane. COUSIN TO HUMAN. Harcourt,
        1960. Story of the maturing of a 15 year old
        girl in a small town in Kentucky in the mid-
        Thirties.

1843   Merrick, Elliott. FROM THIS HILL LOOK DOWN.
        Stephen Daye, 1934. Sketches of life in Vermont
        during the Depression; drought, rain, sick neigh-
        bors, and a CWA job make up part of the story.

1844   Moore, Ruth. SPOONHANDLE. Morrow, 1946.
        Maine coastal town in the middle Thirties.

1845   Morris, Hilda. THE MAIN STREAM. Putnam,
        1939. Contrasting picture of life on a farm in
        New York and life in a factory town.

1846   Newhouse, Edward. YOU CAN'T SLEEP HERE.
        Furman, 1934. Story centering around the move-
        ment for unemployment insurance; a New York
        reporter joins a squatters' colony and becomes
        active in the movement after losing his job during
        the Depression.

1847   Norris, Charles. HANDS. Farrar, 1935. Novel
        showing how the Depression forced many to go
        back to the pioneer ways of working with the
        hands.

1848   -- FLINT. Doubleday, 1944. Conflict between capi-
        tal and labor in the shipbuilding industry in San
        Francisco in the mid-Thirties.

1849   North, Jessica Nelson. ARDEN ACRES. Harcourt,
        1935. Story of a family in a slum section of
        Chicago on relief during the Depression.

1850   Oates, Joyce Carol. GARDEN OF EARTHLY
        DELIGHTS. Vanguard, 1967. Life in a migrant
        work camp and a small town following the Depres-
        sion.

1851   O'Hara, John. THE BIG LAUGH. Random, 1962.
        Centers around theatrical life in New York in
        the 1920's and on to Hollywood movie stardom
        during the Depression.

1852   O'Rourke, Frank. THE BRIGHT MORNING. Mor-
        row, 1963. A young teacher is the central
        character in this pleasant tale of life and love
        in a small Midwestern town in the 1930's.

1853   Palmer, Artes. THERE'S NO PLACE LIKE NOME.
        Morrow, 1963. Picture of family life and the
        construction business in Seattle in the 1930's;
        when the business fails in the Depression the
        family takes up bootlegging, and later, gold
        dredging in Alaska.

1854   Paul, Elliot. THE STARS AND STRIPES FOREVER.
        Random, 1939. Paternalistic owner opposes the
        organization of a labor union in his factory.

1855   Pearce, Donn. COOL HAND LUKE. Scribner, 1965.
        Life on a chain gang in a Florida prison camp.

1856   Perry, Dick. RAYMOND AND ME THAT SUMMER.
        Harcourt, 1964. Summer adventures of two boys
        in Cincinnati, Ohio during the Depression.

1857   -- THE ROUND HOUSE, PARADISE, AND MR.
        PICKERING. Doubleday, 1966. Story of family
        life and railroading, set in Cincinnati, Ohio in
        the heyday of the New York Central.

1858   Pharr, Robert Deane. THE BOOK OF NUMBERS.
        Doubleday, 1969. Negro life and the numbers
        racket in the ghetto of a Southern city in the
        Thirties.

1859	Pierce, Noel. THE SECOND MRS. DRAPER.
	McBride, 1937. Social life among the Long
	Island sophisticated country club set in the
	Thirties.

1860	Raymond, Margaret Thomsen. BEND IN THE ROAD.
	Longmans, 1934. Story of a young girl who
	leaves home and gets a job in a factory.

1861	-- SYLVIA, INC. Dodd, 1938. Story of a young
	girl called home from art school to help her
	father save his failing pottery business during
	the Depression.

1862	Rice, Elmer. IMPERIAL CITY. Appleton, 1937.
	Complex social and financial life of a wealthy
	family in New York City.

1863	Rickett, Frances. A CERTAIN SLANT OF LIGHT.
	Putnam, 1968. Politics and family life in a
	small town in Indiana during the Depression.

1864	Ritner, Ann Katherine. SEIZE A NETTLE. Lip-
	pincott, 1961. Story of a household of women
	and of their efforts to keep going during the
	Depression.

1865	Roberts, Marta. TUMBLEWEEDS. Putnam, 1940.
	Unemployment and gradual demoralization of a
	Mexican couple brought to California as railroad
	laborers; depicts the fear and dislike of relief
	agencies by those who need it most.

1866	Robinson, Dorothy. THE DIARY OF A SUBURBAN
	HOUSEWIFE. Morrow, 1936. Story of a Long
	Island housewife's courage and resourcefullness
	in meeting the Depression.

1867	Roe, Wellington. THE TREE FALLS SOUTH. Put-
	nam, 1937. Kansas farmers facing destitution
	from drought, dust, storms, and the Depression
	march on the county seat for government aid.

1868	Roth, Arthur J. SHAME OF OUR WOUNDS. Cro-
	well, 1961. A grim realistic picture of New
	York City in the 1930's, set around the adventures
	of three boys who run away from a Catholic Home

for Boys.

1869   Rothberg, Abraham.   THE SONG OF DAVID FREED.
        Putnam, 1968.   Story of cultural and family con-
        flicts as a young Jewish boy grows up in New
        York City during the Depression.

1870   Rubin, Louis.   THE GOLDEN WEATHER.   Atheneum,
        1961.   Nostalgic view of a 13 year old boy's
        activities in Charleston, South Carolina before
        and during the 75th anniversary of the fall of
        Fort Sumter in 1936.

1871   Ryan, J. M.   MOTHER'S DAY.   Prentice, 1969.
        Based on the life of the Ma Barker outlaw gang
        from their wild existence in the Ozarks to their
        death in a Florida ambush in the "Bonnie and
        Clyde" tradition.

1872   Sandoz, Mari.   CAPITAL CITY.   Little, 1939.
        Picture of sordid political and social life in a
        Midwestern city; story of conflict between capital
        and labor; the rise of fascism, the tragedy of dis-
        possessed farmers, unemployment, and graft and
        corruption in government.

1873   Saxton, Alexander.   THE GREAT MIDLAND.   Apple-
        ton, 1948.   Economic class struggle and race
        relations in Chicago in the Thirties; a story of
        labor unions, race riots, and Communist activi-
        ties.

1874   Scott, Evelyn.   BREAD AND A SWORD.   Scribner,
        1937.   Story of a writer compromising his crea-
        tive integrity to support his family during the
        Depression.

1875   Scott, Virgil.   THE HICKORY STICK.   Swallow,
        1948.   Economic conditions of a young student and
        teacher in a small Ohio town through the Depres-
        sion years.

1876   Scowcroft, Richard.   FIRST FAMILY.   Houghton,
        1950.   Life in a prosperous middle-class family
        after the 1929 crash.

1877   Shepherd, Jean.   IN GOD WE TRUST, ALL OTHERS

PAY CASH. Doubleday, 1966. Memories of childhood in a small Indiana town recall family life and customs, Tom Mix movies, Sarsaparilla, and other nostalgia.

1878   Simon, Charlie May. SHARE-CROPPER. Dutton, 1937. Picture of the economic problems of an Arkansas cotton farmer during the Depression; story of the tenant farmers union.

1879   Sims, Marian. THE CITY ON THE HILL. Lippincott, 1940. City solicitor of a small Southern city crusades against slums, political graft, and unjust liquor regulations.

1880   Sinclair, Upton. CO-OP. Farrar, 1936. Development of the farmers' self-help co-operatives in California, 1932-1936.

1881   -- DRAGON'S TEETH. Viking, 1942. Period between 1929 and 1934; events in France and Germany during the rise of Hitler, Goering, and Goebbels. Imprisonment in Dachau prison; Lanny Budd series. Sequel to "Between Two Worlds" (1920's).

1882   -- WIDE IS THE GATE. Viking, 1943. Lanny Budd furthers his anti-Nazi activities while posing as a personal friend of Hitler, Goering, and Hess, and witnesses the beginning of the Spanish Civil War. Sequel to "Dragon's Teeth."

1883   -- PRESIDENTIAL AGENT. Viking, 1944. Lanny Budd becomes a secret agent of President Roosevelt reporting on the political situation in Europe from 1937 to 1938 and the Munich Pact between Chamberlain and Hitler. Sequel to "Wide is the Gate."

1884   Skidmore, Hubert. THE HAWK'S NEST. Doubleday, 1941. Senate investigation of the deaths of many workers from silica dust on a West Virginia mountain tunnel project in 1931.

1885   Slade, Caroline. THE TRIUMPH OF WILLIE POND. Vanguard, 1940. Ironic story of a family on relief; thesis is that New Deal relief measures treat symptoms rather than causes.

1886   -- JOB'S HOUSE.   Vanguard, 1941.   Story of unem-
        ployment and relief during Depression years.

1887   Smith, Betty.   JOY IN THE MORNING.   Harper,
        1963.   Young married love in a Midwest college
        town.

1888   Smitter, Wessel.   F. O. B.   DETROIT.   Harper,
        1938.   Story of the automobile industry showing
        the inhuman speedup in the factory and the work-
        ingman's helplessness in the system.

1889   Steinbeck, John.   IN DUBIOUS BATTLE.   Viking,
        1936.   Story of a strike among the fruit pickers
        in the California fruit country during the Depres-
        sion.

1890   -- OF MICE AND MEN.   Covici, 1937.   Life of
        itinerant ranch workers in California.

1891   -- THE GRAPES OF WRATH.   Viking, 1939.   Story
        of Oklahoma farm families seeking relief from
        the dust bowl by following the seasonal fruit
        picking jobs in California.

1892   Storm, Hans Otto.   COUNT TEN.   Longmans, 1940.
        Story of an American trying to find his place in
        life during the Depression.

1893   Stribling, T. S.   THE SOUND WAGON.   Doubleday,
        1935.   Novel of politics; reform candidates
        opposed to the entrenched political machine and
        gangsters.

1894   Swarthout, Glendon.   LOVELAND.   Doubleday, 1968.
        Light hearted tale of a young man's summer dur-
        ing the Depression with references to the music
        and slang of the period.

1895   Taber, Gladys.   A STAR TO STEER BY.   Macrae,
        1938.   Wisconsin mill town torn by a strike
        when a labor organizer incites the workers against
        the paternalistic mill owners.

1896   Tarkington, Booth.   THE HERITAGE OF HATCHER

IDE.   Doubleday, 1941.   Pictures the changes in
a respectable Middle West family as a result of
the Depression.

1897   Thomas, Dorothy.   THE HOME PLACE.   Knopf,
        1936.   Story of a family conflict and hope for
        better times when drought and the Depression
        force three brothers to return with their families
        to the old farm.

1898   Thomas, Mack.   GUMBO.   Grove, 1965.   Sketches
        of boyhood life in Texas in the Thirties.

1899   Thorp, Duncan.   THANKS YER HONOR.   Crown,
        1963.   A college boy and his Fundamentalist
        grandmother live through Prohibition and Depres-
        sion in Cucamonga, California.

1900   Trilling, Lionel.   THE MIDDLE OF THE JOURNEY.
        Viking, 1947.   Life among the summer residents
        and natives in a farming area in Connecticut in
        the late 1930's; agitated by community feeling
        against a Communist in their midst.

1901   Tunis, John.   SON OF THE VALLEY.   Morrow,
        1949.   Story of TVA and the resentment of the
        people whose homes would be flooded by the pro-
        ject.

1902   Turpin, Waters Edward.   O CANAAN!   Doubleday,
        1939.   Follows the lives of the Negroes who
        migrated to Chicago in 1916 and after; through
        prosperity, the crash of 1929, and the Depression.

1903   Villarreal, Jose Antonio.   POCHO.   Doubleday,
        1959.   Childhood of a Mexican migratory worker
        in the Santa Clara valley of California during the
        Depression years.

1904   Vogel, Joseph.   MAN'S COURAGE.   Knopf, 1938.
        Technicalities and red tape of the New Deal
        relief system and the chaotic economic conditions
        faced by a Polish immigrant family in a small
        American city.

1905   Wagner, Tobias.   THE TURBULENT PENDRAYLES.
        Little, 1937.   Family and social life of a Phila-

delphia locomotive manufacturer after the 1929 crash.

1906   Walker, Mildred. FIREWEED. Harcourt, 1934.
        Story of life in a lumber mill town in upper
        Michigan after the Depression closes the mill.

1907   Warren, Robert Penn. ALL THE KING'S MEN.
        Harcourt, 1946. Story of a demagogue based on
        the life and death of Huey Long.

1908   Weaver, John. ANOTHER SUCH VICTORY. Viking,
        1948. Presents both sides of the veterans'
        Bonus March against Washington in 1932. Mc-
        Arthur and Patton appear.

1909   Webber, Gordon. WHAT END BUT LOVE. Little,
        1959. Memories of farm life and industrial
        growth set in the framework of a family reunion
        on a Michigan farm near the automobile factories
        in 1934.

1910   Weller, George Anthony. NOT TO EAT, NOT FOR
        LOVE. Smith and Haas, 1933. Picture of under-
        graduate life at Harvard University in 1933.

1911   White, Milton. A YALE MAN. Doubleday, 1966.
        Realistic sketches of student life at Yale during
        the Depression and New Deal years.

1912   Wickenden, Dan. TOBIAS BRANDYWINE. Morrow,
        1948. A story of family life during nine years
        of the Depression and New Deal relief measures.

1913   -- THE RED CARPET. Morrow, 1952. New York
        in 1936 as a young Illinois college graduate found
        it.

1914   Williams, Ben Ames. TIME OF PEACE. Hough-
        ton, 1942. Novel of American life and political
        thought from 1930 to Pearl Harbor; theme is the
        changing reaction to the threat of war and the
        gradual acceptance of Roosevelt's foreign policy.

1915   Wilson, Gregory. THE VALLEY OF TIME. Double-
        day, 1967. Story of a fundamentalist teacher
        pictures life and religion in eastern Tennessee

before and during the TVA years.

1916 Wilson, S. J. HURRAY FOR ME. Crown, 1964.
      Story of Jewish family life and customs as the
      five-year old son grows up in Brooklyn during
      the Depression.

1917 Wolfe, Thomas. YOU CAN'T GO HOME AGAIN.
      Harper, 1940. Observations on economic and
      political life from the Depression to the spread
      of Nazism; set in New York, Brooklyn, England,
      and Germany.

1918 Wright, Richard. NATIVE SON. Harper, 1940.
      Story of the frustrations and resentment in the
      life of a young Negro in Chicago in the 1930's.

1919 -- LAWD TODAY. Walker, 1963. A day in the
      life of a Negro postal clerk in Chicago during
      the Depression.

1920 Wright, Sarah E. THIS CHILD'S GONNA LIVE.
      Delacorte, 1969. Story of the bleak existence
      of a Negro family in the black ghetto of a small
      town in rural Maryland.

1921 Yaffe, James. NOBODY DOES YOU ANY FAVORS.
      Putnam, 1966. Conflict between father and son
      over the son's lack of interest in the family
      leather wear business.

1922 Zara, Louis. SOME FOR THE GLORY. Bobbs,
      1937. Rise of orphan boy to presidential can-
      didacy; details of ward, state, and national
      politics.

1923 Zugsmith, Leane. TIME TO REMEMBER. Random,
      1936. Story of the conflicts involved in a depart-
      ment store strike, from the standpoint of the
      striking clerks.

1924 Adams, Frank Ramsay. WHEN I COME BACK.
McBride, 1944. Story of a typical small town
mother trying to keep her 17 year old son out
of the army in 1942.

1925 Albrand, Martha. WITHOUT ORDERS. Little,
1943. Story of an American soldier in undercover work for the American army and the
Italian underground.

1926 Allen, Ralph. THE HIGH WHITE FOREST. Doubleday, 1964. Three allied soldiers cut off by the
German offensive at the Battle of the Bulge in
1944.

1927 Appel, Benjamin. FORTRESS IN THE RICE.
Bobbs, 1951. Guerrilla warfare in the Philippines after Pearl Harbor.

1928 Arnold, Elliott. THE COMMANDOS. Duell, 1942.
Story of the purpose, training, and action of
commando guerrilla units culminating in a raid in
Nazi-occupied Norway.

1929 -- TOMORROW WILL SING. Duell, 1945. Story of
Italian-American relations at a U. S. bomber base
in Southern Italy.

1930 -- WALK WITH THE DEVIL. Knopf, 1950. Advance
of the American army in Italy.

1931 Arnow, Harriette. THE DOLLMAKER. Macmillan,
1954. Story of a Kentucky family in wartime
Detroit.

1932 Arthur, Phyllis. PAYING GUEST. Samuel Curl,
1945. Conflicts among an unhappy family are
straightened out by their roomer, an engineer at

the local war plant.

1933   Ashmead, John. THE MOUNTAIN AND THE FEA-
       THER. Houghton, 1961. Story of wartime
       Hawaii and combat in the South Pacific from
       1943 to the Battle of Leyte Gulf.

1934   Atwell, Lester. PRIVATE. Simon and Schuster,
       1958. Story of a middle-aged soldier in the
       Battle of the Bulge and in the invasion of Ger-
       many.

1935   August, John. ADVANCE AGENT. Little, 1942.
       A newspaperman and a soldier expose a secret
       Nazi organization.

1936   Barr, George. EPITAPH FOR AN ENEMY. Har-
       per, 1958. An American sergeant, leading a
       group of French villagers to the beach for evacua-
       tion, gains new understanding of the enemy as he
       sees the influence which a humane German com-
       mander had on the group.

1937   Bassett, James. HARM'S WAY. World, 1962.
       A story of U.S. Navy life during the first year
       of war in the Pacific.

1938   Beach, Edward. RUN SILENT, RUN DEEP. Holt,
       1955. Realistic novel of submarine warfare in
       the Pacific.

1939   Bergamini, David. THE FLEET IN THE WINDOW.
       Simon and Schuster, 1960. Story of the guerrilla
       fighting in the Philippines and life in a Japanese
       internment camp as experienced by the young son
       of an American missionary doctor.

1940   Berk, Howard. THE HERO MACHINE. New Ameri-
       can Library, 1967. Life in a U.S. air base in
       the China-Burma-India theatre in World War II.

1941   Beverley-Giddings, Arthur Raymond. BROAD MAR-
       GIN. Morrow, 1945. An American flier,
       wounded with the RAF, recuperates in Tidewater
       Virginia.

1942   Bonner, Paul Hyde. EXCELSIOR! Scribner, 1955.

Scion of a Swiss banking family faces conflicting
loyalties in America at the outbreak of the war.

1943   Bowman, Peter. BEACH RED. Random, 1945.
        Picture of a landing assault on a Pacific island
        through the thoughts and feelings of a soldier in
        the hour before his death.

1944   Boyd, Dean. LIGHTER THAN AIR. Harcourt,
        Brace and World, 1961. Humorous tale of the
        blimp service in the war.

1945   Boyle, Kay. HIS HUMAN MAJESTY. Whittlesey,
        1949. Ski troopers training in Colorado in
        1944.

1946   Brelis, Dean. THE MISSION. Random, 1958.
        Story of an OSS agent operating behind the
        Japanese lines in Burma in 1943.

1947   Bridge, Ann. A PLACE TO STAND. Macmillan,
        1953. Daughter of an American businessman
        becomes involved with a family of Polish refugees
        and witnesses the brutality of the Nazis when
        they march into Budapest in 1941.

1948   Bright, Robert. THE LIFE AND DEATH OF LITTLE
        JO. Doubleday, 1944. Story of the effect of the
        war on a young Spanish-American from a village
        in New Mexico.

1949   Brinkley, William. DON'T GO NEAR THE WATER.
        Random, 1956. Comedy of a U.S. Navy public
        relations unit on a Pacific island during the war.

1950   -- THE NINETY AND NINE. Doubleday, 1966. Life
        on an LST landing craft at the time of the Anzio
        Beachhead in Italy.

1951   Bromfield, Louis. MR. SMITH. Harper, 1951.
        An American major on a Pacific island reviews
        his fruitless life.

1952   Brown, Eugene. THE LOCUST FIRE. Doubleday,
        1957. Fast paced action story of an Air Trans-
        port Command pilot in China during World War II.

1953   Brown, Harry. WALK IN THE SUN. Knopf, 1944.
        Story of a squad of American soldiers on a beach-
        head in Italy.

1954   Brown, Joe David. KINGS GO FORTH. Morrow,
        1956. Story of two American artillery observers
        in action against the Germans in Italy and Southern
        France.

1955   Buck, Pearl. COMMAND THE MORNING. Day,
        1959. Story of the scientists who developed the
        first atomic chain reaction at the University of
        Chicago, December 2, 1942; set in Chicago,
        Oak Ridge, Washington, and Los Alamos.

1956   Burnett, William Riley. TOMORROW'S ANOTHER
        DAY. Knopf, 1945. A gay young gambler re-
        turns from the war and settles down in the
        restaurant business.

1957   Busch, Niven. THEY DREAM OF HOME. Bobbs,
        1944. Story of five U.S. Marines who face the
        problems of adjusting to civilian life in Los
        Angeles after action in the Pacific.

1958   Caldwell, Janet Taylor. THE FINAL HOUR.
        Scribner, 1944. Conflict in the Pennsylvania
        munitions dynasty from 1939 to 1942; some want
        to do business with Hitler. Sequel to "Eagles
        Gather" (Thirties).

1959   Calmer, Ned. THE STRANGE LAND. Scribner,
        1950. Story of an unsuccessful Allied offensive
        in Europe in 1944.

1960   Camerer, David. THE DAMNED WEAR WINGS.
        Doubleday, 1958. Personality conflicts among a
        group of U.S. pilots on an air base in Italy;
        bombing missions over the Ploesti oil fields.

1961   Camp, William Henry. SKIP TO MY LOU. Double-
        day, 1945. Story of an itinerant Arkansas Ozark
        hill family who migrate to the California ship
        yards during the war.

1962   Camp, William Martin. RETREAT, HELL! Apple-
        ton, 1943. Story of the U.S. Marines fighting in

Shanghai and at Cavite, Bataan, and Corregidor
in the Philippines on December 6, 1941.

1963   Carleton, Marjorie. THE SWAN SANG ONCE.
        Morrow, 1947. A soldier, released from Japanese
        prison camp, seeks proof that his wife was a
        traitor during the war.

1964   Carse, Robert. FROM THE SEA AND THE JUN-
        GLE. Scribner, 1951. Episode on an island in
        the West Indies involving an ex-gangster, German
        submarines and the sinking of American ships.

1965   Caspary, Vera. THE ROSECREST CELL. Putnam,
        1967. Story centers around the activities of a
        Communist group in a Connecticut town from the
        1930's into World War II.

1966   Chamales, Tom. NEVER SO FEW. Scribner, 1957.
        Guerrilla activity in Burma in World War II.

1967   Chambliss, William C. BOOMERANG. Harcourt,
        1944. Story of a new U. S. Navy ship in the
        South Pacific.

1968   Charyn, Jerome. AMERICAN SCRAPBOOK. Viking,
        1969. Story of life in the concentration camps for
        Japanese-Americans set up in California during
        the war.

1969   Chidester, Ann. NO LONGER FUGITIVE. Scribner,
        1943. Story of a draft dodger whose experiences
        give him the conviction he needs to take his part
        in the war effort.

1970   Clagett, John. THE SLOT. Crown, 1958. Story
        of a PT boat and its crew assigned to guard the
        busy channel between Guadalcanal and the Solomon
        Islands in World War II.

1971   Clarke, Arthur C. GLIDE PATH. Harcourt, 1963.
        Story of the early development of radar with
        American and British scientists and technicians
        stationed at an air base in Cornwall.

1972   Clavell, James. KING RAT. Little, 1962. Pic-
        ture of the sordid life of American prisoners-of-

war in a Japanese prison camp in Singapore.

1973   Cochrell, Boyd. THE BARREN BEACHES OF HELL.
        Holt, 1959. Story of a young Marine private
        through the invasions of Tarawa, Saipan, and
        Tinian and occupation duty at Nagasaki, Japan.

1974   Coleman, William Lawrence. THE GOLDEN
        VANITY. Macmillan, 1962. Struggle for
        power aboard a cargo ship during the last stages
        of the war in the Pacific.

1975   Connell, Evan S. THE PATRIOT. Viking, 1960.
        Story of the training of a naval air cadet, of his
        life as a seaman, and of his post-war art studies
        at the University of Kansas.

1976   Cook, Fannie. MRS. PALMER'S HONEY. Double-
        day, 1946. Story of the war work and labor
        union activity of a lovable Negro girl in St.
        Louis.

1977   Cotler, Gordon. BOTTLETOP AFFAIR. Simon
        and Schuster, 1959. A humorous story of the
        search for a lone Japanese holdout on a small
        Pacific island during the war.

1978   Covert, Alice. THE ETERNAL MOUNTAIN.
        Doubleday, 1944. Romance in which a young
        man takes a job in a war plant and gets in
        shape for the army.

1979   Cozzens, James Gould. GUARD OF HONOR. Har-
        court, 1948. Tribulations of the commanding
        officer of an air base in Florida.

1980   Crowley, Robert T. NOT SOLDIERS ALL. Double-
        day, 1967. Story of medics under fire during
        the Italian campaign.

1981   Daniels, Sally. THE INCONSTANT SEASON.
        Atheneum, 1962. A young girl recalls her
        childhood in western New York state during
        World War II.

1982   Davis, Clyde Brion. THE STARS INCLINE. Farrar,
        1946. Career of a Denver newspaper man from

the Spanish Civil War to the campaigns in Africa
and Europe in World War II.

1983   -- PLAYTIME IS OVER. Lippincott, 1949. Day-to-
day life on a small Arkansas farm during the war.

1984   Davis, Paxton. TWO SOLDIERS. Simon and Schuster, 1956. Two novelettes showing the war in
the China-Burma-India theater.

1985   De Pereda, Prudencio. WINDMILLS IN BROOKLYN.
Atheneum, 1960. Story of a young boy growing
up in the Spanish colony of Brooklyn during the
World War II years.

1986   Dibner, Martin. THE DEEP SIX. Doubleday, 1953.
Life aboard a Navy cruiser during the war.

1987   Dixon, Clarice M. THE DEVIL AND THE DEEP.
Scribner, 1944. Stories of life in the U.S.
Merchant Marine in 1941-1942.

1988   Dodson, Kenneth. AWAY ALL BOATS. Little,
1954. Amphibious warfare in the Pacific from
the campaigns in the Gilbert Islands to Okinawa.

1989   -- STRANGER TO THE SHORE. Little, 1956.
Adventurous story centered around a U.S. Merchant Marine sailor and a German raider in the
waters off Chile in 1942.

1990   Dunlap, Katharine. ONCE THERE WAS A VILLAGE.
Morrow, 1941. Story of Americans involved in
war mobilization in a French village at the
beginning of the war.

1991   Eastlake, William. CASTLE KEEP. Simon and
Schuster, 1965. Story of a group of American
soldiers and their relations with the aristocratic
owners of the castle in which they are quartered
in Germany.

1992   Eddy, Roger. BEST BY FAR. Doubleday, 1966.
Reminiscences of World War II veterans at a
reunion on the site of a battlefield in Italy.

1993   Edmiston, James. HOME AGAIN. Doubleday, 1955.

Story of Japanese-Americans in California and their life in relocation camps during the war.

1994 Ellison, James Whitfield. THE FREEST MAN ON EARTH. Doubleday, 1958. Story of what happens when a conscientious objector refuses to answer a call by the draft board.

1995 Eyster, Warren. FAR FROM THE CUSTOMARY SKIES. Random, 1953. Life cycle of an American destroyer from training cruise through action at Guadalcanal and New Guinea to its sinking in a battle.

1996 Falstein, Louis. FACE OF A HERO. Harcourt, 1950. Story of hate, fear, and boredom among the men who flew American bombers based in Italy.

1997 Fast, Howard. THE WINSTON AFFAIR. Crown, 1959. Story of the trial of an American soldier for the killing of a British soldier in the Far East.

1998 Fleming, Berry. COLONEL EFFINGHAM'S RAID. Duell, 1943. Story of a retired army man and a young newspaper man fighting local corrupt politics in a Georgia town until the reporter joins the National Guard on the way to war.

1999 -- THE LIGHTWOOD TREE. Lippincott, 1947. A Georgia teacher, exempt from the draft, works to defend liberty at home when local politicians use undemocratic action in arresting a student.

2000 Forester, C. S. THE GOOD SHEPHERD. Little, 1955. Tale of four U.S. Navy ships escorting a merchant marine convoy from America to England in the face of repeated German submarine attacks.

2001 Fosburgh, Hugh. VIEW FROM THE AIR. Scribner, 1953. Story of the crew of a bomber on forty missions over Truk in the South Pacific.

2002 Frizell, Bernard. TEN DAYS IN AUGUST. Simon and Schuster, 1956. A romance set against the

German occupation of Paris, as the underground
Resistance movement prepares for the advancing
Allies.

2003   Frye, Pearl. THE NARROW BRIDGE. Little,
        1947. Story of the tension and antagonism in
        Honolulu after the attack on Pearl Harbor.

2004   Gabriel, Gilbert Wolf. I GOT A COUNTRY. Double-
        day, 1944. Story of three U. S. Army soldiers
        stationed in Alaska.

2005   Gallico, Paul. THE LONELY. Knopf, 1949. A
        young U. S. flyer must decide between an English
        girl and his girl back home.

2006   Garth, David. BERMUDA CALLING. Putnam, 1944.
        Spy story of World War II.

2007   -- WATCH ON THE BRIDGE. Putnam, 1959. The
        capture of the Remagen Bridge over the Rhine in
        March, 1945, is the central element in a love
        story of an American soldier and a German girl.

2008   Gilpatric, Guy. ACTION IN THE NORTH ATLANTIC.
        Dutton, 1943. Action with the U. S. Merchant
        Marine on the run to Murmansk.

2009   Gionannitti, Len. THE PRISONERS OF COMBINE D.
        Holt, 1957. Story of six American airmen in a
        German prison camp in 1944-45.

2010   Glaspell, Susan. JUDD RANKIN'S DAUGHTER.
        Lippincott, 1945. Story of wartime family life;
        a war-shocked son; isolationist editor in Iowa.

2011   Goertz, Arthemise. DREAM OF JUJI. McGraw,
        1958. Story of a group of Americans interned in
        Japan at the outbreak of the war.

2012   Goethals, Thomas. CHAINS OF COMMAND. Ran-
        dom, 1955. Strategists at the rear headquarters
        of a U. S. army unit ignore warnings of a German
        offensive shortly before the Battle of the Bulge.

2013   Goodman, Mitchell. THE END OF IT. Horizon,
        1961. Story of a field artillery unit of the 5th

Army in Italy.

2014   Gwaltney, Francis Irby.   THE DAY THE CENTURY
        ENDED.   Rinehart, 1955.   Story of the brutality
        of the war in the Philippines which ended on the
        day the atom bomb was dropped at Hiroshima.

2015   Habe, Hans (pseud.)   THE MISSION.   Coward, 1966.
        Story of the conference of 32 nations at Evian-
        les-Bains on Lake Geneva called by President
        Roosevelt to discuss the rescue of Jews in Nazi
        Germany.

2016   Haines, William Wister.   COMMAND DECISION.
        Little, 1947.   The air war over Europe as seen
        by the commanding officer of a bomber division
        based in England.

2017   Hall, James Norman.   LOST ISLAND.   Little, 1944.
        Pictures the destruction of the natives' way of
        life when an army of American experts prepare to
        build an airbase on a small Pacific island.

2018   Hanson, Robert P.   A GLIMPSE OF CANAAN.   Mor-
        row, 1966.   A veteran returns home to Vermont
        after his wife leaves him.   He reminisces about
        his war experiences and about his family back-
        ground through three generations in Vermont.

2019   Hardy, William M.   U. S. S. MUDSKIPPER.   Dodd,
        1967.   A U. S. submarine crew off the coast of
        Japan plan a raid to destroy a freight train which
        runs along the coast.

2020   Hawkins, John and Ward Hawkins.   THE PILEBUCK.
        Dutton, 1943.   Indictment of labor union racketeers
        and slackers in a wartime shipyard in the North-
        west where an FBI spy is sent to investigate
        sabotage.

2021   Haydn, Hiram.   MANHATTAN FURLOUGH.   Bobbs,
        1945.   Story of a young soldier, depressed over
        the death of a friend in training camp, on leave
        in New York City.

2022   Hayes, Alfred.   GIRL ON THE VIA FLAMINIA.
        Harper, 1949.   The last year of the war in Italy;

love affair between an American G. I. and an
Italian girl.

2023   Heggen, Thomas. MISTER ROBERTS. Houghton,
       1946. Story of life on a cargo ship in the Paci-
       fic and the reaction of the crew to the dullness
       of their duty.

2024   Heller, Joseph. CATCH-22. Simon & Schuster,
       1961. A comical novel about a young bombardier
       stationed in Italy and his efforts to avoid flying
       missions.

2025   Hemingway, Leicester. THE SOUND OF THE TRUM-
       PET. Holt, 1953. Two American cameramen
       record the invasion on the Normandy beaches on
       D-Day.

2026   Herber, William. TOMORROW TO LIVE. Coward,
       1958. Set in Hawaii and Saipan in 1944; story
       of the U. S. Marines engaged in island fighting.

2027   Hersey, John. THE WAR LOVER. Knopf, 1959.
       Life of an American Flying Fortress crew on
       missions and on a bomber base in England.

2028   Heyliger, William. HOME IS A ONE-WAY STREET.
       Westminster, 1945. Story of a wounded soldier
       and his problems in readjusting to his wife, job,
       and family.

2029   Heym, Stefan. THE CRUSADERS. Little, 1948.
       Follows an American division from the Normandy
       invasion through France, Germany, the liberation
       of Paris, the Battle of the Bulge, and the occupa-
       tion of the Ruhr.

2030   Hicks, Granville. BEHOLD TROUBLE. Macmillan,
       1944. Story of a conscientious objector and the
       consequences of his stand against the draft board.

2031   Higginbotham, Robert E. WINE FOR MY BROTHERS.
       Rinehart, 1946. Story of the trip of an oil tanker
       from Texas to New York in January, 1942.

2032   Hillyer, Laurie. TIME REMEMBERED. Macmillan,
       1945. Story of normal life disrupted by the war

when a son is caught in the attack on Pearl Harbor; the mother represents pacifist sentiment.

2033   Hilton, James. THE STORY OF DR. WASSELL. Little, 1943. Fictionized account of the heroic efforts of Dr. Corydon Wassell to rescue the wounded men from the H. M. S. Marblehead and lead them from Java to Australia in 1942.

2034   -- NOTHING SO STRANGE. Little, 1947. Story of a young American scientist viewing the war in Europe and England.

2035   Hoffman, William. THE TRUMPET UNBLOWN. Doubleday, 1955. Experiences of an American soldier in a field hospital during the Battle of the Bulge.

2036   -- YANCEY'S WAR. Doubleday, 1966. A sharp operator profits from his deals in the service until he dies a hero's death.

2037   Hough, Henry Beetle. ROOSTER CROW IN TOWN. Appleton, 1945. A Maine coastal town during 1942-43 and the effect on the lives of the people of the fear of invasion, civil defense dimouts, amphibious forces practicing in the neighborhood, price control, rationing, and general war fever.

2038   Howe, George. CALL IT TREASON. Viking, 1949. Story of the training and action of three German prisoners dropped behond German lines as a U. S. Army intelligence team.

2039   Hueston, Ethel. MOTHER WENT MAD ON MONDAY. Bobbs, 1944. Family and home life in a small town in New York during the war; son reported missing; teen-age daughter has romance with an army flier.

2040   Hunt, Howard. EAST OF FAREWELL. Knopf, 1942. Story of a destroyer on convoy duty in the Atlantic.

2041   -- LIMIT OF DARKNESS. Random, 1944. Story of 24 hours in the lives of a group of American fliers based on Guadalcanal.

2042   Jessey, Cornelia. TEACH THE ANGRY SPIRIT.
        Crown, 1949. Life in the Mexican quarter of
        Los Angeles during the war.

2043   Jonas, Carl. BEACHHEAD ON THE WIND. Little,
        1945. Picture of cleanup operations after a
        landing on a beachhead in the Aleutian Islands.

2044   Jones, James. FROM HERE TO ETERNITY.
        Scribner, 1951. Pre-Pearl Harbor army life in
        Hawaii, ending with Japanese attack.

2045   -- THE PISTOL. Scribner, 1958. Follows the
        actions of a soldier who finds a pistol during the
        attack on Pearl Harbor through the plots to take
        it from him.

2046   -- THE THIN RED LINE. Scribner, 1962. Story
        of the campaign and battle to recapture Guadal-
        canal in 1942-43.

2047   Jones, Nard. THE ISLAND. Sloane, 1948. Pic-
        tures the conditions and problems typical of
        American communities during the war in the
        story of three men in Seattle.

2048   Kadish, M. R. POINT OF HONOR. Random, 1951.
        Story of an American artillery battalion in the
        Italian campaign.

2049   Kantor, MacKinlay. HAPPY LAND. Coward, 1943.
        A father saddened by news of his son's death
        reviews the boy's life.

2050   -- GLORY FOR ME. Coward, 1945. Story in
        verse form of three veterans with bitter war
        memories who find themselves misfits in their
        home town.

2051   Kata, Elizabeth. SOMEONE WILL CONQUER THEM.
        St. Martins, 1962. American girl married to a
        Japanese in Tokyo in 1944 hides an American air-
        man, shot down in a bombing raid; life in war-
        time and occupation in Japan.

2052   Keefe, Frederick L. THE INVESTIGATING OFFICER.
        Delacorte, 1966. Suspenseful story of the inquest

into the killing of two German prisoners of war
by an American officer.

2053   Kehoe, Karon. CITY IN THE SUN. Dodd, 1946.
        Story of a Japanese-American family in California
        and in a relocation camp during the war.

2054   Kelly, Jack. THE UNEXPECTED PEACE. Gambit,
        1969. Story of an army infantry unit in the
        Philippines during the war and in Japan as part
        of the occupation forces.

2055   Kendrick, Baynard H. LIGHTS OUT. Morrow,
        1945. Reaction of a blinded soldier to his
        rehabilitation to daily routine living, and to his
        discovery that two of his new friends are a
        Negro and a Jew.

2056   Keyes, Frances Parkinson. ALSO THE HILLS.
        Messner, 1943. Story of the war effort in a
        New Hampshire village.

2057   Killens, John Oliver. AND THEN WE HEARD THE
        THUNDER. Knopf, 1963. A Negro from New
        York City encounters racial discrimination in
        the army; story leads up to a bloody race riot
        in Australia.

2058   Klaas, Joe. MAYBE I'M DEAD. Macmillan, 1955.
        Story of the forced march of 10, 000 prisoners-
        of-war from a German prison camp just before
        the liberation in 1945.

2059   Knowles, John. A SEPARATE PEACE. Macmillan,
        1959. Story of life at a New Hampshire boarding
        school in 1942, showing the restlessness caused
        by the war.

2060   Kolb, Avery. JIGGER WITCHET'S WAR. Simon and
        Schuster, 1959. Humorous story of a Negro sol-
        dier in England and behind the German lines in
        France in World War II.

2061   Kubeck, James. THE CALENDAR EPIC. Putnam,
        1956. Life aboard a U.S. Merchant Marine ship
        in World War II; emphasis on amorous adventures
        during shore leave.

2062   Lamott, Kenneth. THE STOCKADE. Little, 1952.
        Pictures the inhuman treatment of 5, 000 Okina-
        wans and Koreans in an American prison camp on
        a Pacific island near the end of the war.

2063   Landon, Joseph. ANGLE OF ATTACK. Doubleday,
        1952. Story of air warfare and the effects of an
        unethical act on the crew of a bomber based in
        Italy.

2064   Lasswell, Mary. HIGH TIME. Houghton, 1944.
        Three beer drinking warmhearted old ladies
        contribute to the war effort.

2065   Lawrence, Josephine. THERE IS TODAY. Little,
        1942. A story of the wartime home front repre-
        senting typical types; the young couple who marry
        in spite of the draft, the glory-seeking volunteer
        worker, and the middle-aged patriotic veteran.

2066   -- A TOWER OF STEEL. Little, 1943. Story of
        women in wartime, represented by four young
        women who work in a law office.

2067   Lay, Beirne and Sy Bartlett. TWELVE O'CLOCK
        HIGH. Harper, 1948. Story of a demoralized
        bomber group based in England in 1942; pic-
        tures the strain and tension of the war in the
        air.

2068   Leckie, Robert. ORDAINED. Doubleday, 1969.
        Story of a Catholic priest, ordained in 1936,
        who serves as an Army Chaplain in the Pacific
        theatre.

2069   Leeming, John. IT ALWAYS RAINS IN ROME.
        Farrar, 1961. A lighthearted tale revolving
        around the question of whether or not to destroy
        an ancient bridge in Italy.

2070   Leggett, John. WHO TOOK THE GOLD AWAY.
        Random, 1969. Story of two Yale roommates
        from college days in 1938 through the war and
        to success and failure in the electronics industry.

2071   Leonard, George. SHOULDER THE SKY. McDowell,
        1959. Story of two young flight instructors

assigned to a Georgia base instead of being sent
into combat duty in 1944; picture of the training
of bomber pilots.

2072   Lewisohn, Ludwig. BREATHE UPON THESE. Bobbs,
       1944. Story of a typical American family shocked
       into awareness of the world by the experiences of
       a German refugee scientist.

2073   Long, Margaret. LOUISVILLE SATURDAY. Ran-
       dom, 1950. Story of eleven girls and the crises
       they meet one Saturday night in Louisville,
       Kentucky, in 1942.

2074   Loomis, Edward. END OF A WAR. Ballantine,
       1957. Follows an infantryman from training in
       France, through the Belgian offensive in the
       winter of 1944, and the occupation of Germany.

2075   MacCuish, David. DO NOT GO GENTLE. Double-
       day, 1960. Story of a young man who grows up
       in a Montana mining town; joins the Marine
       Corps, and after boot camp survives the heavy
       fighting on Guadalcanal.

2076   Mackay, Margaret. FOR ALL MEN BORN. John
       Day, 1943. Story of life at Pearl Harbor on the
       day of the Japanese attack.

2077   McLaughlin, Robert. THE SIDE OF THE ANGELS.
       Knopf, 1947. The reactions of two brothers to
       their army experiences in the Mediterranean area.

2078   MacLeish, Archibald and Robert De San Marzano.
       INFERNAL MACHINE. Houghton, 1947. Satire
       of official Washington during the war.

2079   Mailer, Norman. THE NAKED AND THE DEAD.
       Rinehart, 1948. Picture of amphibious assault
       and jungle fighting in the capture of a Japanese-
       held island in the Pacific.

2080   Mandel, George. THE WAX BOOM. Random,
       1962. Story of an American platoon in the fore-
       front of the December, 1944 offensive against
       Germany.

2081   Mandel, Paul, and Sheila Mandel. THE BLACK
        SHIP. Random, 1969. An American PT boat
        crew assigned to a British base on the North
        Sea survive a sinking and join the Dutch under-
        ground.

2082   Marmur, Jacland. ANDROMEDA. Holt, 1947.
        An American freighter, one of the last to leave
        Singapore before the Japanese arrive, carries a
        young romantic girl and an American who turns
        out to be a Japanese agent.

2083   Marquand, J. P. SO LITTLE TIME. Little, 1943.
        Satire of the contemporary scene of theatrical
        and literary life centering around a World War I
        veteran whose son is nearing draft age.

2084   -- REPENT IN HASTE. Little, 1945. Story of
        the marital problems of a flier in the Pacific.

2085   Master, Dexter. THE ACCIDENT. Knopf, 1955.
        Novel about the making and using of the atomic
        bomb told during the eight days it takes a young
        atomic scientist to die from exposure to radiation;
        setting is Los Alamos in 1946.

2086   Matheson, Richard. THE BEARDLESS WARRIORS.
        Little, 1960. Story of the battle experiences of
        a squad of U. S. riflemen made up chiefly of 18
        year old replacements; set in Germany in Decem-
        ber, 1944.

2087   Matthiessen, Peter. RADITZER. Viking, 1961.
        Character study of two non-combatant sailors,
        set in Honolulu during World War II.

2088   Mayo, Eleanor R. TURN HOME. Morrow, 1945.
        Story of a veteran trying to find a place in his
        home town.

2089   Merrick, Gordon. THE STRUMPET WIND. Mor-
        row, 1947. Story of an American intelligence
        officer working with the French underground.

2090   Miller, Dallas. FATHERS AND DREAMERS.
        Doubleday, 1966. Life in a small town near
        Cleveland, Ohio in 1943 reflects the feeling of

the period; F. D. R., ration books, slang, and the things boys talked about as they reached maturity.

2091 Miller, Merle. ISLAND 49. Crowell, 1945. Picture of the home background and the action of a group of men attacking a coral atoll in the Pacific.

2092 Moon, Bucklin. THE DARKER BROTHER. Doubleday, 1943. Story of a Southern Negro facing northern intolerance; Pearl Harbor makes him aware of his country, and he goes willingly to fight for it.

2093 Morris, Terry. NO HIDING PLACE. Knopf, 1945. Story of the problems faced by wives who follow their husbands in the army.

2094 Mydans, Shelley. THE OPEN CITY. Doubleday, 1945. Picture of life in Santo Tomas prison camp at Manila after the Japanese invaded the Philippines.

2095 Myrer, Anton. THE BIG WAR. Appleton, 1957. Story of the U. S. Marines in action in the Pacific, and in love on the home front.

2096 Newhafer, Richard L. THE LAST TALLYHOO. Putnam, 1964. Story of five U. S. Navy pilots and of their exploits in the war.

2097 Nichols, John Treadwell. THE WIZARD OF LONELINESS. Putnam, 1966. Life of a lonely 11-year-old boy spending the last year of the war with his grandparents in a small Vermont town.

2098 Nordhoff, Charles and Norman Hall. THE HIGH BARBAREE. Little, 1945. Iowa farm-boy pilot shot down in the Pacific finds his dream island, but it is only in death he has found his dream.

2099 Ogilvie, Elisabeth. STORM TIDE. Crowell, 1945. Life of lobster fishermen on an island off the Maine coast; the coming of war brings the submarine menace. Sequel to "High Tide at Noon."

2100 -- EBBING TIDE. Crowell, 1947. Bennett's Island off the coast of Maine during the war. Sequel to "Storm Tide" (above).

2101   O'Rourke, Frank. 'E' COMPANY. Simon and
       Schuster, 1945. Formation, training, and action
       of an infantry company from December 17, 1941
       to first action in Africa a year later.

2102   Patterson, Mary. THE IRON COUNTRY. Houghton,
       1965. A young couple matures in the Minnesota
       mining country during World War II.

2103   Paul, Louis. THIS IS MY BROTHER. Crown,
       1943. Story of five U. S. soldiers, their thoughts
       and feelings, as they await death as spies after
       capture by the Japanese.

2104   Perrin, Ursula. GHOSTS. Knopf, 1967. Memories
       of life in a small mill town in upstate New York
       in 1945.

2105   Plagemann, Bentz. THE STEEL COCOON. Viking,
       1958. Story of a ship and its crew at war in
       the Pacific.

2106   Popkin, Zelda. THE JOURNEY HOME. Lippincott,
       1945. A train wreck forces a combat veteran
       to reconsider his ideas about the civilians with
       whom he had been traveling.

2107   Powell, Richard. THE SOLDIER. Scribner, 1960.
       Story of the heroic evacuation of U. S. forces from
       a small unstrategic island in the Pacific.

2108   Pratt, Rex. YOU TELL MY SON. Random, 1958.
       Story of the annihilation of a Regular Army pla-
       toon during a patrol action in the South Pacific
       and of the survivors' efforts to whip the inex-
       perienced Guard unit, to which they were
       assigned, into shape for the coming battle.

2109   Pratt, Theodore. MR. WINKLE GOES TO WAR.
       Duell, 1943. Humorous story of a hen-pecked
       husband who is drafted and returns home a hero.

2110   Reed, Kit. AT WAR AS CHILDREN. Farrar,
       1964. Picture of the daily life and routine of
       three children whose fathers are away at war

in the submarine service.

2111   Ripperger, Henrietta. 112 ELM STREET. Putnam,
        1943. Story of family life on the home front;
        father works in a war plant, one son is in the
        army, and the family is keeping a young English
        boy for the duration.

2112   Robertson, Don. THE GREATEST THING SINCE
        SLICED BREAD. Putnam, 1965. Authentic
        feeling of the period, based on the gas explosion
        in Cleveland, Ohio in 1944; nostalgic references
        to sports, music, movies. Followed by "The
        Sum and Total of Now" (Tense Years).

2113   Robinson, Wayne. BARBARA. Doubleday, 1962.
        Follows the fortunes of a U. S. Army tank bat-
        talion from the landing in Normandy to the fall
        of Berlin.

2114   Rosenhaupt, Hans. THE TRUE DECEIVERS.
        Dodd, 1954. Story of a German-born intelligence
        officer in the American army assigned the job of
        interrogating German prisoners of war.

2115   Ross, James E. THE DEAD ARE MINE. McKay,
        1963. The lone survivor of a squad decimated
        in the Anzio beachhead refuses further combat
        duty and is assigned to a graves registration
        unit.

2116   Routsong, Alma. A GRADUAL JOY. Houghton,
        1953. Story of a World War II veteran and his
        ex-Wave wife, and of their life in a trailer camp
        while attending Michigan State College.

2117   Rubinstein, S. Leonard. THE BATTLE DONE.
        Morrow, 1954. Prisoners, guards, and camp
        personnel in a prisoner-of-war camp in South
        Carolina shortly after the war.

2118   Rylee, Robert. THE RING AND THE CROSS.
        Knopf, 1947. Racial philosophies of democracy
        and fascism in a Texas town during World War II.

2119   Sapieha, Virgilia Peterson. BEYOND THIS SHORE.
        Lippincott, 1942. Story of an American girl

married to a Polish count who finds Americans
indifferent to the Nazi threat after fleeing the
Germans in Austria and Poland.

2120   Saroyan, William. THE HUMAN COMEDY. Harcourt, 1943. Story of family life in wartime;
one son away in the army and the young ones
working at odd jobs.

2121   Saxton, Alexander. BRIGHT WEB IN THE DARK-
NESS. St. Martins, 1958. Story of the San
Francisco shipyards centering around the labor
issues involving Negroes in war work.

2122   Searls, Hank. THE HERO SHIP. World, 1969.
Story centers around an act of cowardice on a
U. S. Navy aircraft carrier in the final days of
the war against Japan; scenes of Navy flight
training, of Pearl Harbor on December 7, 1941,
and the final destruction of the ship; based on
the actual loss of the U. S. S. Franklin.

2123   Shapiro, Lionel. SIXTH OF JUNE. Doubleday,
1955. An American paratrooper and an English
commander take part in the D-Day invasion of
Normandy.

2124   Shaw, Charles. HEAVEN KNOWS, MR. ALLISON.
Crown, 1952. After the fall of Bataan a nun and
a marine are marooned on an island behind
Japanese lines.

2125   Shaw, Irwin. THE YOUNG LIONS. Random, 1948.
Two Americans and a German seen in their pre-
war life and in episodes of army training and on
war duty.

2126   Sheean, Vincent. A CERTAIN RICH MAN. Random, 1947. Story of the wartime experiences,
as a bomber pilot, of a rich man and of its
effect on his home life and social responsibility
after the war.

2127   Sinclair, Upton. DRAGON HARVEST. Viking,
1945. Lanny Budd in Europe as the secret agent
of President Roosevelt, meets Hitler and Chamberlain, and takes part in the evacuation of Dun-

kirk. Sequel to "Presidential Agent" (The Thirties).

2128 -- A WORLD TO WIN. Viking, 1946. As agent of
President Roosevelt, Lanny Budd reports on German plans to attack Russia, is tutored by Ein-
stein for a mission to learn about German atomic
energy research, and lands in Hong Kong at the
outbreak of the war. Covers the years 1940-1942.
Sequel to "Dragon Harvest."

2129 -- PRESIDENTIAL MISSION. Viking, 1947. Lanny
Budd acts as Roosevelt's secret agent in Africa
before the American invasion, and later, in
Germany. Sequel to "A World to Win."

2130 -- ONE CLEAR CALL. Viking, 1948. Lanny Budd,
as Roosevelt's secret agent, operates in Italy,
France, Spain, and Germany from the invasion
of Sicily to the invasion of France; story ends
with Roosevelt's reelection in 1944. Sequel to
"Presidential Mission."

2131 -- O SHEPHERD, SPEAK! Viking, 1949. Lanny
Budd takes part in the Nuremburg war trials in
1946, acts as President Truman's representative
in Moscow, and uses his trust fund to promote
world peace. Sequel to "One Clear Call."

2132 Sire, Glen. THE DEATHMAKERS. Simon and
Schuster, 1960. Story of war and death during
General Patton's armored battalion push into
Bavaria in the last days of the war.

2133 Skidmore, Hobert Douglas. VALLEY OF THE SKY.
Houghton, 1944. Story of the experiences of a
youthful bomber crew in the South Pacific.

2134 Slaughter, Frank. A TOUCH OF GLORY. Doubleday, 1945. Army medical officer returns home to
find an industrial boom town; forms group medicine plan in opposition to a compensation racket.

2135 -- SURGEON, U.S.A. Doubleday, 1966. Romantic
story about a heart surgeon who volunteers
after Pearl Harbor and serves in the army during
World War II.

2136   Slote, Alfred. STRANGERS AND COMRADES.
        Simon and Schuster, 1964. Pictures various as-
        pects of life on the homefront and in the service
        from Pearl Harbor to the end of the war.

2137   Smith, William Dale. NAKED IN DECEMBER.
        Bobbs, 1968. Events in the lives of three fami-
        lies with a background of the period leading up
        to the American entry into the war.

2138   Sparks, Dorothy Elizabeth. NOTHING AS BEFORE.
        Harper, 1944. Isolationist sympathies in a
        small Illinois town shattered by the attack on
        Pearl Harbor.

2139   Statham, Leon. WELCOME, DARKNESS. Crowell,
        1950. Guerrilla warfare in the Philippines.

2140   Stein, Gertrude. BREWSIE AND WILLIE. Random,
        1946. Postwar responsibilities of young Ameri-
        cans brought out in the form of bull sessions
        among a group of soldiers in France after the
        armistice.

2141   Stephens, Edward. ROMAN JOY. Doubleday, 1965.
        Story of a jazz drummer and draft-dodger in the
        music and big band business during the war.

2142   Stevens, William. THE GUNNER. Atheneum,
        1968. Story of the adventures of a young aerial
        gunner with the Fifteenth Air Force in Italy in
        1944, who goes A. W. O. L. after seeing too much
        action.

2143   Stong, Philip. ONE DESTINY. Reynal, 1942.
        Story of a rural Iowa community awakening to
        world events; farmer's son gives up his medical
        education to become a pilot.

2144   Swarthout, Glendon. THE EAGLE AND THE IRON
        CROSS. New Amer. Lib. , 1966. Story of two
        German prisoners-of-war who escape from an
        Arizona prison camp and join an Indian tribe
        on the reservation.

2145   Syers, William Edward. THE SEVEN. Duell,
        1960. Story of the action of a U. S. Navy sub-

marine chaser off the coast of Central America
and in the Pacific.

2146　Taylor, Ward. ROLL BACK THE SKY. Holt,
1956. Story of a member of a B-29 bombing
crew based on Saipan. Tense picture of low
level bombing missions over Japan.

2147　Thatcher, Russell. THE CAPTAIN. Macmillan,
1951. Pressures and frustrations of the commander of a landing craft in the Pacific.

2148　Tillett, Dorothy. ANGRY DUST. Doubleday, 1946.
Story of conflict between management and labor
in a metal working plant in New York where the
C. I. O. is trying to strengthen its position.

2149　Tregaskis, Richard. STRONGER THAN FEAR.
Random, 1945. Picture of street fighting tactics
in the story of an army patrol clearing out Nazi
snipers.

2150　Uris, Leon. BATTLE CRY. Putnam, 1953. Life
among the Marines at Guadalcanal, Tarawa, and
Saipan.

2151　Van de Water, Frederic. THE SOONER TO SLEEP.
Duell, 1946. Story of women without men in a
Vermont town during the war.

2152　Van Pragg, Van. DAY WITHOUT END. Sloane,
1949. Story of an exhausted platoon in the hedge-
rows of Normandy.

2153　Wallace, Francis. EXPLOSION. Morrow, 1943.
Story of the heroism of men trapped in a mine
explosion and of retribution when the Nazi agent
responsible for the explosion is identified.

2154　Warrick, LaMar. YESTERDAY'S CHILDREN.
Crowell, 1943. Story of a family with a draft-
age son in college as the war approaches; set in
a suburb of Chicago.

2155　Weismiller, Edward. THE SERPENT SLEEPING.
Putnam, 1962. Activities of an American intelligence unit stationed in Cherbourg, France in

late 1944; story involves action with German spies
and French collaborators.

2156   Wendt, Lloyd. A BRIGHT TOMORROW. Bobbs,
        1945. Pacifist sentiment in rural South Dakota in
        1940-1941.

2157   Wernick, Robert. THE FREEBOOTERS. Scribner,
        1949. Adventures of three soldiers in an Ameri-
        can unit in North Africa and Italy.

2158   Westheimer, David. SONG OF THE YOUNG SENTRY.
        Little, 1968. Story of two American airmen as
        prisoners of war after being shot down over Italy
        in 1942.

2159   White, Theodore. THE MOUNTAIN ROAD. Sloane,
        1958. Story of an American demolition squad
        assigned to delay a Japanese advance in China in
        1944.

2160   Wilder, Margaret. SINCE YOU WENT AWAY.
        Whittlesey, 1943. Letters from a wife to her
        soldier husband telling of life on the home front.

2161   Wilhelm, Gale. THE TIME BETWEEN. Morrow,
        1942. Story of the ten days leave of an heroic
        American flyer after hospitalization before he
        returns to the war.

2162   Williams, George. THE BLIND BULL. Abelard,
        1952. An American major in a Saipan hospital
        reviews his past life and his battle experiences.

2163   Williams, Thomas. WHIPPLE'S CASTLE. Random,
        1969. Home life in a small town in New Hamp-
        shire in the 1940's.

2164   Williams, Wirt. THE ENEMY. Houghton, 1951.
        Story of the tedium and detail of life aboard a
        warship during wartime.

2165   Wouk, Herman. THE CAINE MUTINY. Doubleday,
        1951. Life aboard a minesweeper in the Pacific
        under a tyrannical skipper.

2166   Yates, Richard. A SPECIAL PROVIDENCE.   Knopf,
       1969.   Story of an 18 year old soldier reaching
       maturity in training camp and in action in Belgium.

THE TENSE YEARS -- 1945 TO THE SIXTIES

2167   Abbey, Edward. FIRE ON THE MOUNTAINS. Dial,
        1962. Story of a New Mexico rancher and his
        struggles to prevent government confiscation of
        his land to expand the White Sands Proving
        Grounds.

2168   Albrand, Martha. NIGHTMARE IN COPENHAGEN.
        Random, 1954. An American scientist attempts
        to thwart the Russians from getting a secret
        explosive recovered from a German submarine
        sunk off Denmark in World War II.

2169   Anders, Curtis. THE PRICE OF COURAGE. Saga-
        more Press, 1957. Realistic battle scenes as
        experienced by an infantry company in the Korean
        War.

2170   Anderson, Thomas. YOUR OWN BELOVED SONS.
        Random, 1956. Authentic setting and military
        detail revolving around a dangerous mission by
        six volunteers in the Korean War.

2171   Anderson, William C. THE GOONEY BIRD. Crown,
        1968. Pictures the lighter side of life among a
        helicopter crew, a female war correspondent,
        and some friendly natives in Vietnam.

2172   Annixter, Jane and Paul. PEACE COMES TO CAS-
        TLE OAK. Longmans, 1961. Story of family
        life in the Carolina and Georgia coastal lowlands
        complicated by the return of the eldest son from
        the Korean War and the encroachment of hill
        people in the area.

2173   Barbeau, Clayton. THE IKON. Coward, 1961.
        Story of a young American soldier who undergoes
        a religious conversion during the Korean War.

2174 Barry, Jane. GRASS ROOTS. Doubleday, 1968.
Story of a political campaign for a Congressional
seat in which the issues are contemporary American problems of Vietnam, civil rights, and big
government versus private enterprise.

2175 Bartholomew, Cecilia. THE RISK. Doubleday,
1958. Story of the tragic effect on the family of
a man who is declared a security risk because
of his friendship with a known subversive. Re-
creates the uncertainties and suspicions of the
McCarthy era in the early 1950's.

2176 Beaumont, Charles. THE INTRUDER. Putnam,
1959. Story of events in a Southern city when
a few courageous citizens react to the trouble
stirred up by an outside rabble rouser who came
in to form a prosegregation organization.

2177 Bittle, Camilla R. A SUNDAY WORLD. Coward,
1966. Picture of life in a small Southern university town faced with rapid social and economic
changes.

2178 Boles, Paul Darcy. DEADLINE. Macmillan, 1957.
Story of a Southern newspaperman's decision to
take a stand against segregation, and of the
effects of his decision.

2179 Bonner, Paul Hyde. SPQR. Scribner, 1952.
Sophisticated romance centering around a first
secretary of the American Embassy in Rome,
involving a spy hunt.

2180 -- HOTEL TALLEYRAND. Scribner, 1953. Story
of American diplomatic personnel in Paris in
1950; background is the American effort to check
the growth of Communism in Europe.

2181 Botsford, Keith. THE MARCH-MAN. Viking,
1964. Picture of life in Southern California in
the 1940's as viewed by an Italian of more traditional background.

2182 Bourjaily, Vance. THE MAN WHO KNEW KENNEDY.
Dial, 1967. A story set in the tense years of
the early 1960's, and of the effect of the assasi-

nation of President Kennedy on the leading character.

2183   Boyle, Kay. GENERATION WITHOUT FAREWELL.
       Knopf, 1959. Story of the relationship between
       victor and vanquished, set in the American
       occupation zone of Germany in 1948.

2184   Briley, John. THE TRAITORS. Putnam, 1969.
       Story of five GI's, captured by the Viet Cong,
       and of the consequences of their anti-war campaign.

2185   Brooks, Gwendolyn. MAUD MARTHA. Harper,
       1953. Story of a Negro girl growing up from
       childhood to motherhood facing discrimination
       on the South Side in Chicago during the 1940's.

2186   Brown, Frank London. TRUMBULL PARK. Regnery, 1959. Fictional account of the race riots
       in Trumbull Park, a Chicago housing development,
       in the 1950's.

2187   Bryan, C. D. B. P. S. WILKINSON. Harper, 1965.
       Adventures of an army lieutenant set against the
       background of events from the Korean War to
       the Berlin Blockade.

2188   Buckley, David. PRIDE OF INNOCENCE. Holt,
       1957. Story of the moral and intellectual disillusionment of a young American soldier on occupation duty in Germany after World War II.

2189   Burgess, Jackson. THE ATROCITY. Putnam,
       1961. Story of a brutal incident and its effect
       on one U. S. soldier in an ordanance company
       stationed in Italy at the end of World War II.

2190   Burnett, Hallie. WATCH ON THE WALL. Morrow,
       1965. An American girl visiting in Berlin becomes involved in a plot to help an East German
       escape to the West over the Berlin Wall.

2191   Carruth, Haydn. APPENDIX A. Macmillan, 1963.
       Experiences of the editor of a literary magazine
       depicts the publishing and social world of Chicago in the 1950's.

2192   Chastain, Thomas. JUDGMENT DAY. Doubleday,
        1962. Documentary story of a Southern town
        torn by racial violence following a lynching. A
        white minister attempts to lead his congregation
        in some constructive action proposed by a Black
        militant leader.

2193   Chatterton, Ruth. THE BETRAYERS. Houghton,
        1953. Story of the investigation by a Congres-
        sional committee of a young scientist suspected
        of subversive activity.

2194   Chaze, Elliott. TIGER IN THE HONEYSUCKLE.
        Scribner, 1965. Story of a civil rights demon-
        stration in a small Mississippi town, as witnessed
        by a local white newspaper reporter.

2195   Chevalier, Haakon Maurice. THE MAN WHO WOULD
        BE GOD. Putnam, 1959. An FBI agent is won
        over to the Communist Party by the scientist he
        is investigating; the scientist, cleared for atomic
        bomb research, changes his convictions.

2196   Clark, Alan. THE LION HEART. Morrow, 1969.
        Raw picture of life and action in the Vietnam
        War.

2197   Cobb, William E. AN INCH OF SNOW. Blair
        (private press), 1964. Political satire of the
        1960 Presidential campaign in a Southern town.

2198   Coon, Gene L. MEANWHILE, BACK AT THE
        FRONT. Crown, 1961. Humorous account of
        life in the public information unit of the First
        Marine Division in the Korean War.

2199   Coppel, Alfred. A LITTLE TIME FOR LAUGHTER.
        Harcourt, 1969. Follows the fortunes of three
        friends from graduation in 1940 through World
        War II, the McCarthy era of the 1950's, and
        into a settled life in the 1960's.

2200   Crawford, William. GIVE ME TOMORROW. Put-
        nam, 1962. Story of a U.S. Marine officer in
        the Korean War; flashbacks show the discrimina-
        tion faced by Mexican-Americans in El Paso,
        Texas, and the public apathy toward the war.

2201   Daniels, Lucy. CALEB, MY SON. Lippincott,
        1956. Tragic story of the effect of segregation
        upon a family of Southern Negroes.

2202   Davis, Christopher. FIRST FAMILY. Coward,
        1961. Story of the effects of a white suburban
        community when a Negro family moves into the
        neighborhood.

2203   Davis, Dorothy. THE EVENING OF THE GOOD
        SAMARITAN. Scribner, 1961. A review of
        recent history from the 1930's to the 1950's;
        story centers around a liberal professor, an
        atomic scientist, and a "professional" Jew in
        a large Midwestern city patterned after Chicago.

2204   Drury, Allen. ADVISE AND CONSENT. Doubleday,
        1959. Picture of the workings of the U. S. Senate;
        story of political and personal conflicts set in
        motion as the Senate debates confirmation of the
        President's nomination for Secretary of State;
        issue is the nominee's association with a student
        Communist group.

2205   Dykeman, Wilma. THE FAR FAMILY. Holt, 1966.
        Story of race relations in the southern Appala-
        chians, with flashbacks to life in the South Caro-
        lina highlands in an earlier day.

2206   Edwards, Junius. IF WE MUST DIE. Doubleday,
        1963. Story of what happened when a young
        Negro Korean War veteran tries to vote in an
        unidentified Southern town.

2207   Ehle, John. MOVE OVER, MOUNTAIN. Morrow,
        1957. Novel of Negro life in North Carolina
        complicated by family rivalries and dreams of
        "up north. "

2208   Elegant, Robert S. A KIND OF TREASON. Holt,
        1966. Story of intrigue and suspense in Saigon
        set against a background of the Vietnam War in
        1964.

2209   Fair, Ronald L. HOG BUTCHER. Harcourt, 1966.
        Life in a Negro ghetto in Chicago seen through
        the eyes of two ten year old boys.

2210   Fairbairn, Ann. FIVE SMOOTH STONES. Crown,
        1966. Story of the struggle of a New Orleans
        Negro who works his way through Harvard Law
        School and returns to the South to become involved
        in the civil rights movement.

2211   Fleming, Thomas J. ALL GOOD MEN. Doubleday,
        1961. Realistic picture of big city politics,
        party machinery, and petty ward heelers in an
        Eastern city in 1951.

2212   Flood, Charles Bracelen. A DISTANT DRUM.
        Houghton, 1957. Story of a young man, grad-
        uate of Harvard '51, writing a first novel and
        growing to maturity; enlists in the Army at the
        time of the Korean War and goes through basic
        training before discharge because of a congenital
        defect.

2213   -- MORE LIVES THAN ONE. Houghton, 1967.
        Hardships of life in a Chinese Communist pri-
        soner-of-war camp in the Korean War contrasted
        with life going on normally back home.

2214   Ford, Jesse Hill. THE LIBERATION OF LORD
        BYRON JONES. Little, 1965. Story of racial
        conflict and crisis in a Tennessee town.

2215   -- THE FEAST OF SAINT BARNABAS. Little,
        1969. Race relations in a small town in Florida
        in 1966 as tension mounts, leading up to a race
        riot.

2216   Ford, Norman R. THE BLACK, THE GRAY, AND
        THE GOLD. Doubleday, 1961. Picture of the
        pressures of life at West Point based on the
        cheating scandal at the academy in 1951.

2217   Frank, Pat. HOLD BACK THE NIGHT. Lippin-
        cott, 1952. Story of a U.S. Marine unit in
        Korea covering the retreat from the Changjin
        Reservoir to Hungnam on the coast.

2218   Frankel, Ernest. BAND OF BROTHERS. Macmil-
        lan, 1958. A story of the Marine retreat from
        the Yalu River to Hungnam when the Chinese
        entered the war in Korea.

2219   -- TONGUE OF FIRE. Dial, 1960. Story of a cru-
        sading Congressman who achieves quick fame
        through his Congressional committee investigating
        supposed Communists; patterned on the career of
        Senator Joseph McCarthy.

2220   Franklin, Edward Herbert. IT'S COLD IN PONGO-
        NI. Vanguard, 1965. Combat novel of the Korean
        War.

2221   Gallico, Paul. TRIAL BY TERROR. Knopf, 1952.
        Story of an American newspaperman captured
        behind the Iron Curtain and tried as a spy.

2222   Gann, Ernest. SOLDIER OF FORTUNE. Sloane,
        1954. Picture of Communist China as seen by
        two Americans searching for the photographer-
        husband of one of them.

2223   Garfield, Brian. THE LAST BRIDGE. McKay,
        1966. Story of a combat team on a suicide mis-
        sion in the Vietnam War.

2224   Garrett, George. WHICH ONES ARE THE ENEMY.
        Little, 1961. Set in Trieste after World War II,
        this is a love story told against a background of
        U. S. occupation forces and the underground of
        soldier-gangsters and black market operators.

2225   Geer, Andrew Clare. RECKLESS, PRIDE OF THE
        MARINES. Dutton, 1955. Story of a mule mas-
        cot of the Fifth U. S. Marine Regiment who be-
        came famous as an ammunition carrier and morale
        builder in the Korean War.

2226   Gilden, K. B. (pseud.). HARRY SUNDOWN. Double-
        day, 1965. Two World War II veterans, a Negro
        and his white neighbor, work together to save
        their farms from the avaricious citizens of their
        small Georgia community.

2227   Gilman, Peter. DIAMOND HEAD. Coward, 1960.
        Recreates the historical background and the strug-
        gle for Hawaiian statehood from the viewpoint of
        a present-day family.

2228   Gordon, Arthur. REPRISAL. Simon and Schuster,

1950. Story of race violence in a Georgia town when a young Negro whose wife had been murdered takes things into his own hands.

2229 Graham, Lorenz. NORTH TOWN. Crowell, 1965. Story of a Negro family's escape from the violent racial bigotry of the South to face the subtle bigotry of the North.

2230 Greene, Harris. THE 'MOZART' LEAVES AT NINE. Doubleday, 1960. A U. S. Army security service chief in American-occupied Austria is busy keeping track of surviving Nazis and Russian agents in the year after the end of World War II; story of the effect of the U. S. decision to return a Russian defector.

2231 Gregor, Manfred. TOWN WITHOUT PITY. Random, 1961. Story of German-American relations in a small German town still occupied by American troops in the late 1950's.

2232 Groninger, William. RUN FROM THE MOUNTAIN. Rinehart, 1959. Story of the army experiences of a young American soldier in occupied Japan from 1946 to 1949.

2233 Gurney, Hal. FIFTH DAUGHTER. Doubleday, 1957. Story of the interactions of the Okinawans and Americans during the occupation following World War II.

2234 Gwaltney, Francis Irby. THE NUMBER OF OUR DAYS. Random, 1959. A World War II veteran leads a revolt against radical segregationists in his home town in Arkansas following the Supreme Court decision in 1954.

2235 Haas, Ben. LOOK AWAY, LOOK AWAY. Simon and Schuster, 1964. Story of racial strife in a Southern community through the experiences of three World War II veterans, once boyhood friends; one is a politician, one a Negro who turns to non-violent protest, and one a newspaperman who suffers because of an editorial against racism.

2236   -- THE LAST VALLEY. Simon & Schuster, 1966.
       A World War II and Korean War veteran fights
       to save his Appalachian valley and its people from
       destruction when a power company proposes to
       construct a hydroelectric dam; picture of Southern
       society at all levels.

2237   Habe, Hans. OFF LIMITS. Fell, 1957. Story of
       the relations between Americans and Germans
       in the U. S. occupied zone of West Berlin, 1945-
       1951.

2238   Halberstam, David. ONE VERY HOT DAY. Hough-
       ton, 1967. Story of one day in heavy battle action
       of a small American unit in Vietnam.

2239   Hardy, William. THE JUBJUB BIRD. Coward,
       1966. A good humored account of a civil rights
       drive in a Southern college town, involving white
       and black liberals, segregationists, militants, and
       a student from the North.

2240   Hempstone, Smith. A TRACT OF TIME. Houghton,
       1966. Story of the war in Vietnam in 1963,
       written by a correspondent for the Chicago Daily
       News.

2241   Hercules, Frank. I WANT A BLACK DOLL. Simon
       and Schuster, 1967. Tragic story of the mixed
       marriage of a white girl from Kentucky and a
       Negro medical student.

2242   Hersey, John. A BELL FOR ADANO. Knopf, 1944.
       Story of the efforts of an understanding American
       occupation administrator to rebuild a devastated
       Italian village according to his own democratic
       ideals.

2243   Hill, Weldon. THE LONG SUMMER OF GEORGE
       ADAMS. McKay, 1961. Picture of ordinary,
       everyday events of life in small Oklahoma town
       in the 1940's and 1950's.

2244   Hooker, Richard. MASH. Morrow, 1968. Story
       of the crew of a mobile army surgical hospital
       unit in action and in play during the Korean War.

2245   Hoffman, William. A PLACE FOR MY HEAD.
       Doubleday, 1960. A small town Virginia lawyer
       successfully defends a Negro's insurance claim
       but finds the Negro hoped to lose as a propaganda
       weapon in his race agitation; presents the case
       of the whites who care for the Negro welfare but
       want to keep the status quo.

2246   Horwitz, Julius. THE W. A. S. P. Atheneum, 1967.
       Sordid story of Negro-white relations in Harlem.

2247   Jackson, Felix. SO HELP ME GOD. Viking, 1955.
       Story of a young lawyer who sends an anonymous
       letter to a Congressional committee accusing him-
       self of being a Communist in an effort to expose
       the dangers of condemning a man as subversive
       on the basis of hearsay evidence; an indictment
       of the fear and suspicion aroused by the McCarthy
       investigations.

2248   Jones, Leroi. THE SYSTEM OF DANTE'S HELL.
       Grove, 1965. Grim story of childhood and adoles-
       cence in the Negro slums of Newark, experiences
       as an Air Force serviceman in a small Southern
       town, and later scenes of Negro life in New York
       City.

2249   Kaplan, Arthur. HOTEL DE LA LIBERTE.
       Dutton, 1964. Sketches of the humorous activities
       of American students living in Paris under the
       G. I. Bill in the late 1940's.

2250   Karp, David. THE LAST BELIEVERS. Harcourt,
       1964. Story of a playwright pictures the history
       of Communism in the United States from the 1920's
       to the Hollywood blacklisting of the 1950's.

2251   Kennedy, Jay Richard. FAVOR THE RUNNER.
       World, 1963. Story of a liberal activist involved
       in various movements from the Spanish Civil War
       to the civil rights movement.

2252   Kern, Alfred. THE WIDTH OF WATERS. Houghton,
       1959. Story of the preparations for a sesquicen-
       tenial celebration in a Pennsylvania town, and of
       the effect of news that one hometown boy had been
       killed and another had become a turncoat in the

Korean War.

2253   Kerouac, John. BIG SUR. Farrar, 1962. Auto-
        biographical novel of the beat generation groping
        for meaning and a role in life.

2254   -- DESOLATION ANGELS. Coward, 1965. Philo-
        sophical novel of the life of the "beat generation"
        of the 1950's; scenes in New York City and San
        Francisco.

2255   Kiker, Douglas. THE SOUTHERNER. Rinehart,
        1957. Story of a school segregation case in a
        fictional Southern city.

2256   Killens, John Oliver. 'SIPPI. Trident, 1967.
        Negro life in the rural South before and after
        the Supreme Court decision of 1954; civil
        rights movement, Ku Klux Klan, Southern liberals,
        and Northern hippies.

2257   King, Larry L. THE ONE-EYED MAN. New Ameri-
        can Library, 1966. Picture of Southern politics
        centering around the efforts of a demagogic
        governor to cope with integration at the State
        university.

2258   Knebel, Fletcher. THE ZINZIN ROAD. Doubleday,
        1966. Story of life of the Peace Corps volun-
        teers in Africa.

2259   Kolpacoff, Victor. THE PRISONERS OF QUAI DONG.
        New American Library, 1967. The brutalizing
        effect of war shown by the treatment of a prisoner
        at a military base in Vietnam.

2260   Lorraine, John. MEN OF CAREER. Crown, 1960.
        Story of the U.S. State Department diplomatic
        corps in Vienna in 1953; theme is how the mem-
        bers of the Foreign Service reacted to the McCar-
        thy loyalty investigations.

2261   Lynch, Michael. AN AMERICAN SOLDIER. Little,
        1969. Story of the horrors of war as seen by a
        sensitive Army corporal in the Korean War.

2262   McGivern, William P. ODDS AGAINST TOMORROW.

Dodd, 1957. Story of two bank robbers, one
white, one Negro, and of their friendship growing
out of enmity during their flight and refuge in an
isolated farmhouse.

2263   McGovern, James. THE BERLIN COURIERS. Abelard, 1960. Story of a U.S. intelligence agent in
Berlin during the East German uprising of 1953,
sent to interview a defecting scientist; captured by
the Russians, he escapes with important documents.

2264   McIlwain, William. THE GLASS ROOSTER. Doubleday, 1960. Story of violence following the false
accusation that a young Negro had raped a white
woman; set around a survey of white and Negro
recreational facilities in a Southern town.

2265   MacInnes, Helen. I AND MY TRUE LOVE. Harcourt, 1953. A Washington hostess and a Communist Czech official are caught between Communist spies and the hysterical fear of Communists
in government.

2266   Maddux, Rachel. ABEL'S DAUGHTER. Harper,
1960. Story of a Northern couple who move to
a small Southern town during World War II and
come to understand the practical aspects of the
color question in the South through their friendship with the leader of the Negro community.

2267   Malliol, William. A SENSE OF DARK. Atheneum,
1968. Story of combat in the Korean War and in
training with the U.S. Marines at Parris Island.

2268   Mankiewicz, Don. TRIAL. Harper, 1955. Story
of the trial of a young Mexican in a West coast
city; Communists exploit the possibilities of
racial prejudice.

2269   Marquand, J. P. STOPOVER: TOKYO. Little,
1957. American intelligence agents attempt to
break up a Communist plot to stage anti-Ameri-
can riots in Japan.

2270   Marshall, Paule. BROWN GIRL, BROWNSTONES.
Random, 1959. Story of a Negro girl coming to
grips with herself and with life and its prejudices

in Brooklyn.

2271   Mayfield, Julian. THE GRAND PARADE. Van-
       guard, 1961. Story of the racial crisis in a
       Southern city centering on the school segregation
       issue.

2272   Meiring, Desmond. THE BRINKMAN. Houghton,
       1965. A story of American involvement in Viet-
       nam and Laos.

2273   Mercer, Charles. THE MINISTER. Putnam, 1969.
       Story follows a rebellious Protestant minister in
       the Civil Rights movement, in jail, in relief
       work with a Catholic priest in Korea, and on to
       his break-up with the organized Church; set at
       the time of the Korean War.

2274   Michener, James. BRIDGES AT TOKO-RI. Ran-
       dom, 1953. Story of a U.S. Navy aircraft car-
       rier task force assigned the mission of bombing
       enemy supply lines in the Korean War.

2275   Miller, Warren. THE SLEEP OF REASON. Little,
       1960. A satire on politics in Washington during
       the McCarthy era; story of a young man hired to
       ferret out subversion for a Senate investigating
       committee.

2276   -- FLUSH TIMES. Little, 1962. Picture of life
       in the American colony in Cuba as they witness
       the change from flush times under Batista to a
       new life under Castro.

2277   Moll, Elick. SEIDMAN AND SON. Putnam, 1958.
       Picture of the New York dress industry following
       the Korean War.

2278   Moore, Col. Gene D. THE KILLING AT NGO-THO.
       Norton, 1967. Story of the life and actions of a
       U S. Army colonel sent as an advisor to the
       Vietnamese Army early in the war.

2279   Moore, Robin. THE GREEN BERETS. Crown,
       1965. Sketches of combat life with the U.S.
       Special Forces in Vietnam.

2280   Morressy, John. THE ADDISON TRADITION. Dou-
       bleday, 1968. Story of a student rebellion at a
       small liberal arts college, showing the student
       unrest and revolt of the nineteen-sixties.

2281   Morris, Edita. THE FLOWERS OF HIROSHIMA.
       Viking, 1959. An American realizes the horror
       of the atomic bomb when he discovers that the
       Japanese family with whom he is lodging lost
       their wife and mother in the 1945 bombing and
       that the father is dying of radiation sickness.

2282   Newman, Charles. NEW AXIS. Houghton, 1966.
       Family life in a Midwestern suburban city follow-
       ing the Korean War; reflects their reaction to the
       launching of the first Russian satellite.

2283   O'Donnell, M. K. YOU CAN HEAR THE ECHO.
       Simon & Schuster, 1966. Follows the activities
       of the members of family in a small town near
       Dallas, Texas on the day President Kennedy was
       assassinated.

2284   Pollini, Francis. NIGHT. Houghton, 1961. Life
       of American prisoners captured by the Chinese
       during the Korean War; centers around the
       efforts at brainwashing, and the conflict and
       violence between "reactionaries" and "progres-
       sives."

2285   Polonsky, Abraham. A SEASON OF FEAR. Cam-
       eron, 1956. Story of the conflicts arising out of
       the signing of a loyalty oath by a civil engineer.
       Convincing picture of the fear and suspicion made
       possible by the climate of opinion in the early
       1950's at the time of the McCarthy investigation.

2286   Powell, Richard. DON QUIXOTE, U. S. A. Scrib-
       ner, 1966. Comic novel about the life of a
       Peace Corps volunteer sent to a Caribbean Island.

2287   Press, Sylvia. CARE OF DEVILS. Beacon, 1958.
       Story of the efforts of a woman agent in Washing-
       ton to clear her name from the accusations made
       against her in a security investigation.

2288   Rex, Barbara. VACANCY ON INDIA STREET.

Norton, 1967. Story of middle class suburban
life and the effects of a Negro family moving
into the neighborhood.

2289   Robertson, Don. A FLAG FULL OF STARS. Putnam, 1964. Story of politics, family and home
life in 1948 on the day Truman defeated Dewey.

2290   -- THE SUM AND TOTAL OF NOW. Putnam, 1966.
Picture of family life in a small Ohio town as
Morris Bird III as a teenager faces up to the
death of his grandmother. Sequel to "Greatest
Thing Since Sliced Bread" (WW II.)

2291   Rogers, Lettie Hamlett. BIRTHRIGHT. Simon
and Schuster, 1957. Story of the reactions when
a teacher in a small Southern town praises the
Supreme Court decision of 1954.

2292   Romula, Carlos P. THE UNITED. Crown, 1951.
Picture of international diplomacy at work in
the United Nations; story of an alternate U. S.
delegate standing up for his principles against
the arguments of a newspaper columnist and a
Boston Brahmin.

2293   Roripaugh, Robert A. A FEVER FOR LIVING.
Morrow, 1961. Tragic love story set in U. S.
occupied Japan, giving details of life in an army
camp.

2294   Ross, Walter. COAST TO COAST. Simon and
Schuster, 1962. Story of the Senate investigation
into the 1959 television quiz show payola scandals.

2295   Ross, Glen. THE LAST CAMPAIGN. Harper,
1962. Adventures of an army bandsman in the
First Cavalry Division in the first year of the
Korean War.

2296   Roth, Philip. LETTING GO. Random, 1962.
Story of Jewish family life and the college scene
in the 1950's; set in New York City and the University of Chicago.

2297   Rubin, Michael. WHISTLE ME HOME. McGraw-
Hill, 1967. Story of Jewish family life in Brook-

lyn from 1946 to 1953.

2298   Russell, Ross. THE SOUND. Dutton, 1961.
       Story of a Negro trumpeter and the jazz and
       drug scene in the years following World War II.

2299   Salter, James. THE ARM OF FLESH. Harper,
       1961. Vivid picture of life of the members of
       a fighter squadron in an American air base in
       occupied Germany after World War II.

2300   Scott, Robert L. LOOK OF THE EAGLE. Dodd,
       1955. Story of jet warfare in the Korean War,
       and of a scheme to fly a Russian jet out of
       North Korea.

2301   Shaw, Irwin. THE TROUBLED AIR. Random,
       1951. Story of the disastrous results when a
       radio program director is ordered to fire five
       actors suspected of being Communists.

2302   Sheldon, Walter. TOUR OF DUTY. Lippincott,
       1959. Story of Japanese-American relations in
       occupied Japan after World War II; set on a U. S.
       Air Force base near a small Japanese village.

2303   Sidney, George. FOR THE LOVE OF DYING.
       Morrow, 1969. A depressive anti-war novel
       centering around a U. S. Marine unit in their
       last days in the Korean War.

2304   Sinclair, Jo. THE CHANGELINGS. McGraw, 1955.
       Story of a Jewish community in a Midwestern
       city being pressed by a growing Negro population;
       teenagers lead their parents toward tolerance and
       understanding in the face of threatening race riots.

2305   Sinclair, Upton. RETURN OF LANNY BUDD. Vik-
       ing, 1953. Events since the end of World War II
       bring back Lanny Budd in this story of the growth
       of the Russian menace; takes him to the troubled
       spots of Europe, from 1946 to 1949. Sequel to
       "O Shepherd Speak" (World War II).

2306   Singer, Howard. WAKE ME WHEN IT'S OVER.
       Putnam, 1959. Humorous story of an Air Force
       radar man who builds an island resort hotel on

his off-duty hours for servicemen on leave from
the Korean War.

2307   Slaughter, Frank. SWORD AND SCALPEL. Double-
       day, 1957. Story of an American army officer in
       the Korean War; experiences in battle, as a pris-
       oner of the Chinese, and on trial for collaborating
       with the Communists.

2308   Smith, William Dale. A MULTITUDE OF MEN.
       Simon and Schuster, 1960. Conflict between a
       company union and outside labor organizers in a
       West Virginia steel mill in the period after the
       Korean War.

2309   Sneider, Vern. THE TEAHOUSE OF THE AUGUST
       MOON. Putnam, 1951. Humorous story of an
       American occupation team and its efforts to
       "rehabilitate" and democratize Okinawa after the
       war.

2310   -- A PAIL OF OYSTERS. Putnam, 1953. Story
       of an American newspaperman on Formosa, de-
       termined to find the facts behind official camou-
       flage.

2311   Spencer, Elizabeth. THE VOICE AT THE BACK
       DOOR. McGraw, 1956. Story of life in a small
       Mississippi community, showing the changing
       pattern in race relations.

2312   Stark, Irwin. THE SUBPOENA. New American
       Library, 1966. A shrill recreation of the witch
       hunting era of the McCarthy investigations during
       the early 1950's.

2313   Stephens, Edward. BLOW NEGATIVE. Doubleday,
       1962. Story of the development of the nucleur
       submarine; fictional treatment of the career of
       Admiral Rickover and the U. S. Navy's opposition
       to his ideas.

2314   Styron, William. THE LONG MARCH. Random,
       1968. Story of life in a U. S. Marine training
       base in South Carolina, centering around the
       effects of a forced march on officers and men.

2315   Thayer, Charles Wheeler. MOSCOW INTERLUDE.
        Harper, 1962. Story of life in the U. S. embassy
        in Moscow during the time of Stalin's power,
        plagued by Soviet red tape and spies.

2316   Tiede, Tom. COWARD. Trident, 1968. Story of
        soldiers at war in Vietnam filled with cruelty,
        blundering, and sudden death.

2317   Ullman, James Ramsey. WINDOM'S WAY. Lippin-
        cott, 1952. An American doctor in a hospital
        near a rubber plantation in Southeastern Asia
        sympathizes with the natives in a strike over
        their need for more rice land; strong-arm official
        action drives some of the people into the Com-
        munist camp.

2318   Uris, Leon. ARMAGEDDON. Doubleday, 1964.
        Story of the American occupation forces in Ber-
        lin from the end of World War II to the Berlin
        airlift in 1948.

2319   Von Hoffman, Nicholas. TWO, THREE, MANY MORE.
        Quadrangle, 1969. Based on the student rebellion
        and riots in American universities in the Sixties,
        similar to the Columbia University affair in 1968.

2320   Voorhees, Melvin. SHOW ME A HERO. Simon and
        Schuster, 1954. Story of the Korean War and of
        the moral dilemma of three men, a general, a
        newspaper reporter, and a private.

2321   Wallis, Arthur and Charles Blair. THUNDER ABOVE.
        Holt, 1956. Story of adventure behind the Iron
        Curtain when an American plane participating in
        the Berlin Airlift of 1948-49 is shot down.

2322   Weeks, William Rawle. KNOCK AND WAIT AWHILE.
        Houghton, 1957. Story of American counteres-
        pionage in postwar Europe, involving an American
        girl reporter's efforts to hide behind the Iron
        Curtain.

2323   West, Morris. THE AMBASSADOR. Morrow, 1965.
        Story based on U. S. political and military involve-
        ment in Vietnam in 1963.

2324   Wheeler, Keith. SMALL WORLD. Dutton, 1958.
        Story revolving around world affairs from World
        War II through the Korean War to the Cold War
        and Communist East Germany as they effect two
        American newspaper foreign correspondents.

2325   -- PEACEABLE LANE. Simon and Schuster, 1960.
        Story of prejudice in a suburban community near
        New York when neighbors unite in an effort to
        block the sale of a house to a Negro family.

2326   Wilson, John Rowan. THE SIDE OF THE ANGELS.
        Doubleday, 1968. Story of a Russian scientist
        who defects to the United States.

2327   Wilson, William. THE L. B. J. BRIGADE. Apoca-
        lypse, 1965. Anti-war story of a recent college
        graduate who is drafted and sent to Vietnam.

2328   Wouk, Herman. YOUNGBLOOD HAWKE. Double-
        day, 1962. Picture of the publishing and enter-
        tainment world of New York and Hollywood,
        1945-1951.

2329   Wright, Richard. THE OUTSIDER. Harper, 1953.
        Story of a Negro's search for an ethical identity
        in Chicago.

2330   -- THE LONG DREAM. Doubleday, 1958. Story
        of a Negro boyhood in a Mississippi town; the
        father became powerful in the Negro community
        by working with corrupt officials, and in the end
        the son escapes by flight to France.

2331   Young, Jefferson. A GOOD MAN. Bobbs, 1953.
        Story of the trouble aroused when a Mississippi
        Negro tenant farmer planned to paint his house
        white.

2332   Zarubica, Mladin. SCUTARI. Farrar, 1967.
        An American CIA agent faces the Chinese
        Communists at a missile base in Albania.

CHRONICLES

2333   Aaron, Chester. ABOUT US. McGraw, 1967.
Story of Jewish family life in a coal mining town
near Pittsburg from the Depression through WW II.

2334   Adelson, Ann. THE LITTLE CONQUERORS. Random, 1960. Story of an Italian-American family
settling and growing up in a New England town
dominated by Irish politicians; time is 1930's to
the 1950's.

2335   Aldrich, Bess Streeter. MISS BISHOP. Appleton,
1933. Story of an English teacher in a Midwestern
college facing life from the 1880's to the 1930's.

2336   Appel, Benjamin. A BIG MAN, A FAST MAN.
Morrow, 1961. Story of a labor leader's interviews with a public relations man hired to project a better public image of him; ranges from
the drives to organize labor in the 1930's to the
era of the big unions in the 1950's.

2337   Auchincloss, Louis. HOUSE OF FIVE TALENTS.
Houghton, 1960. Family chronicle of the rich in
Newport and New York from 1873 to 1948; pictures
mansions on Fifth Avenue, garden parties, the
opera, and architecture.

2338   -- PORTRAIT IN BROWNSTONE. Houghton, 1962.
Social and business life in New York City from
1901 to 1951.

2339   Bacon, Josephine. ROOT AND THE FLOWER.
Appleton, 1936. Development of the position of
women in American life from 1860 to the 1930's.

2340   Banister, Margaret. TEARS ARE FOR THE LIVING.
Houghton, 1963. Panorama of one hundred years
in the life of a Virginia town from before the

Civil War to the 1950's.

2341   Banning, Margaret Culkin. THE QUALITY OF MER-
        CY. Harper, 1963. Story of a Midwestern
        family and of their involvement in various chari-
        table organizations--Red Cross, U. N. R. R. A.,
        and volunteer hospital work--from 1910 through
        WW II.

2342   Benjamin, Harold. THE SAGE OF PETALUMA.
        McGraw, 1965. Autobiographical novel of a
        school teacher and administrator from childhood
        through his teaching career from pre-WW I days
        to the present.

2343   Blassingame, Wyatt. LIVE FROM THE DEVIL.
        Doubleday, 1959. Story of the Florida cattle
        country and the development of the modern cattle
        industry from 1900 to the 1950's.

2344   Boles, Paul Darcy. GLENPORT, ILLINOIS. Mac-
        millan, 1956. Portrays average community life
        in a small town near Chicago from 1929 to 1944;
        the son of an Irish baker grows up to be a suc-
        cessful band leader until his death in World War II.

2345   Bourjaily, Vance. THE VIOLATED. Dial, 1958.
        Follows the lives of four Americans from the
        prosperous Twenties, through the Depression and
        World War II, to the prosperous Fifties.

2346   Boyd, James. ROLL RIVER. Scribner, 1935.
        Story of four generations of a Pennsylvania river
        town family.

2347   Brace, Gerald Warner. THE GARRETSON CHRONI-
        CLE. Norton, 1947. Story of three generations
        of a New England family in a village not far from
        Boston.

2348   Brandon, Evan. GREEN POND. Vanguard, 1955.
        Story of the medical profession, set in the Caro-
        lina red lands from the Civil War to the present.

2349   Bromfield, Louis. THE FARM. Harper, 1933.
        Ohio farm and small town life from 1815 to 1915;
        depicts the changing manners and patterns of rural

social life and the development of a small Midwestern industrial town.

2350   Burlingame, Roger.   THREE BAGS FULL.   Harcourt, 1936.   Panorama of life in the Mohawk Valley of New York from the days of the Holland Land Company to the present; picture of the change from the log cabins of pioneer days to mansion and town house as communities developed.

2351   Carleton, Jetta.   THE MOON FLOWER VINE. Simon & Schuster, 1963.   History of a family in rural Missouri from 1900 to the Korean War; father is a teacher, the youngest child becomes a television writer in New York City.

2352   Carroll, Gladys Hasty.   DUNNYBROOK.   Macmillan, 1943.   Fictional biography of the author's family from Revolutionary War days.   Setting is a Maine village.

2353   -- SING OUT THE GLORY.   Little, 1957.   Panorama of United States history from the turn of the century as it affects an isolated community in Maine.

2354   Cheever, John.   THE WAPSHOT CHRONICLE.   Harper, 1957.   Picture of family life in an old New England town from the turn of the century to the present.

2355   Clad, Noel.   LOVE AND MONEY.   Random, 1959. Chronicle of the social and economic history of the United States from 1917 to 1948; includes anti-German feeling during World War I, the growing movie industry, the jazz age, the Florida boom, the Depression, the rise of Hitler, World War II, the housing boom following the war, and the Congressional investigations of the McCarthy era.

2356   Clune, Henry.   BY HIS OWN HAND.   Macmillan, 1952.   Story of a small segment of American society from 1906 through the Twenties and the post-Depression years of the Thirties.

2357   Davis, Paxton.   THE SEASON OF HEROES.   Morrow,

1967. Three generations of a Virginia family
from the Civil War to 1912, when the children
witness a Negro lynching.

2358   Deal, Babs H. HIGH LONESOME WORLD. Doubleday, 1969. Story of the life and death of a
country music singing star; based on the life of
Hank Williams.

2359   Delmar, Vina. THE BIG FAMILY. Harcourt, 1961.
Story of the Slidell family and of the social and
political events of the country from the Revolutionary War through the 1870's; centers around
John Slidell, Southern political leader and Confederate representative to France during the
Civil War.

2360   Dos Passos, John. MID-CENTURY. Houghton,
1961. A panoramic documentary of the labor
movement in the United States, tracing the
growth of big unions; includes short biographies
of representative people in the movement.

2361   Douglas, Ellen. A FAMILY'S AFFAIRS. Houghton,
1962. Story of simple family customs, births,
and deaths in three generations of a Creole
family in a small Mississippi town from the
early 1900's to post-World War II days.

2362   Downes, Anne Miller. THE EAGLE'S SONG.
Lippincott, 1949. Story of a strong-willed
family clan and a growing community in the Mohawk River valley of New York from the Revolution to World War I.

2363   Espey, John Jenkins. THE ANNIVERSARIES. Harcourt, 1963. Pictures the rapid growth of
Southern California through the story of three
generations of a Pasadena family.

2364   Ferber, Edna. AMERICAN BEAUTY. Doubleday,
1931. Chronicle of the build-up, the gradual
disintegration, and the rejuvenation of a large
estate in Connecticut from 1700 to 1930.

2365   -- COME AND GET IT. Doubleday, 1935. Story
of the rise and fall of the lumber industry in

in Wisconsin and Michigan from 1850 to the 1930's.

2366 -- GIANT. Doubleday, 1952. Sweeping story of land and oil rich Texas; 1920's to the present.

2367 -- ICE PALACE. Doubleday, 1958. Tale of Alaska from pioneering days to the movement for statehood.

2368 Fields, Jonathan. THE MEMOIRS OF DUNSTAN BARR. Coward, 1959. Picture of the changing patterns of farm and small town life and the growth of little business in Illinois from 1890 to the crash of 1929.

2369 Goddard, Gloria. THESE LORDS' DESCENDANTS. Stokes, 1930. Story of changing American life from Colonial times to World War I through the fortunes of the descendants of an English migrant to Colonial America.

2370 Grau, Shirley Ann. THE KEEPERS OF THE HOUSE. Knopf, 1964. Story of three generations of Negro-white relationships in a Southern community.

2371 Hebson, Ann. THE LATTIMER LEGEND. Macmillan, 1961. Story of the break-up of a marriage in the post-Korean War period, with a flashback to the Civil War on the West Virginia border when a Gettysburg widow is won over by one of Morgan's Raiders.

2372 Hergesheimer, Joseph. THE LIMESTONE TREE. Knopf, 1931. Chronicle of Kentucky family life from the time of Daniel Boone through the Civil War to the 1890's.

2373 Holt, Isabella. THE GOLDEN MOMENT. Random, 1959. Story of a woman's marriages set against a background of American political life from the 1920's through the Roosevelt era and World War II to the Congressional loyalty investigations in the 1950's.

2374 Horgan, Paul. MEMORIES OF THE FUTURE. Farrar, 1966. Story of two sisters married to U. S. Navy men, and of their life from World War I through the 1920's and 1930's to World War II.

2375 Horowitz, Gene. HOME IS WHERE YOU START FROM.

Norton, 1966. Story of a Jewish family in New York
City from the early 1920's through the Depression to
World War II.

2376   Hough, Henry Beetle. LAMENT FOR A CITY. Atheneum, 1960. Reporter and editor of a New England
newspaper from 1900 to the present describes
the decline of his paper.

2377   Hummel, George Frederick. JOSHUA MOORE,
AMERICAN. Doubleday, 1943. Episodes in
American history from colonization, the American
Revolution, settling in Ohio, anti-slavery riots
in Kansas, and expansion in California.

2378   Humphrey, William. THE ORDWAYS. Knopf, 1965.
Story of four generations of a Tennessee family
adapting to a new environment in an East Texas
border town.

2379   Hunter, Evan. SONS. Doubleday, 1969. Story of
three generations of a Wisconsin family set
against a background of participation in World
War I, World War II, and Vietnam by a grand-
father, father, and son.

2380   Hunter, Rodello. A HOUSE OF MANY ROOMS.
Knopf, 1965. Episodes in the life of a Mormon
family in Utah from the 1890's to post World
War I days.

2381   Jenks, Almet. THE SECOND CHANCE. Lippincott,
1950. Story of a man who missed fighting in
World War I, recovered from near disaster during
the Depression after entering the financial life of
Wall Street in the 1920's, and is killed in action
in World War II.

2382   Jessup, Richard. SAILOR. Delacorte, 1966. Life
and times of a career sailor from his early life
in Savannah, Georgia during World War I through
the Depression to World War II when his freightor
is sunk by a German U-Boat in the North Atlantic.

2383   Kern, Alfred. MADE IN U.S.A. Houghton, 1966.
Portrait of a union leader and of his drive to the
top.

2384   Keyes, Frances Parkinson.   CRESCENT CARNIVAL.
        Messner, 1942.   New Orleans during fifty years
        from the 1890's to the 1940's; details of the car-
        nival season, Louisiana lottery, fireman's parade,
        architecture, and social and political life.

2385   -- THE RIVER ROAD.   Messner, 1945.   Picture of
        political, financial, and social conditions in the
        bayou country of Louisiana from World War I
        through World War II.

2386   -- STEAMBOAT GOTHIC.   Messner, 1952.   Family
        chronicle which reflects fluctuations in the econ-
        omic life and describes the customs and manners
        of plantation and river life on the lower Mississippi
        River from 1870 to 1930.

2387   Knickerbocker, Charles H.   THE DYNASTY.   Dou-
        bleday, 1962.   A realistic medical novel which
        follows a young doctor through medical school
        and through most of his professional career.

2388   Lockridge, Ross.   RAINTREE COUNTY.   Houghton,
        1948.   Story of Raintree County, Indiana from
        1844 to 1892, showing current events as the hero
        saw them on his visits back to his home county.

2389   Longman, M. B. (pseud.).   THE POWER OF BLACK.
        Globus, 1961.   Epic story of three generations of
        a Southern family who lose everything in the
        Civil War, begin over in the Texas oil fields, and
        follow the fluctuations of the oil industry through
        the post-World War I era.

2390   McConkey, James.   CROSSROADS.   Dutton, 1967.
        Recollections of events in a Depression era
        childhood and service in World War II, and how
        they effect the present life of an ordinary family
        man.

2391   Maier, William.   THE TEMPER OF THE DAYS.
        Scribner, 1961.   A slow-moving novel, set in
        New England, shows the feeling of the times from
        the flambouyant 1920's through the Depression of
        the 1930's and later.

2392   Marquand, J. P.   HAVEN'S END.   Little, 1933.

Chronicle of a New England town through three
generations of a family whose prosperity was based
on slave running.

2393   -- THE LATE GEORGE APLEY.   Little, 1937.
        Life story of a member of a Beacon Hill family.
        Pictures the life and customs of aristocratic
        Boston in the period from the 1880's to 1933.

2394   -- SINCERELY, WILLIS WADE.   Little, 1949.
        Story of the rise of a successfull industrialist,
        picturing the impact of changes in the American
        economic scene from the turn of the century to
        the 1940's.

2395   Meaker, M. J.   HOMETOWN.   Doubleday, 1967.
        Three generations of a family in the grocery
        business in a small town in the New York Fin-
        ger Lakes region from 1914 to 1941.

2396   Mercer, Charles E.   GIFT OF LIFE.   Putnam,
        1963.   Picture of small town life in Pennsylvania
        from World War I to World War II; story of a
        determined woman raising her illegitimate daugh-
        ter.

2397   Michener, James.   HAWAII   Random, 1959.   An
        epic history of the Hawaiian Islands from ancient
        times to the successful struggle for statehood.

2398   Mills, Charles.   THE ALEXANDRIANS.   Putnam,
        1952.   Panorama of the changing patterns of life
        in a small Georgia town from its first settlement
        in 1839 until the day of its centennial celebration
        in 1939.

2399   Moody, Minnie Hite.   LONG MEADOW.   Macmillan,
        1941.   Chronicle of the Hite family from 1705 to
        the 1860's when two of the cousins died in the
        Civil War, one fighting for the South, the other
        for the Union.

2400   Moore, Ruth.   SPEAK TO THE WINDS.   Morrow,
        1956.   Three generations of the families who,
        in 1844, developed a town on an island off the
        Maine coast to exploit the granite found there.

2401 -- THE GOLD AND SILVER HOOKS. Morrow, 1969.
Story of a New England woman and her family
problems from the early 1900's through the Prohibition era of the Twenties, when her husband
is involved in rum-running.

2402 Morris, Hilda. THE LONG VIEW. Putnam, 1937.
A three-generation family chronicle showing
the changing patterns of life from the Civil War
through the Depression; New Jersey, rural New
York, Indiana, Chicago, and Europe.

2403 Myrer, Anton. ONCE AN EAGLE. Holt, 1968.
Saga of army life from World War I through
World War II and after; story of a career sol-
dier as he rises from private to general.

2404 Norris, Frank. TOWER IN THE WEST. Harper,
1957. Picture of American social and economic
life from the Twenties to World War II through
the life history of a revolutionary skyscraper
hotel in St. Louis; Prohibition, the crash of
1929, the Depression, recovery, and prosperity
through World War II.

2405 O'Hara, John. FROM THE TERRACE. Random,
1958. Study of the life of a member of the wealthy class from boyhood through service in
World War I, career in the early aviation industry and in Wall Street financial circles, and
government service in World War II.

2406 Ozick, Cynthia. TRUST. New American Library,
1966. Intellectual, political, and social life
of the rich in Europe and New York from the
1930's to the present.

2407 Petrakis, Harry Mark. THE ODYSSEY OF KOSTAS
SOLAKIS. McKay, 1963. An account of life
in the Greek-American community of Chicago
from 1919 to 1954.

2408 Powell, Richard. THE PHILADELPHIAN. Scribner, 1956. Story of social life and customs seen
through four generations of a Philadelphia family
from 1857 to the present.

2409   -- I TAKE THIS LAND. Scribner, 1963. Social
       and business life, railroad building, land booms,
       and orange growing industry in Southwest Florida
       from the 1890's to the 1920's.

2410   Rawlings, Marjorie Kinnan. THE SOJOURNER.
       Scribner, 1953. Life on a farm in upstate New
       York from 1880 to World War II.

2411   Rejan, Edwin. ONE CLEAR CALL. Macmillan,
       1962. Recollections of an eighty-two year old
       priest on his forty-five years in a Brooklyn
       parish; covers events during the polio epidemic
       of 1916, World War I, World War II, the New
       York dock strike in 1936, and the immigration of
       the Puerto Ricans into the neighborhood.

2412   Robinson, Henry Morton. WATER OF LIFE. Simon
       & Schuster, 1960. American social and political
       events from the post-Civil War period through
       Prohibition in the background of this history of
       the whiskey making industry.

2413   Rooney, Frank. THE COURTS OF MEMORY. Van-
       guard, 1954. Story of modern family life from
       1930's to the present; set in Los Angeles and
       New York.

2414   Sandburg, Carl. REMEMBRANCE ROCK. Harcourt,
       1948. Panorama of American history from the
       days of the Pilgrims to the end of World War II.

2415   Saunders, Winifred Crandall. TO SPAN A CONTI-
       NENT. Caxton, 1965. Family saga of a New
       York State farmer who wanders westward to the
       Pacific in 1839; after settling on an Illinois home-
       stead his sons are active in the Underground
       Railroad and later fight in the Civil War. Fron-
       tier life, family and social customs, and the
       Abolition movement.

2416   Scanlon, John. DAVIS. Doubleday, 1969. Bio-
       graphy of a military genius from West Point
       cadet before World War II, through action in
       the Burma campaign with Wingate's Raiders,
       promotion between wars, and on to his death in
       the Korean War.

2417   Seton, Anya. THE HEARTH AND EAGLE. Hough-
       ton, 1948. Story of Marblehead, Massachusetts
       from its earliest settlement to the present.

2418   Shaw, Irwin. VOICES OF A SUMMER DAY. Dela-
       corte, 1965. The son of immigrant Russian
       parents looks back on his family life from 1927
       to the present.

2419   Siebel, Julia. THE NARROW COVERING. Har-
       court, 1956. Life in a small town in Kansas
       from before World War I to the years following
       Pearl Harbor.

2420   Sigal, Clancy. GOING AWAY. Houghton, 1961.
       Memoir of an angry young man experiencing the
       changes, reforms, and Leftist agitation in Ameri-
       can society from the 1930's to the present.

2421   Simmons, Herbert. MAN WALKING ON EGGSHELLS.
       Houghton, 1962. Story of the economic and
       social struggles of a Negro family from 1927
       to the present.

2422   Sourian, Peter. THE GATE. Harcourt, 1965.
       Three generations of an Armenian-American
       family; the son becomes a successful architect.

2423   Stegner, Wallace. THE BIG ROCK CANDY MOUN-
       TAIN. Duell, 1943. Life in the Far West
       and in Saskatchewan Province of Canada from
       1906 to 1942.

2424   Stern, Richard Martin. BROOD OF EAGLES.
       New American Library, 1969. Story of a family
       and their business empire in the aircraft industry
       from pre-World War I to the present.

2425   Stevens, Louis. DAYS OF PROMISE. Prentice,
       1948. Panorama of American society from the
       Civil War to the 1940's told through the chronicle
       of a Kansas newspaper family.

2426   Streeter, Edward. HAM MARTIN, CLASS OF '17.
       Harper, 1969. Success story of a Harvard grad-
       uate, through World War I, the Depression, and
       World War II, who sees his son become the

creative writer he had wished to be.

2427   Sulkin, Sidney. THE FAMILY MAN. Luce, 1962.
        A Russian-Jewish immigrant struggles for finan-
        cial success from the Depression years to the
        McCarthy era in the 1950's.

2428   Tute, Warren. LEVIATHAN. Little, 1959. A
        story of the steamship industry; the building and
        operating of a great liner from its launching in
        the 1930's to its sinking in service as a troop
        carrier during World War II.

2429   Vidal, Gore. WASHINGTON, D. C. Little, 1967.
        Private life and politics of a U. S. Senator
        from the early days of the New Deal to the period
        of the Cold War and the McCarthy era.

2430   Walker, Mildred. CURLEW'S CRY. Harcourt,
        1955. Picture of ranch life in Montana from
        1905 to the 1940's.

2431   Watson, Virginia. MANHATTAN ACRES. Dutton,
        1934. Picture of the growth of New York City;
        chronicle of a Dutch family from the 1630's to
        1933.

2432   Weeks, Jack. SOME TRUST IN CHARIOTS. Mc-
        Graw, 1964. Three generation saga of a family
        empire growing with the automobile industry
        from the invention of a gas buggy in 1895 to the
        1940's.

2433   Wescott, Glenway. THE GRANDMOTHERS. Har-
        per, 1927. Chronicle of a Wisconsin family,
        one of those who helped settle the frontier, from
        the 1840's through the Civil War to the turn of
        the century.

2434   White, William Allen. A CERTAIN RICH MAN.
        Macmillan, 1909. Story of a millionaire indus-
        trialist and the growth of his Kansas town from
        the Civil War to the turn of the century.

2435   Wight, Frederick. CHRONICLE OF AARON KANE.
        Farrar, 1936. Story of the long life of a Scotch-
        Irish Cape Cod sailor from 1838 through the

post-Civil War years.

2436   Wilder, Robert. THE SUN IS MY SHADOW. Put-
        nam, 1960. Story of a woman's career in news-
        paper work; economic and political events from
        the late 1920's through the Depression, the
        Roosevelt era, the rise of Hitler, and World
        War II.

2437   -- THE SEA AND THE STARS. Putnam, 1967.
        Saga of the growth of Florida from undeveloped
        scrub land through the boom days of World War I
        and the Twenties, the collapse of the bubble, and
        rebuilding the fruit and trucking industry, motel
        development, and the building of new communities.

2438   Williams, Ben Ames. THE STRANGE WOMAN.
        Houghton, 1941. Story of a wicked but beautiful
        woman, extending in time from the War of 1812
        through the Civil War with Maine as its scene.

2439   Williams, John. STONER. Viking, 1965. Life
        story of a poor Missouri farm boy who worked
        his way through the University of Missouri and
        stayed on as a teacher until driven away by a
        scandal; 1891 to 1956.

2440   Wilson, Mitchell. LIVE WITH LIGHTNING. Little,
        1949. Story of the career of a young physicist,
        from his years as laboratory assistant during the
        Depression of the Thirties, to industrial scien-
        tist, to atomic research worker during World
        War II and after.

Subject Index

New Jersey   195, 272, 341, 1497, 1653, 2402
New Madrid Earthquake, 1811   588
New Mexico   521, 600-601, 610, 612, 614, 624, 631, 646,
   651, 659, 663, 672, 680, 687, 694-695, 705, 710, 726,
   760, 1072, 1241, 1948, 1955, 2085, 2167
New Orleans, La.   28, 68, 86, 89, 92, 106, 167, 308, 317,
   345, 351, 357, 360, 362, 379, 381, 383, 397, 405, 480,
   482, 621, 724, 808, 974, 981, 1040, 1105-06, 1123,
   1125, 1147, 1154, 1194, 1197, 1199, 1222, 1228-29,
   1321-22, 1332, 1358, 1460, 1472, 1689, 1726, 1780,
   2210, 2384
New Salem, Ill.   584
New South   see   Southern Life Following Reconstruction
New York (City)   25, 71, 73, 75, 90, 120, 136, 163, 169,
   212-213, 216, 231, 235, 269, 297, 299, 322, 325, 327,
   342, 347, 354, 357, 365, 370, 378, 727, 770, 1074,
   1122, 1232, 1236, 1246, 1260-61, 1267, 1276, 1307,
   1327, 1329, 1341-44, 1363-64, 1389, 1397, 1409, 1413,
   1438-39, 1453-54, 1461, 1471, 1485, 1527, 1538, 1549,
   1565, 1587, 1592, 1596, 1602, 1608, 1612, 1624, 1638,
   1667, 1671, 1674, 1676, 1679, 1682, 1689, 1720, 1728,
   1731, 1735-36, 1755, 1775, 1782, 1785, 1790-91, 1798,
   1800, 1816, 1832, 1846, 1851, 1862, 1868-69, 1917,
   2021, 2057, 2246, 2248, 2254, 2277, 2296, 2325, 2328,
   2337-38, 2351, 2375, 2406, 2411, 2413, 2431
   see also   Brooklyn; Long Island; Staten Island
New York (State)   21-24, 73, 94, 132-134, 147, 149, 153,
   155, 159-162, 169, 179-180, 220-221, 236, 251, 271-272,
   278, 294-296, 302, 305-307, 369, 378, 386, 399, 413-
   416, 426, 428-431, 438, 453, 500, 555, 863, 1010, 1012,
   1034, 1037, 1080, 1148, 1164, 1189-90, 1251, 1269, 1312,
   1322, 1325, 1328, 1339, 1387, 1397, 1415, 1607-08, 1623,
   1673, 1686, 1732, 1736, 1751, 1776, 1845, 1859, 1866,
   1981, 2039, 2104, 2148, 2350, 2362, 2395, 2402, 2410,
   2415
New York Central Railroad   1857
New York State University   1790
Newport, R.I.   77, 143, 288, 1454, 1741, 2337
Newspapers and Newspapermen   25, 235, 271, 389, 686,
   727, 993, 1072, 1112, 1127, 1140, 1464, 1474, 1476,
   1550, 1560, 1595, 1641, 1739, 1846, 1935, 1982, 1998,
   2010, 2171, 2178, 2194, 2221, 2235, 2292, 2310, 2320,
   2324, 2376, 2425, 2436
Nez Perce Indians   761, 897, 930, 937
Niagara Falls   431
Niagara Peninsula in the War of 1812   387
Nineteen-Thirties   826, 882, 1243-44, 1270, 1338, 1348,